Evgenia Iliopoulou
Because of You: Understanding Second-Person Storytelling

Lettre

Evgenia Iliopoulou born in 1986, lives in Zurich, Switzerland, and specializes in narratology, theory of literature and interdisciplinary approaches within Comparative Literature. She holds an undergraduate degree in Greek Philology from her hometown University of Patras, Greece, and an MA in Comparative Literature from Ludwig Maximilian University of Munich, Germany. In 2014, during her doctoral studies, Zurich University sponsored her participation in the summer session of School of Theory and Criticism at Cornell University in the US.

Evgenia Iliopoulou

Because of You: Understanding Second-Person Storytelling

[transcript]

This work was accepted as a PhD thesis by the Faculty of Arts and Social Sciences, University of Zurich in the fall semester 2017 on the recommendation of the Doctoral Committee: Prof. Dr. Thomas Fries «main supervisor», Prof. Dr. Sandro Zanetti.

Published with the support of the Swiss National Science Foundation.

Bibliographic information published by the Deutsche Nationalbibliothek
The Deutsche Nationalbibliothek lists this publication in the Deutsche Nationalbibliografie; detailed bibliographic data are available in the Internet at http://dnb.d-nb.de

Cover layout: Maria Arndt, Bielefeld
Typeset by Francisco Bragança, Bielefeld
Printed by Majuskel Medienproduktion GmbH, Wetzlar
Print-ISBN 978-3-8376-4537-8
PDF-ISBN 978-3-8394-4537-2
https://doi.org/10.14361/9783839445372

Preface

This thesis is the result of a critical investigation that began in April 2011. It started as a study of interactive fiction that aspired to contribute to the topic by exploring the reader's active participation and involvement in the text. Necessitating constant modification over the years, the research has generated in me an abiding interest in second-person storytelling that evolved to become the actual theme of this thesis. This research aims to improve our understanding of the phenomenon within the literary paradigm.

Because of You: Understanding Second-Person Storytelling had its origins in open text formats and experimental narratives along the lines of "choose your own adventure" stories such as Italo Calvino's *Se una notte d'inverno un viaggiatore* and extended to cyber texts. This wide range of narrative typologies offered grounds for exploring interactivity in a multidisciplinary manner, afforded by the dialogic dimension of the second person in other media as well as in non-fiction employments. Once the research centred on fiction and second-person narratives, the question regarding the grade and nature of the reader's interaction with the text proved to be indicative of the richness of second-person storytelling.

Italo Calvino's novel marked a transition in my research. Thematising reading and the reader-author relationship in a unique and emphatic way, his novel immersed me in the concept of address-dominated narratives. It introduced me to the richness and dynamics of the second-person narrative technique by revealing some of its main characteristics such as its ludic character, self-reflexivity and intertextuality. Though *Se una notte d'inverno un viaggiatore* was not selected for the close-reading part of this thesis, it still needs to be mentioned as a benchmark and catalyst for my research and the formulation of key ideas and assumptions.

One major challenge that I faced in defining the actual focus of my research was the angle and perspective I should most profitably employ. Since neither theory nor criticism were offering satisfactory answers or ideas, neglecting as they were the rich history of second-person examples in literature and the adaptation of the technique in lyrics and drama, I often reached dead ends having embarked on misleading cognitive routes. Once I had decided to follow a more inductive method towards drawing my conclusions by focussing on the fundamentals of person, pronoun, grammar and rhetoric, the texts themselves provided the answer. One key observation I made was that though second-person texts have been continually present and diverse in the history of literature, they also reflected an intriguing uniqueness as they always appeared only once in the oeuvre of their authors.

This observation generated questions about the kind of stories that authors prefer to tell in the second person. Exploring their methods and reasons for doing so, as well as studying the implications of the technique, helped to define the aims of my study. Instead of ambitiously seeking homogeneity and common characteristics that would enable me gradually to model a *theory* of second-person fiction, I was fascinated to notice some affinities between prayers and postmodern texts, texts from medieval times and the *nouveau roman*, epic poems and recent prose: it seemed as if second-person texts belonged to a literary history that involves an eternal dialogue between texts and authors. My focus then moved to intertextuality but only so as to establish a dialogue as I was reluctant to impose any generalisations or groupings. Examples such as Christa Wolf's *Kindheitsmuster,* Michel Butor's *La Modification,* Georges Perec's *Un homme qui dort,* Ilse Aichinger's *Spiegelgeschichte,* Günter Grass's *Katz und Maus,* Frederick Barthelme's stories in *Moon Deluxe* and Paul Auster's *Winter Journal,* though all written in the second person, are different enough from each other to require examination as individual case studies.

Choosing autobiographical and pseudo-autobiographical examples written in the second person, I have strengthened my focus on the *I–you* relationship and orientated my research onto the possible reasons why the first person is missing, is disguised, silenced or implied in these second-person novels. Reflecting on my readings, observations and my selection of texts and trying to transform these reflections into writing, I encountered elements that were decisive for my study even at a later stage of my doctorate: the alternating power of every process of representation; the dynamics of language and self-reflexivity; the constant transformations and modifications of the narrative; the idea of multiple versions of a life, of a self, of an *I*, one that could be better expressed by a *you* as, for example, in Butor's *La Modification*, revealing the close though important distance between the evolving poles of the *I–you* constellation.

On completing my readings and having articulated all my thoughts and speculations, I managed to explain the second-person enigma as a liminal technique that reflects liminal narrative circumstances while always engaging the reader in a role that's not merely passive. I found that I had reached my aim of understanding second-person storytelling better. This is reflected in the understanding of the textual examples and in the analysis of the four texts of the second part, in revisiting the fundamentals of grammar and rhetoric and in listing the origins, implications and rich elaborations of the phenomenon. It was further proved by my writing of the first and final chapters of this thesis only when I had finished the part on the texts themselves, treating them not only as the object but also as the source of my research.

In undertaking this research and writing this thesis I benefited from the advice and encouragement of many people. First and foremost, I would like to thank Prof. Dr. Thomas Fries and Prof. Dr. Sandro Zanetti for supervising my work. Their example, teaching and support helped me realise the project. Thanks to my friends for the fruitful discussions and interest.

Special thanks to Christine; Michael, Lucia, Cameron; to Tairi, Popi, Hara, Maria, Irene, Fania, Vivi.

I would also like to offer sincere thanks and gratitude to my family for their unstinting support over all these years. Mom, Dad, Ilia, our *we*, no matter the constellation it took over the years, has been always safeguarding my *I*, and the development of my thoughts on *you*. Thank you for giving me the courage to embark on this journey, remain on that path and complete what I started.

to that person

Table of Contents

Part 1
Introduction

Prologue

The writing of this dissertation was occasioned by a constellation of contradictory aspects: the existence of various fascinating texts written in the second person, each a unique and remarkable work of art, combined with a general lack of understanding of second-person novels on the part of critics and theorists not to mention publishers who tend to treat second-person texts either with extreme doubt and suspicion or, on the contrary, believing in their success irrespective of the quality of the book. Subsequently, the aim of this project is to clarify aspects of second-person storytelling as an enigmatic literary phenomenon associated with a narrative technique that has certain key properties and is appropriate on certain narrative occasions.

It hopes to further support the understanding of this technique by focussing on the grammatical, poetic and rhetorical implications that accompany it and to clarify elements that are often overlooked. These elements may appear obvious to deal with at the very beginning, since they are related to fundamental categories of storytelling and language like, for example, person and pronoun, but they are nonetheless still complicated, especially when used in fictional narratives. This overview aspires to shed light on what the second person stands for in storytelling.

My dissertation, entitled *Because of You: Understanding Second-Person Storytelling*, approaches second-person narratives not as a group that needs to be classified as a genre, but as separate narratives that each feature the same technique but with different poetic and rhetorical connotations. The project is not a theoretical attempt aspiring to culminate in a strict definition of what the second-person narrative technique is. Rather it approaches the technique in an inductive way: observations on the texts themselves form the basis for assumptions and any conclusions are the stronger for it as they are drawn with regard to the enigmatic and poetic character of the technique, aiming to clarify its essential elements and rhetorical tropes that are used in numerous ways within a particular narrative.

The Second-Person Enigma

> Prendi la posizione più comoda: seduto, sdraiato, raggomitolato, coricato. Coricato sulla schiena, su un fianco, sulla pancia. In poltrona, sul divano, sulla sedia a dandolo, sulla sedia a sdraio, sul pouf.[1]

Italo Calvino's *Se una notte d'inverno un viaggiatore* is perhaps the best recognised and well-known second-person text among contemporary readers. Published in 1979, the novel is a strange narrative collage composed of the beginnings of ten different novels which are interrupted by a second narrative strand in which a Reader (the protagonist of the novel) is in search of some missing pages of the book he is reading, the same book that the actual reader (*you* or *I*) has in hand. Thematising the composition of his own book and addressing the Reader directly, Calvino surprised both the readers and critics of his time with the striking way in which he addressed formal questions of narration through the operation of *address*, a gesture that caused a long-lasting debate on the style and literary virtues of *Se una notte d'inverno un viaggiatore* in general and second-person storytelling in particular.

Indeed, the suspicion and doubt expressed in relation to Calvino's book is not something new when it comes to second-person fiction. Second-person novels have frequently been treated as experimental novelties that either deter a readership from engaging with them or, on the contrary, attract the attention of readers by their *catchy* technique irrespective of their literary virtues. Paradoxically this technique that is often seen as tricky or even unpopular has been a narrative mode continuously employed throughout the history of literature, and in many instances even acclaimed in prize-winning novels such as Ilse Aichinger's *Spiegelgeschichte* that was honoured

1 | Italo Calvino, *Se una notte d'inverno un viaggiatore*. 1979. (Milano: Oscar Mondadori, 1994) 3.

with the Group 47 prize in 1952. Also puzzling is the fact that while many authors have reported problems getting their books published due to the employment of the second-person technique in the past, the situation lately seems to be completely reversed as we witness a rapid growth of second-person texts emerging on the literary scene, especially in the Anglophone world.

In an attempt to defend his work, Calvino in December 1979 published an essay in the "Alfabeta" journal in which he rephrased the title of the novel as *Se una notte d'inverno un narratore*[2] in response to Angelo Guglielmi's criticism of his novel's challenging style and form. Five years later, at a conference held at the Institute of Italian Culture in Buenos Aires in 1984, he defended his novel and his compositional choices, emphasising the self-reflective character of his book, the pleasure of reading and, of course, that of writing.

> L'impressa di cercare di scrivere romanzi "apocrifi", cioè che immagino siano scritti da un autore che non sono io e che non esiste, l'ho portata fino in fondo nel mio libro *Se una notte d'inverno un viaggiatore*. È un romanzo sul piacere di leggere romanzi; protagonista è il Lettore, che per dieci volte comincia a leggere un libro che per vicissitudini estranee alla sua volontà non riesce a finire.[3]

As a patchwork of literary beginnings of books that the author could have written but didn't, *Se una notte d'inverno un viaggiatore* not only reveals vital components of the writing process but it also highlights the reading process by exposing it to the reader and making it a central theme of the novel. Calvino's book is a marginal self-reflexive text in which the employment of the second-person narrative voice establishes the unique reader-author relationship that the author treats as a major theme of the book. The playful way in which Calvino decides to address his readership and the fragmented char-

2 | Calvino (1979/1994), v-xiv.

3 | Italo Calvino, *Il Libro, i Libri.* (Buenos Aires: Nuovi quaderni italiani, 1984) 19.

acter of his narrative not only challenge the norms of traditional storytelling but also any reading of the book itself, as readers have to deal with having their position put under scrutiny in various ways: through the theme of reading, by being addressed by and identified with the Reader of the narrative, by struggling with a work of fragments and missing pages that constantly gets interrupted just as the main character of the story (the Reader) is.

Se una notte d'inverno un viaggiatore puts a double emphasis on the Reader, firstly by presenting him as the main character of the narrative and secondly by its composition in the second-person narrative mode in which the concept of address dominates. The second-person technique presupposes, or demands, *active* readers who continually accept or reject their involvement in the story. The continual challenge and ambiguity outlined above presented by reading *Se una notte d'inverno un viaggiatore* can be described as the enigma of second-person storytelling. It is an enigma that can also be found, to varying degrees, in response to other second-person texts. In Calvino's novel, however, since the reading challenge also dominates the plot, the enigma is expanded from rhetoric to a more theoretical and metatextual context. *Se una notte d'inverno un viaggiatore* is unique as it discusses theory (that of the second person and Reader Response theory) by being it.

This novel has been the foundational text of my research and its starting point, giving rise to concepts and thoughts on second-person narrative technique and how the concept of address operates. It establishes revealingly the link between the employment of the second person and the reader (the addressee) as well as the association of the technique with self-reflexivity and intertextuality, and it does so in a ludic and hence experimental narrative. These are all features that belong to second-person storytelling. However, though *Se una notte d'inverno un viaggiatore* has been essential to setting the cognitive grounds of this study, as my research evolved it proved to be a less good example for understanding the second person as it emphasises the Reader-Author constellation at the expense of the rhetoric of the second person *per se*.

With the aim of understanding the second-person technique, this project has developed a basic typology of address. It reflects a continuous shifting between different addressees which is derived from the classic notion of *apostrophe* and expressed rhetorically as such; it also reflects a mid-distance between narrator and narrated as seen in narratives in which the narrator is not alienated from the narrative but neither is he/she involved the actual moment of narration; it further reflects the second person as an open and ambiguous form, a placeholder for the indefinite and undetermined in the discourse thus, in many cases, enabling narrative depth and complexity.

The above typology is the result of reading and attempting to classify, or at least identify, common features in the long history of second-person literature. In the second part of this project four narratives have been selected for a detailed analysis. They reflect this basic typology and classification and offer the grounds to explore vital aspects of the technique in detail. The texts chosen belong to German and French cold- and post-war period literature, and by addressing different themes they employ the second person in different forms (*tu* and *vous, du*) and narrative modes.

The first novel discussed, *Kindheitsmuster* by Christa Wolf (1976), is the story of a narrator who, after several failed attempts at composing her childhood autobiography in the traditional first-person narrative form, decides to do so in the third, making a narrative persona out of her past self and conducting a continual self-inquisitive (second-person) dialogue while writing. Wolf's *Kindheitsmuster* is a fine example of the different levels of distance the pronominal forms reflect in the discourse. Her example is followed by *La Modification* by Michel Butor (1957), a novel reflecting the *nouveau roman* period and showing the process of decision-making on a train journey that coincides with the main narrative in progress. In Butor's self-reflexive narrative the second-person technique is employed to depict the making of a narrative persona and a novel. Here the second-person technique reveals in detail the character's surroundings, and through the consistent use of the polite *vous* it invites the reader into the fictional world, which is being composed the moment it is read. The generation of the novel in Butor reflects the generation of its key persona as the plot chronicles a process of self-awareness and story of re-establishing self-authority.

The third novel discussed is *Un homme qui dort* by George Perec (1967), a text often associated with Butor's *La Modification* due to their temporal and linguistic proximity and the employment of the second-person technique. Perec presents a *tu*-narrative rich in intertextual implications that shows a student performing an experiment in social detachment by abandoning his own *I*, which is constantly addressed in the second person. Perec's narrative echoes earlier texts that summarised indifference or that involved similar narrative modes and offers a basis for focussing on intertextuality and its role in understanding the second-person technique. What is important to mention here is that in Perec, the second person functions as a narrative figure throughout the narrative; it generates a constant shifting towards different addressees – the heroes and references from other texts – and designates a narrative *topos* that includes all references and literary influences that coexist in Perec's narrative persona until the latter becomes concrete and can be referred to with the pronoun used (*tu*).

The last text discussed in the project is Ilse Aichinger's *Spiegelgeschichte* (1949), a most enigmatic and complex text that challenges the reader with its theme as it shows episodes from the life of a dying woman in a hospital bed in reverse and is interrupted by a narrative level external to the woman (third person). Ilse Aichinger presents a rather short text in which an indeterminate voice, undefined until the end of the narrative, keeps addressing the woman throughout her situation and tells these life episodes in reverse order. Striking is the fact that this reversed flow affects the meanings of the events and their relationship, hence reasons appear as results and connotations of happiness or sadness have a reverse implication. Aichinger, like Perec, creates a story without a legitimate narrative figure, introducing a voice narrator and a dying main narrative figure who is a passive recipient of the narrative. Intriguing also is the fact that in

Spiegelgeschichte, the analysis is subject to this reversal as well, since the main question to be answered here is not the referent of the second person but its origin as well as the relationship the woman shares with this voice.

The texts outlined above are not presented in chronological order but according to the complexity of the narrative strategy of the second person they employ; this order of presentation aims to clarify the various issues and questions associated with or arising from the use of the second-person narrative mode and serves the understanding of the technique gradually. It is the ambivalence and contradiction inherent in second-person narrative that deserves further discussion. Intriguing, moreover, is the fact that second-person narrative is possible in all forms of storytelling, and for reasons related to its audience-oriented character and its effect on the *I* it is found in different media, even in non-fiction: Theatre, Cinema, Video Games, Advertising, Social Media platforms and Hypnosis. Its versatile appearance in different media and in literature and its ambiguous though resilient nature *per se* make the second person an exciting phenomenon to study, though it is rather challenging to choose an appropriate angle from which to do so.

The fundamentals for pursuing this close-reading analysis and the basic tools of this inductive research are listed in the first part of this project. This part focuses on establishing a fundamental understanding of the second person, starting from the essentials of grammar and rhetoric and discussing the fundamental category of person and pronoun, gesturing towards understanding more precisely what the second *person* and the second-person *pronoun* are. To explain this review and methodology, the first part involves a brief and selective summary of theoretical contributions that centre on second-person fiction but that have proven insufficient for this research since they do not reflect the historical continuity of the phenomenon and its versatile employment in different poetic forms. Hence in this part of the project a historical overview of the phenomenon is included, one that traces its development through the years: based on a rich anthology of second-person narratives, the rhetorical tropes and figures that appear systematically within the technique are summarised. This section stresses the continuity and importance of the technique and the problems associated with its study which are linked to the fact that often the obvious, for example the problem of *person* considered as (purely) grammatical or not,[4] is the most difficult to talk about.

The thesis ends with a chapter that outlines and elaborates on what was discussed so far and compares the four narrative examples expanding on some of the major assumptions mentioned only briefly along the way and listing the final conclusions regarding the poetic value and rhetorical impact of the second person in fiction. *Because of You: Understanding Second-Person Storytelling* aims to show the potential of employing the narrative *you* in a text and improve its understanding. By doing so it aspires to draw some conclusions on what it is about the second-person perspective that makes it so appealing and intriguing for readers and writers alike, despite being discouraging at times.

Theory

Attempts to theorise the second-person narrative technique have so far proved ill advised due to the nature of the research object, which is too resilient and broad to be classified as a genre. Given that the second-person narrative technique participates in different genres involving numerous employments, functions and characteristics, it is hard to formulate a summary (theory) based on a single example that would reflect the mode as a whole. Another obstacle to the theorising process is the binary thinking of traditional theorists (and their successors) that bases thoughts and assumptions on pairs of oppositions that can only show the second person as a special case, an experimental and exceptional narrative phenomenon.

---

4 | Émile Benveniste. *Problèmes de linguistique générale I.* (Paris: Gallimard, 1966) 226.

It is striking that major theorists such as Gérard Genette and Franz Stanzel play down the second person as a narrative mode, devoting just a few lines to it. Though Genette deals with many of the issues related to the second-person narrative mode and even acknowledges the problem of distance within the narrative (problem with the self over time, perspective, point of view within storytelling), he fails to examine it in connection with the second-person technique, since his study focuses on first- and third-person narratives only, handling the second person as a special case that appears to be an exception. Where he focuses on the opposition between *diegesis* and *mimesis* (*telling* and *showing*), second-person narratives remain unmentioned and are omitted from his triadic notional model, based on the concepts of distance, point of view and person.

This is because Genette's theory is based on dichotomies, such as that of *hetero-* and *homodiegesis,* which are not applicable to second-person narratives that are treated in his work as a special form, a sub-category of *heterodiegesis.* Genette fails to cover the numerous other cases of second-person texts in which, for example, the narrator as well as the narratee participate in the actions recounted at the level of plot and which therefore cannot be defined as *heterodiegetic.* The theorist prefers the terms *heterodiegetic* and *homodiegetic* rather than *person* to determine the position of the narrator in the narration, which depicts clearly that narrative voices tend to designate the roles within the narrative and are strongly associated with pronouns, functioning as placeholders. Consequently, Genette's terminology addresses the relatedness or even identification/tautology of the experiencing and narrating self rather than that particular persona per se. When writing about the second person, his theoretical assumption tends to refer to an elaboration or expansion of the *intradiegetic* narrator, thus undermining and reducing the phenomenon.

Un narrateur intradiégétique, narrataire intradiégétique, et le récit des Grieux ou de Bixiou ne s'adresse pas au lecteur de *Manon Lescaut* ou de la *Maison Nucingen*, mais bien au seul M. de Renoncourt, aux seuls Finot,

Courture et Blondet, que désignent seuls les marques de "deuxième personne" éventuellement présentes dans le texte, tout comme celles qu'on trouvera dans un roman par lettres ne peuvent désigner que le correspondant épistolaire. Nous, lecteurs, ne pouvons pas plus nous identifier à ces narrataires fictifs que ces narrateurs intradiégétiques ne peuvent s'adresser à nous, ni même supposer notre existence.[5]

Franz Stanzel based his theory on the realms of existence, and he offered an elaborated depiction of the narrative issues puzzling readers and theorists with his famous typological circle (*Typenkreis*). Here again, the second-person narrative cannot be correctly positioned, because of the broad character of the second-person technique and the potential inherent in the pronoun to take over several roles and functions in the discourse. However, even taking into account this drawback, Stanzel's concept, pictured in a theoretical circle, is more applicable to the second-person technique than Genette's since it implies the notion of gradation.

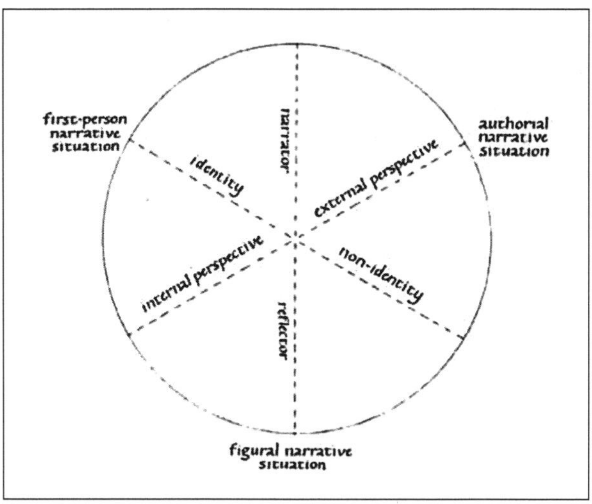

5 | Gérard Genette, *Figures III*. (Paris: Édition du Seuil, 1972) 265.

Like Genette, Stanzel classifies literature in terms of binary opposites, with the second person failing to fit in. Second-person fiction involves dual narrative personae with double qualities – both figural and authorial – and therefore should always be treated on a case-by-case basis. The same is true for the narrative perspective: it is not quite clear where examples such as Perec's *Un homme qui dort* should be located, that may portray the internal perspective of the narrated, but present it as if it were external. Stanzel's typological circle is not applicable to second-person narratives as a whole as it doesn't depict their cohesive elements. However valuable it may be for the study of second-person storytelling as a reflection of the *Other,* he defines second-person narrative more as a self-dramatised *I,* a negation of the first-person narrator constellation that relates to other narrative modes:

> Der Ich-Erzähler von J.D. Salingers *The Catcher in the Rye,* Holden Caulfield, steht als Hauptfigur der Erzählung mitten in der fiktionalen Welt, die der Roman darstellt. Die Identität der Seinsbereiche des Erzählers und der übrigen Charaktere ist also unzweifelhaft gegeben, sie bleibt auch aufrecht angesichts der Neigung dieses Ich- Erzählers, sich mit seinem Anliegen direkt an den Leser zu wenden.[6]

Stanzel uses the term *Transponierungsziel*[7] to describe the modifying process that an *extrovertierter* (probably second-person) narrator creates between the two main poles: the first-person narrator of the events and the more distanced narrator who is at a remove from the narrated incidents and dramatic time. The gap between these two narrative territories could be covered by the second-person mode, but for Stanzel it designates one of the major properties of the original text as a basic story in the author's mind. According to Stanzel, it should not be considered an open slot for an additional narrative

6 | Franz K. Stanzel, *Theorie des Erzählens.* 1979. (Göttingen: Vandenhoeck and Ruprecht, 2001) 82.

7 | Stanzel (1979/2001), 83.

mode but rather a literary achievement, viewed as an exceptional narrative performance of an elevated and remarkable narrative style.

By converting the dramatised *I*, as Stanzel describes second-person narrators, into a third-person narrator, the experience and the inner world of the hero can be projected without discontinuities in the appropriate mode. Consequently, whereas Stanzel reveals the narrative territory covered by the second-person transgressive form, he avoids describing it in words and thus fails to cover the second-person phenomenon in his theoretical work. Of course, the reason why both theorists didn't devote more analysis or thought to the second-person phenomenon is the period during which they wrote their essays. At that time, second-person texts were only beginning to appear on the literary scene with the works of Butor and Aichinger, which were still viewed as exceptional and experimental cases of fiction.

> [...] der Zusammenhang zwischen Erlebnis und Erzählung, der durch die Identität der Seinsbereiche des Erzählers und der dargestellten Wirklichkeit gegeben ist, ohne schwerwiegende Eingriffe in das Sinngefüge des Romans nicht gelöst werden kann. Eine Transponierung der Ich-Erzählung in eine Er-Erzählung würde aber die Lösung dieses Zusammenhangs voraussetzen.[8]

As the second-person narrative came to enjoy increasing popularity especially in the Anglophone world after the 1950s, recent theorists, principally Monika Fludernik, Brian Richardson and Irene Kacandes, approached the narrative phenomenon more systematically than their predecessors. However, their work emphasised very specific issues such as reader identification and the transgressive character of literature, restricting their view to the experimental aspect of the technique and missing vital parts of its rhetorical and poetic sense.

8 | Stanzel (1979/2001), 83.

Eine besonders auffällige Konstellation ist die Du-Erzählung, in der die Geschichte einer Leserfigur geschildert wird. Im Deutschen ist diese Variante des Figurenverhältnisses zwischen Erzählebene und Geschichtsebene eher selten, während in der englischsprachigen Literatur und in den romanischen Sprachen eine Vielzahl von Werken dieser Machart existiert.[9]

Up to this point, second-person theory, while reflecting on a larger number of texts and richer in examples than the older theorists, could be characterised as a rather multi-generic discipline that mixed methods and schools and focused above all on determining the pronoun's reference. This paradoxical attempt is in vain, however, because it contradicts the shifting nature of reference made possible by the pronoun. Recent views also tend to search for ways in which to apply existing theory; as a result, new theories tend to propose neologisms rather than produce fresh, innovative and more elaborate readings of the texts themselves. Despite these problems and potential flaws, this project appreciates the conclusions drawn in theory so far, expanding on them in order to enhance an understanding of the second-person narrative technique and present it in the most precise and enlightening way.

Monika Fludernik combines aspects of the theories of Stanzel and Genette and develops her own account of second-person storytelling. She radicalises the dichotomy between *homodiegetic* and *heterodiegetic* fiction (Genette), complicates the (non)-coincidence of the realms of existence between narrator and narratee (Stanzel), and finally proposes mapping the area of narrative *you*-s by expanding them from a narratological object of study to a communicational one. Her approach may be seen as an attempt at bridging the two incompatible methodologies of Genette and Stanzel.

Fludernik's observations on second-person narrative are based on the transgressive case of Italo Calvino's *Se una notte d'inverno un viaggiatore* but they refer also, among other texts, to Ilse Ai-

9 | Monika Fludernik, *Erzähltheorie: eine Einführung.* (Darmstadt: WBG, Wissenschaftliche Buchgesellschaft, 2010) 42f.

chinger's experimental *Spiegelgeschichte.* Fludernik classifies both texts as experimental narratives of postmodern literature (*Experimente mit Personalpronomina in postmoderner Literatur*), the sense of which isn't restricted to the fictional use of the second-person pronoun but includes other pronouns (used even less frequently) as well. After acknowledging the morphological diversity of the second person, Fludernik's major contribution is her insight that the second person should be regarded as a territory in which to expect not only second-person grammatical forms. Her argument regarding second-person variants and equivalents echoes a grammatical approach that will be discussed later and that is based on languages such as German and Italian where second-person forms can be substituted in function by other pronominal forms like *Sie* or *Lei*. It also implies the understanding of the second-person storytelling technique in a broader sense than as a grammatical phenomenon emphasising more its properties and characteristics.

Nevertheless address remains the central irreplaceable characteristic constituent of so-called second person fiction. The term second person fiction in fact needs to be revealed as a misnomer of major proportions. What is called second person fiction does not in any way have to employ a second person pronoun in reference to the protagonist. What it needs to employ is a pronoun of address, and in some languages such a pronoun can be in the third person (e.g. the German "polite" Sie, a third person plural form, or the Italian Lei, a third person singular). [...] The addressee function of the pronoun is crucial in structuring the make-up of second person fiction because it combines a "conative" (Jakobson 1958) level of address, there must be an addressor, an I (implicit or explicit), and hence a narrator, and this narrator can be a mere enunciator or also a protagonist sharing the *you*'s fictional existence on the story level.[10]

10 | Monika Fludernik, "Second Person Fiction: Narrative You as Addressee And/Or Protagonist". In *Arbeiten aus Anglistik und Amerikanistik* 18/2 (1993) 219.

Fludernik classifies second-person fiction cases in three groups according to the function of address: first, "explicit address *you* or means of imperatives;" second, "the addressee as actant," where the addressee is an intradiegetic narratee though not as in the Genettian metaleptic mode; and third, "the non-address function," where the second person appears in reference to a fictional protagonist, designating a narrator divorced from the fictional *you*, described by Stanzel as a reflector narrative situation in the second person where the sense of an experiencing self dominates.[11] Fludernik refuses the metaleptic function of the pronoun, at least in its Genettian sense in the second class of second-person texts, with the argument that it signals a situation of verisimilar identity between the addressed *you* and the protagonist *you*.

Apparently, her ideas relate more closely to the teller and reflector dichotomy that Stanzel introduced, indicating that the communicative level of the function of address is more dominant in second-person fiction than any other. Consequently, according to Fludernik, the narrative *you* can function precisely like a narrative *I* or *he/she* in the reflector-(al) mode, whereas in the teller mode *you*, the protagonist can have a similar relationship with the addressee as is the case in traditional first-person (*homodiegetic*) narratives.

In order to overcome possible overlaps in terminology Monika Fludernik, expanding on Genette, introduces the terms *homocommunicative* and *heterocommunicative* to depict the relationship between story and level of communication in fiction, arranging the categories accordingly as central or peripheral depending on the grade of involvement that narrators and addressees have in the narrated stories.[12] A flaw in Fludernik's mapping model arises from the sorting out of the narrative examples, because many of the case examples fail to qualify as *pure* second-person narratives. Rather, they depict types of pseudo-oral narratives, involving characters that are partially produced and originated by *apostrophe*.

11 | Fludernik (1993), 220f.

12 | Fludernik (1993), 223f.

It appears also that the process of inventing slots for these "special" cases to fit into her theory leads to an excessive map of *homocommunicative* and *heterocommunicative* narratives, which could be significantly reduced.[13] Her account is further unsettled by the fact that not all second-person narratives should be thought of as experimental; Fludernik's theory is selective and fails to cover all second-person texts. As an example, apart from experimental examples, second-person narratives may also present common, linear plots, for example in autobiographies or other non-metatextual narratives with an ordinary and familiar structure.[14]

Irene Kacandes, the second major second-person theorist, introduces the term "talk fiction" and emphasises the apostrophe rhetoric of second-person storytelling. She contributes to the theorisation of second-person narratives with complementary observations deriving from other socially-oriented disciplines such as psychology. Kacandes connects talk-fiction with trauma and "narrative memory" inscribed in the language of testimony. Consequently, narratives in her theory are seen as "statements" depicting past experiences with which the subjects of thought are dealing. Important is the fact that she recognises the process of distancing as key to understanding the use of the second person in autobiography since it enables this productive interaction with the past. What Kacandes calls "intrapsychic witnessing," referring to a form of self-talk where the character acts as witness to his or her own experience, provides a particularly elucidating reading strategy for second-person autobiographies or autobiographical narratives involving traumatic experiences.[15]

13 | Rolf Reitan, "Theorizing Second-Person Narratives: A Backwater Project?". In *Strange Voices in Narrative Fiction.* Eds. Per Krogh Hansen, Stefan Iversen, Henrik Skov Nielsen and Rolf Reitan. (Berlin: De Gruyter, 2011) 152-154.

14 | Fludernik (2010), 43.

15 | Irene Kacandes, *Talk Fiction: Literature and the Talk Explosion (Frontiers of Narrative).* (Lincoln and London: University of Nebraska Press, 2001) 97.

Kacandes discusses Christa Wolf's *Kindheitsmuster* in detail, a key text for the study of the second-person technique in this project. However, she emphasises a psychological rather than a narratological or poetic perspective as she interprets the employment of the second-person technique as part of the healing process, in this case when dealing with a guilty past:

> These novels concern themselves with the stage directly prior to witnessing to trauma, prior to the creation of the story of what happened to the self, when the mind heals by consciously incorporating the traumatic memory into existing mental schemas [...] reader co-witnesses deduce the infliction of trauma by the main evidence of the unintegrated psyche of the respective protagonists. The overwhelming task of integrating the self is at heart of Christa Wolf's *Patterns of Childhood.* [...] The interrogative self who is trying to figure out the relationship of her adult self to the child's psyche is addressed directly as "you". [...] To be a *Mensch* would be to be able to remember, to be able to conduct a dialogue by creating an interlocutor, a "you" with whom to witness to what happened.[16]

Such an approach is very focused on the theme of the War and the traumatic past and it could not apply to other texts, not to mention the fact that it doesn't suggest a rhetoric or narratological analysis on the text itself, though it is based on the way the author uses the pronouns. Brian Richardson, the third major second-person theorist, labels second-person texts in storytelling "unnatural voices." He defines "pure" second-person fiction (with protagonists completely designated by the second-person pronoun) and classifies it further into three groups involving standard, hypothetical/subjunctive and autotelic forms.[17]

---

16 | Kacandes (2001), 101.

17 | Brian Richardson, *Unnatural Voices: Extreme Narration in Modern and Contemporary Fiction.* (Columbus: The Ohio University Press, 2006) 18.

Standard second person narration oscillates between third and first person perspectives, with each narrative usually settling toward one or the other, while repeatedly if briefly seeming to include the reader as the object of the discourse. Hypothetical second person texts fuse a heterodiegetic depiction of an ever more specific individual with an imagined future of the reader, thus merging a third person perspective with a hypothetical "you" that is the virtual equivalent of "one". Autotelic texts have the greatest share of direct address to the actual reader and superimpose this onto a fictional character designated by "you" that tends to be treated from an external perspective as if in the third person. This intensifies one of the most fascinating features of second person narrative: the way the narrative "you" is alternately opposed to and fused with the reader - both the contracted and the actual reader.[18]

Richardson succeeds in theorising second-person texts without delegating them to sub-cases of the other two pronouns, acknowledging the uniqueness of the form which for him can be described as "playful ... transgressive, and illuminating," "always conscious of its unusual own status and often disguis[ing] itself, playing on the boundaries of other narrative voices."[19] Richardson's method of mapping narrative cases distinguishes the narrative examples from other second-person narratives that employ the pronoun only at the level of narration. His method is inductive and informative though based on delimiting the field and emphasising any deviations he observed, always classifying the cases starting from a structural/ pronominal interpretation of the second-person pronoun.[20]

It should be noted that my account enumerates tendencies rather than stipulates invariant conditions; this is because second person narration is an extremely protean form, and its very essence is to eschew a fixed essence.[21]

18 | Richardson (2006), 32f.

19 | Richardson (2006), 23.

20 | Reitan (2011), 151.

21 | Richardson (2006), 19.

Richardson's labelling of second-person narrative as "unnatural" in contrast to so-called "natural" narratives is disturbing. He claims that the employment of the second person "defamiliarizes"[22] the narrative whereas arguably the very opposite happens: second-person address evokes an oral, everyday, familiar tone in the discourse and therefore functions more likely as a hypnotising voice. Richardson's evaluation could be considered as supporting an argument that second-person narrative employment is a popular ploy. Such an implication is unfair to the literary properties of second-person narratives and is completely contrary to the perspective adopted by the present project which attempts to show how "natural" and fundamental this narrative mode is for certain literary occasions.

Building on the groundwork of traditional and post-traditional theorists, increasing numbers of readings of second-person fictions have been undertaken; they form a palimpsest of ideas and testify to the long-lasting discussion of the enigma of the second person in the field of literature and narratology. Other theorists like Steven Cohan and Linda Shires refer only to specific novels when discussing second-person narratives in their theoretical analyses of narrative fiction. Cohan and Shires use Calvino's second-person novel to expose "the limitations of classifying agents according to pronouns, for [– as they argue –] pronouns in narration refer for their antecedents to the characters performing the action being narrated," avoiding any generic overview of the technique.[23]

The fact that theory fails to reflect the evolution and continuous presence of the phenomenon in the history of literature or its significant appearances in non-epic forms such as the *lyrisches du* in poetry and the *monologue* in drama, led the project to a more inductive approach that aspires to drawing concepts and conclusions on second-person storytelling based on its primary sources, the texts themselves. Starting from an understanding of the fundamentals of

22 | Richardson (2006), 28.

23 | Steven Cohan and Linda M. Shires, *Telling Stories: A Theoretical Analysis of Narrative Fiction.* (London and New York: Routledge, 1998) 92.

grammar (person/pronoun), rhetoric and storytelling, this project aims to show how second-person narrative has developed over time and it introduces some of its qualities that appear consistently through time and that define the technique.

Acknowledging the above is a vital point that is missing from narratological and second-person research. Monika Fludernik is the only exception; she has dealt with the second-person narrative form extensively, taking into account the history of second-person storytelling and forming a theoretical model. Though the latter is problematic, it represents a significant contribution to the matter. Furthermore, in terms of studies and research, scholars have treated the second-person phenomenon mostly from a linguistic point of view, as a secondary feature in studies focussing on other topics or on the authors' work as a whole, or as a case study in studies focussing on single authors and works. This project aims to contribute to the present state of research and, by further reviewing the case studies, provide assumptions and conclusions that would benefit the discussion of second-person storytelling as a whole in narratology.

The enigma of second-person storytelling will not be solved in this project. This would be impossible given its resilience and versatility as expressed in different narratives. However, it will be better understood in terms of its appealing and intriguing aspects that make readers love or hate it and authors use it almost always only once.

Person

To understand the essentials of the second-person narrative technique and its dynamics, we first need to focus on the fundamental category of *person*. We thus aim to clarify its grammatical meaning and reference, and we aspire to conclude which aspect of the person is dominant. Does second-person storytelling reflect the grammatical choice of composing a text using second-person grammatical forms or does it rather reflect a certain nominal reference and the concept of address?

Linguists define *person* as a deictic category, interpreted relative to the speaker and encoding the participants in a speech situation. The cognitive foundation of *person* reflects the basic structure of a speech act and distinguishes the participants – the speaker and the addressee – and what is spoken about.[24] Fundamentally, the second person reflects the role of the addressee and it is reflected in the utterance not only by way of the second-person pronominal form (*you*) but also by the verbal form (*are*).

What **are** *you* doing?
I am reading a book.

An important observation to add here is that in terms of reference and meaning the person designated as the *you*-addressee in the first sentence shifts to the role of the *I*-speaker in the second. This shows that while the grammatical role of the (second) person is concrete in the utterance, the person of reference shifts together with the input-output system of the utterance.

The category of *person* has to be expressed linguistically through morphology in order to be considered a feature, be it morpho-syntactic or morpho-semantic. Investigation of morpho-syntactic expressions of person reveals that languages with personal inflection differ greatly with respect to which and how many of the available person values are expressed in a single predication. The choice of the expression of the person value – how the person is referred to within the communication stream – may be determined by the relative position of the participant in a person hierarchy. One possible hierarchy of this type has been formulated as follows and it reflects the speaker-addressee or absent person classification:

$1^{st}/2^{nd}$ person > 3rd person

24 | Benveniste (1966), 227f.

A person hierarchy captures the fact that participants can be referred to by person values independently of their semantic or syntactic status. However, the person-based reference to arguments in a clause can also be controlled by syntactic functions that are directly associated with grammar and grammatical rules:

Subject > Direct Object > Indirect Object

or semantic roles:

Agent > Recipient/Experiencer > Patient

This is important when we are confronted with different roles and positions that the second person employs within a narrative, especially in cases where the elevated style of the author and the poetics of the text make for a discourse of structural depth, rich in rhetoric.

The (cognitive) category of *person* exists in a language if it is possible to make a distinction between at least two of the basic principles/participants in a speech act. In languages with a declined verbal system the morpho-syntactic feature of person reflects the grammaticalisation ("sous des *personae* se réalise la notion verbale"[25]) of the category of person in the language, as we have seen in the previous example with the change of the verb from *are* to *am* according to the person *you* and *I*.[26]

Consequently, when referring to the category of person, questions of dominance or emphasis arise: "peut-il exister un verbe sans distinction de personne?"[27]; is the person rather a marker of hierarchy and position in a speech act or is it more a category that

25 | Benveniste (1966), 225.

26 | "Dans toutes les langues qui possèdent un verbe, on classe les formes de la conjugaison d'après leur référence à la personne, l'énumération des personnes constituant proprement la conjugaison; et on en distingue trois, au singulier, au pluriel, éventuellement au duel." Benveniste (1966), 225.

27 | Benveniste (1966), 226.

reflects grammatical values and rules? Therefore, given our interest in second-person narrative, we might ask whether the choice of the second-person pronoun as the main narrative agent would reflect a *variant* personal reference (shifting continuously in a dialogue) rather than *a certain verbal function* that highlights the concept of address itself or maybe both, and if so – what would be the emphasis in each use?

In addition to this ambiguity, there is an analytical problem arising for the category of person, one that comes from the involvement of each person in participant groups associated with the speech act. The category of person can contain a plurality of positions. Within the speech act, there is an inclusive/exclusive distinction (typically applied with regard to the first person that designates the speaker) and a proximate/obviate distinction (typically applied with regard to the third person that designates the *non-person* of the speech act). While the inclusive/exclusive distinction is typically defined as expressing the inclusion of the addressee in the first person, the proximate/obviate distinction concerns the degree of remoteness of the non-participant.

It is worth considering how both distinctions can be applied to the second person, where no such distinction can be determined for definite. By designating the addressee role within the speech act, the second person can take on all possible syntactic and semantic roles. It serves more precisely as a placeholder within the speech situation, fulfilling a role (that of the hearer/the addressee) in which the participants will be switching according to the natural needs of communication. Hence one could argue that the person category within the speech act is more of a position or role in speech, one which the participants exchange during the act of communication – hence its appearance comes more as a grammatical reference rather than a nominal one (an actual reference to a *person*), since that is ambiguous and changes between the persons involved in the speech act.

What are *you* doing?
I am reading a book, what about *you*?

In terms of the involvement of a distinction between "you-excluding-them" and "you-including-them" a logical contradiction exists since in the case of the second person the standard definition of inclusive/exclusive as either involving the addressee or not is not determined. Given the fact that the addressee, the second person, can be both inclusive and exclusive on different occasions as well as both proximate or obviate in relation to the object of the speech act, we understand why dichotomous approaches of any kind or discipline are not applicable in the case of the second person.

An interesting alternative approach to the category of person is offered by Anna Kibort. She presents in her work another possibility for the second person, namely that of a general concept involving the degree of remoteness relative to a speech act participant according to which the person reflects the meeting of these two poles in a more generalised concept. In this view, the separation between inclusive/exclusive can be understood as the "intersection" of the second person, just as the proximate/obviate may be seen as the intersection of the third person.[28]

The notion of relative involvement (distance) that Kibort introduces in her study of the category of person is significant for the current approach as it introduces an additional element linked to the use of pronouns in narratives. If the first person is considered *too close* and the third person *too distant*, the second person is the one that reflects a moderate degree of distance in the speech act, an "intersection". This concept of a gradation of distance and of the levels of involvement in the narrative is essential for an understanding of second-person storytelling and will be discussed later and in more detail.

The expression of the person contrary to its system, which normally involves three grammatical persons and two numbers, is more complicated since it is more abstract and diverse and reflects

28 | Anna Kibort, *Grammatical Features Inventory: Person.* (University of Surrey, 2008) Date accessed 21 September 2017. http://dx.doi.org/10.15126/SMG.18/1.03.

relationships and associations between the three. This will now be discussed with reference to the category of the pronoun.

PRONOUN[29]

Personal reference can be expressed in various ways: depending on the occasion it is possible to refer both to oneself and to one's addressee using common nominal phrases, nouns and, of course, pronouns. Hence pronouns are one of the means of expressing the category of the person and the participants in a speech act.

Nouns and nominal phrases define the person descriptively while verbs reflect it formally in their conjugation and number; in the case of pronouns, however, the expression of person is more complicated. Pronouns mainly serve to replace (previously or later mentioned) names or nouns and are used in the interest of the economy[30]of the text[31] often by helping the author to avoid the repetition

29 | "Pronom, empr. du lat. pronomen, de pro, à la place de, et nomen, nom. Cette dénomination de pronom, qui nous vient des Latins, lesquels l'avaient empruntée aux Grecs (αντωνυμία), n'est pas adéquate à son objet; elle se trouve en contradiction avec les enseignements de linguistes éminents: "L'espèce de mot qui a dû se distinguer d'abord de toutes les autres, écrit M. Bréal, c'est, selon nous, le pronom." Je crois cette catégorie plus primitive que celle du substantif." Maurice Grevisse, *Le Bon Usage. Grammaire française avec des remarques sur la langue française d'aujourd'hui.* 1936. (Gembloux: Éditions J. Duculot, 1975) 448.

30 | "Die Pronomen tragen wesentlich zur Ökonomie der Sprache, d.h. zum sparsamen Gebrauch der sprachlichen Mittel, bei, indem sie unnötige Wiederholungen nicht nur vermeiden helfen, sondern häufig sogar unterbinden." Günther Drosdowski, *Duden: Grammatik der deutschen Gegenwartssprache.* (Mannheim: Dudenverlag, 1995) 326.

31 | "Le pronom est un mot qui souvent représente un nom, un adjectif, une idée ou une proposition exprimés avant ou après lui." Grevisse (1936/1975), 448.

or declaration of the subject. Operating in the discourse as a noun substitute, the pronoun can fulfil all its possible functions,[32] but the fact that it can appear in the text additionally or indirectly by other indicators or text markers also proves that a pronoun can involve information or textual elements that a noun cannot.[33] Therefore, the way a pronoun functions primarily in a discourse defines its grammatical classification.

Likewise, we have reflexive pronouns, personal pronouns, demonstrative pronouns, possessive pronouns and so on; the second person designating a personal reference belongs to the largest category, that of the personal pronouns, hence it is associated with the paradigm of person as mentioned in the previous section. The fact that the person reflects a certain role in the speech act affects the second-person pronoun as well as it is associated more with the role of the addressee inherent in the second person than a specific non-altering actual person.

Additional uses and functions of pronouns, apart from those already listed and classified, may vary, designating, among other

---

32 | "Pronouns are a closed class of words. Pronouns may substitute for or stand for the references to entities which full noun phrases make. [...] The interpretation of the meaning of individual pronouns depends heavily on the context in which they occur. Like nouns, pronouns can act as the heads of noun phrases and function as subject, object or complement of the clause, or as the complement of a proposition." Ronald Carter and Michael McCarthy, *Cambridge Grammar of English: A Comprehensive Guide: Spoken and Written English Grammar and Usage.* (Cambridge: Cambridge University Press, 2006) 375.

33 | "Le pronom est parfois employé absolument: il ne représente alors aucun mot, aucun adjectif, aucune idée, aucune proposition exprimée, et c'est improprement qu'il est appelé "pronom": l'appellation qui lui convient est celle de nominal." Grevisse (1936/1975), 448.

things, distance expressed as politeness/modesty,[34] impersonal/ collective entities[35]or even generic notional categories like those of generic person (French *on*) or gender (*who, they*).[36] Pronouns suggest a closed category of words;[37] as a class they tend towards reduction and never the other way round. Still, we rarely acknowledge the social and political implications of roles and stances that this evolvement of reduction really entails. To this extent, understanding second-person pronouns may be a process connected not only to canonised systems of grammar and syntax, but as briefly mentioned before, it should also include observations related to the richness of rhetoric that reflect social connotations and move beyond simple denotation.

Many determining factors of pronouns are shared with other nominal units such as rank, number, case or person while they may have similar syntactic functions; they are well understood as indicators, requiring contextual identification in order to acquire full meaning.[38] The presence of pronouns in the speech act may also be indirect and implied by other contextual elements such as the presence of a sub-noun or the functionality of a co-noun or may even be hidden. For example, in languages that decline their verbal units there may be no pronoun at all, as it is understood and inherent in

34 | "Quoique représentant un nom singulier, le pronom se met parfois au pluriel, selon l'usage du pluriel de majesté, de politesse ou de modestie." Grevisse (1936/1975), 451.

35 | "Le pronom représentant un mot collectif (ou générique) singulier s'accorde parfois, par syllepse du nombre, non pas avec ce nom, mais avec le nom pluriel suggéré par lui." Grevisse (1936/1975), 451.

36 | Otto Jespersen, *Selected Writings of Otto Jespersen*. (London: George Allen and Unwin Ltd, 1962) 516.

37 | "Die Pronomen haben einen Bestand von ungefähr 100 Wörtern. Dieser Bestand vermehrt sich kaum; er verringert sich eher, da einige Pronomen als veraltet empfunden und daher nur noch selten gebraucht werden." Drosdowski (1995), 326.

38 | Carter and McCarthy (2006), 375.

the ending of the verb.[39] Or when we use imperatives, second-person pronouns are not required and can be omitted since they are the only pronouns applicable to the verbal form; the same happens in the case of direct, face-to-face communication, where pronouns are omitted for profound reasons of necessity as the participants are in direct communication hence, often enough, the imperative is preferred to the indicative.

The location and frequency of pronouns in oral and written communication is different; more precisely the second person associated with direct communication and dialogue is more often omitted in non-mediated forms of the speech act, so when it is present in written form, it adds to a sense of contemporaneity and actuality.

To understand the impact of employing the second-person narrative technique in a given discourse we need to focus on why it was chosen over other options, i.e. the first- or third-person pronouns. Understanding the second-person narrative technique depends on understanding the relationship between the three pronouns available including their connotations. Benveniste discussed this in his *Problèmes de linguistique générale* from a linguistic point of view:

Dans les deux premières personnes, il y a à la fois une personne impliquée et un discours sur cette personne. "Je" désigne celui qui parle et implique en même temps un énoncé sur le compte de "je": disant "je", je ne puis ne pas parler de moi. À la 2e personne, "tu" est nécessairement désigné par "je" et ne peut être pensé hors d'une situation posée à partir de "je"; et, en même temps, "je" énonce quelque chose comme prédicat de "tu". Mais de la 3e personne, un prédicat est bien énoncé, seulement hors du "je-tu"; cette forme est ainsi exceptée de la relation par laquelle "je" et "tu" se spé-

39 | "Sometimes the subject is not expressed: Thank you! Confound it! Etc., and even more the subject may be left out (by "prosiopesis", an expression which however is not used in "Essentials"): (Have you) got a match? (I shall) see you again tomorrow. Very often a sentence consists only of a predicative: Splendid! How annoying!" Jespersen (1962), 501.

cifient. Dès lors, la légitimité de cette forme comme "personne" se trouve mise en question. [...]
La conséquence doit être formulée nettement: la "3e personne" n'est pas une "personne"; c'est même la forme verbale qui a pour fonction d'exprimer la *non-personne*.[40]

Benveniste argues that the second-person pronoun is dependent on the first and cannot be validly isolated from it because both pronouns reflect specific pre-conditioning roles within communication that are themselves interdependent. The two first personal pronouns reflect participation in the speech act and they stand in a closer relationship of interchange, whereas the third person that signifies the total opposite, the absent agent from this speech act, is actually their negation and could also be understood as the *non-person* pronoun.

On voit maintenant en quoi consiste l'opposition entre les deux premières personnes du verbe et la troisième. Elles s'opposent comme les membres d'une corrélation, qui est la corrélation de personnalité: "je-tu" possède la marque de personne; "il" en est privé:[41]

The first and second person function as personal role markers in the context and scheme in which they are involved, building a relationship of reversibility since an exchange of roles is expected for the continuity of the speech act: speakers become addressees and the other way round. Given that people actually interchange the positions of first- and second-person pronouns for the corresponding roles in the speech act, second person and first person are interchangeable in terms of the person they mark but not in the role they stand for, functioning as placeholders in the text that may apply to different people at different times.[42] However, it is also relevant that different people are associated with different degrees of depth:

40 | Benveniste (1966), 228.

41 | Benveniste (1966), 231.

42 | Benveniste (1966), 230.

whereas the first person stands for the authorial *I*, the second person can reflect depersonalised and generic instances (narrative entities) as well.[43] The ability of the second person to reflect more than one addressee simultaneously is reflected in the rhetoric of apostrophe, which enables the shifting in a given discourse between different referents of *you*. This will be analysed in more detail later in the chapter on rhetoric.

Therefore, it is widely used in articles and advertising texts and can suggest a certain social proximity as well as being appropriate for certain social circumstances when used, for example, in the polite form.

La définition de la 2e personne comme étant la personne à laquelle la première s'adresse convient sans doute à son emploi le plus ordinaire. Mais ordinaire ne veut pas dire unique et constant. On peut utiliser la 2e personne hors de l'allocution et la faire entrer dans une variété d'impersonnel. Par exemple "vous" fonctionne en français comme anaphorique de "on" [...] En mainte langue, *tu (vous)* sert de substitut à *on* [...] Il faut et il suffit qu'on se représente une *personne* autre que "je" pour qu'on lui affecte l'indice "tu", tout particulièrement - mais non nécessairement - la personne interpellée. Le "tu" ("vous") peut donc se définir: "le personne non-*je*".[44]

Apart from the correlation of person, the two first pronouns signify a certain gradation in subjectivity. Within the speech act, the referent using the first person opens up and gestures towards the referent, who is positioned in the role of second-person communication. This process of transcendence is linked to a process of objectifying the subjectivity of what is communicated from one to the other; it

43 | "*You* refers most frequently to the immediate addressee(s). But it can also refer more generally to any potential listener(s) or reader(s). This is especially so in advertising texts and public notices. *You* can also have generic reference (to people in general, including the speaker/writer." Carter and McCarthy (2006), 377.

44 | Benveniste (1966), 232.

connotes, in other words, the interchange from the *personne-je* to the *personne-non-je,* who, by being external to that which is narrated, suggests a filter of objectivity.[45] This forms an input/output relationship fundamental to the dialogue and essential for its value and benefit to the interlocutors, as the ideas being discussed are formed and shaped cooperatively by both agents.

Au couple je/tu appartient en propre une corrélation spéciale, que nous appellerons, faute de mieux, corrélation de subjectivité. Ce qui différencie "je" de "tu", c'est d'abord le fait d'être. Dans le cas de "je", intérieur à l'énoncé et extérieur à "tu", mais extérieur d'une manière qui ne supprime pas la réalité humaine du dialogue. [...] [E]n outre, "je" est toujours transcendant par rapport à "tu". [...] Ces qualités d'intériorité et de transcendance appartiennent en propre au "je" et s'inversent en "tu". On pourra donc définir le "tu" comme le personne non-subjective, en face de la personne subjective que "je" représente; et ces deux "personnes" s'opposeront ensemble à la forme de "non-personne" (="il").[46]

The third person doesn't participate in this opposition of subjectivity and non-subjectivity (objectivity) that the first and the second person share since it reflects the *non-person* and acquires no attributes of this kind. Being anchored together, context-dependent and designating actuality and temporal synchronisation, the first two pronouns form a system of direct communication that cannot be experienced or shared by a third-person agent that designates the absence of personal, temporal or spatial determination. Moreover, this process of transcendence and interchangeability is linked to a general sense of ambiguity and lack of determination and specification. Suggesting the addressee, in a communicated discourse irrespective of the different persons adopting the role, the second person acquires an indefinite sense, designating the non-first-person to which the always fixed and determined *I* gestures.

45 | Benveniste (1966), 232.
46 | Benveniste (1966), 232.

Placeholders and relationship or role marker pronouns function as deictic forms and they enable shifting references to different extra-linguistic entities particular to each communicational setting. This shifting quality explains why Jakobson labelled the pronouns "shifters," after Jespersen.

Any linguistic code contains a particular class of grammatical units, which Jespersen labelled SHIFTERS: the general meaning of a shifter cannot be defined without a reference to the message.[47]

Shifters are considered grammatical units, which are contained in linguistic codes and cannot be understood without reference to the message. Combining both functions of representation and index, they belong to the class of "indexical symbols" according to Jakobson.[48] Although some might argue that the shifting character of pronouns may result in a disastrous lack of consistent, specific meaning, making the communication weaker and less successful, Jakobson maintains that pronouns do have a general meaning which is, however, met only in context, in actual existential relation between the speaker and the hearer participating in the utterance.

The inherent interchangeability that pronouns incorporate and presuppose results in a shifting dynamic of reference. This dynamic in the literary paradigm is associated with the rhetoric of apostrophe in its classic sense and it allows not only for narrative duplicity and added depth but also for ambiguity and openness with reference to an addressee. This lack of reference-determination also justifies in part the pronoun's obscurity as an object of research. These undefined and ambiguous reference shifters make a given message different from any other constituent of the linguistic code.[49] An additional quality of pronouns which determines their shifting nature

47 | Roman Jakobson, *Russian and Slavic Grammar. Studies 1931-1981.* (Berlin, New York, Amsterdam: Mouton Publishers, 1984) 42.

48 | Jakobson (1984), 42f.

49 | Jakobson (1984), 43.

is their efficiency, which relies on the paradox of amplification the more reduced their semantic depth is. Put differently, the less information they reveal about their referents, the more accomplished their shifting role.[50]

The key to understanding the second-person pronoun reference and function lies in its relationship to the first-person pronoun. The transformation of the *I* and its transition to a *you* builds a scheme that derives from the roles the pronouns have in the speech act and by their lack of determination in terms of reference as lexical placeholders. When exposing oneself to a *you*, the exposure to the other alters the perspective from the personal and internal to the external and more objective second-person perspective. Such a need of a different perspective that allows a certain distance from the narrated without, however, alienating the person from it, is vital to the poetics of second-person storytelling. It is reflected as *prosopopoeia* in the rhetoric of the text and expresses certain conditions where the continuity and authority of the *I* are challenged.

A good example of what is outlined above is offered by Jim Grimsley's childhood memoir *Winter Birds* (1994), which is written from various narrative perspectives including the second person:

> Today is Thanksgiving and you are freed from school. You can lie in your bed of honeysuckle vine and dream all day beside the river. Walking there, you hug yourself with thin arms, your dark hair blown by the wind. Overhead the branches sway back and forth.[51]

The narrator (the authorial *I*) uses the second person to narrate his boyhood traumatic past, personified by little Danny (who, by the time he is named, has transcended into the third person). *Winter Birds* turned out to be a successful publication but as the author

50 | Beata Stawarska, *Between You and I. Dialogical Phenomenology.* (Athens: Ohio University Press, 2009) 62.

51 | Jim Grimsley, *Winter Birds*. 1984. (Chapel Hill: Algonquin Books, 1994) 6.

comments in a personal communication: "... making the decision to keep *Winter Birds* in the second person was very difficult;"[52] he describes the process of writing the book in the second person as quite challenging both in terms of composition and in terms of getting published and argues that the choice of the second person actually was what established his autobiographical relationship to the protagonist (Danny) and to his book.

I tried three different versions of *Winter Birds*; the first two were in first person and third person, though I forget the order in which I tried them. **The first person version felt false because I was writing as if I were still that age in that family; it put me too far inside the pain of the story. The third person version felt false because it imposed too much distance between the narrative and me.** Since I was writing an autobiographical story, I felt I needed the form of the book to acknowledge my personal connection to Danny.
The third version eventually became the published book**; I tried the second person and found that it had the right voice, and embodied the true connection between writer and material.** I felt as if I were telling the story to myself at the age of eight. It was also in this story that I settled on the idea of confining the book to the Thanksgiving holiday.
In short, **the second person acknowledged the autobiographical nature of the relationship between me, as the author, and Danny as the protagonist, and that's why the book finally worked.** This decision cost me some years in terms of finding a publisher, however; very few publishers were comfortable with a book written in the second person.
I would like to use that point of view again, but I'm not sure where. *Dream Boy*, my second novel, would have worked well in this point of view.[53]

52 | Jim Grimsley, "The second person employment in *Winter Birds*." Email to Evgenia Iliopoulou, 10 October 2014.

53 | Jim Grimsley, "The second person employment in *Winter Birds*." Email to Evgenia Iliopoulou, 10 October 2014.

What Grimsley describes above is key to an understanding of second-person narrative technique and the reasons it is preferred on certain narrative occasions. Grimsley explains that it was ideal for expressing his autobiographical relationship to Danny as it also secured the distance created by the time that had passed, thus avoiding both the proximity of the first person and the alienation of the third.

Moreover, Grimsley emphasises the way autobiographical writing and second-person narrative perspective are related to each other, and he states that he could also have used the second-person perspective for his second semi-/pseudo-autobiographical novel *Dream Boy*. The author's statement implies that second person might be more appropriate in (certain) autobiographical writing. The phenomenon apparently derives from the fact that the second person reflects the aforementioned middle distance from the narrated, and hence it is linked to autobiography, in cases where a semi-distant/semi-close approach to the narrated is desired. Taking also into account the frequent appearance of second-person autobiographical narratives in general, the association of autobiography with second-person storytelling appears to be an aspect of the technique that needs to be discussed in detail, also in view of the concept of self and always in comparison with the other pronouns.

This observation is closely connected to a different concept of the self, namely to the perspective of the *Other*. Levinas and Clarkson have discussed this point in detail. Influenced by and expanding on Levinas' thoughts on the pronominal depiction of the *Other*, Clarkson claims that the second person is the most appropriate choice (instead of the third person) to reflect it. To think of the *Other* as *you* is a step forward from Levinas' thinking. To do so suggests that this *Other*, in a grammatical sense, is closer to the second person as an opposition to our *I* and it is to understand the *Other* as the non-*I* rather than as a person outside the context of our ego. For Clarkson, this dynamic efficiency occurs not just because of the *I-you* polar structure but more so because of the infinite (ceaseless) encounter with the actual shifting *you* at the cultural (real) level.[54] What Clarkson cleverly points out is the fact that the relationship between speech and narrated event fulfils the condition of the *Saying* as stated by Levinas – "the relation proceeding from me to the other"[55] – though he insisted on the third person being the encounter of the invocation rather than the second.[56]

This association of the second person with the indefinite *Other* – the counter pole – reflects ambiguity and openness in the narrative and explains further the frequent use of the second-person narrative technique in autobiography. This phenomenon will be discussed in more detail later based on the narrative examples of Christa Wolf's *Kindheitsmuster* and Ilse Aichinger's *Spiegelgeschichte.* The second person serves as a voice of objectivity and authenticity and reflects the aspiration to improve and amplify self-awareness. By exposing or articulating the autobiographical – traditionally – first-person story in the second person, a persona is made out of the authorial *I* that can be better analysed and observed from a distance, thus confirming the unreliability of memory and the transformation of the self in time.

This change of perspective even within the self and the focussing on the perspective of others as a depiction of the not-self is a common theme not only in second-person autobiographies and storytelling but also was radically thematised by Jean-Paul Sartre in *Huis Clos (No Exit)*, a play that tells the story of four individuals trapped in the hell of the other characters' exclusive views, and that is in the second-person perspective. The characters of Sartre's play are not able or allowed after death to access the first-person perspective so as to see themselves in a mirror, hence they are sentenced to experience their perception of their selves only from the second-person

54 | Carrol Clarkson, "Embodying 'you:' Lévinas and a Question of the Second Person." In *Journal of Literary Semantics* 34/2 (2005) 95.

55 | Emmanuel Levinas, *Totality and Infinity: An Essay on Exteriority.* Trans. Alphonso Lingis. (Dordrecht, Kluwer Academic Publishers, 1991) 121.

56 | Clarkson (2005), 99.

point of view, the angle of the others, those who are trapped with them in the same room. What is described as an extreme state of agony and torture is what characters and narrators of the texts discussed in the project have to deal with deliberately so as to restore the past image, the relationship with their selves and self-awareness.

Le bronze... (Il le caresse.) Eh bien, voici le moment. Le bronze est là, je le contemple et je comprends que je suis en enfer. Je vous dis que tout était prévu. Ils avaient prévu que je me tiendrais devant cette cheminée, pressant ma main sur ce bronze, avec tous ces regards sur moi. Tous ces regards qui me mangent ... (Il se retourne brusquement.) Ha! vous n'êtes que deux? Je vous croyais beaucoup plus nombreuses. (Il rit.) Alors, c'est ça l'enfer. Je n'aurais jamais cru ... Vous vous rappelez: le soufre, le bûcher, le gril ... Ah! quelle plaisanterie. Pas besoin de gril: l'enfer, c'est les Autres.[57]

A last comment on the pronouns concerns the variations they show within the different language systems. For example in Modern English the second person pronoun has one form, *you*, used everywhere for singular and plural reference, moreover it does not have different forms for the nominative and the accusative case but has the same for both. The lack of singular/plural distinction in the use of the second person sometimes makes for ambiguity, especially taking into account the fact that second person can also be used to refer to people in general, like *du* in German or *vous* in French. In such cases the use of the second person deflects attention from the actual addressee of the utterance, and makes the reference non-specific and open-ended. Like the generic pronoun *one*,[58] *man* in German and *on* in French, it projects a third-person referent. The

57 | Jean-Paul Sartre, *Huis Clos suivi de Les mouches*. (Paris: Gallimard, 1947), 93.

58 | "One is rare in modern usage, especially in speech, and is confined to formal styles. It may refer to people in general including the speaker/writer, or, more rarely, as an oblique reference to the speaker/writer but excluding the listener/reader." Carter and McCarthy (2006), 379.

generic *you* is surprisingly frequent in spoken discourse and in non-fiction use such as in advertisements, press-headlines (imperative form) and guidebooks.

> Die Vertautheitsform *du* gebrauchen demgegenüber alle Personen, die miteinander blutsverwandt oder verschwägert sind, auch bei entfernterem Verwandtheitsgrad. [...]
> Unter Erwachsenen, die nicht miteinander verwandt sind, ist die gegenseitige Du-Anrede ferner allgemein üblich bei all denen, die sich der Arbeiterklasse zurechnen. Das Duzen ist hier ein Signal der Klassensolidarität. Dieses "solidaritäts-Du" oder "Genossen-Du" hat sich von seiner sozialen Basis auch in vielen politisch links orientierten Parteien, Gewerkschaften und anderen Gruppierungen dieser politischen Richtung ausgebreitet. Unter den skizzierten Bedingungen hat die Vertrautheitsform *du* also eine bestimmte politische Konnotation und ist in ihrem Vordringen oder Zurückweichen in der deutschen Sprachgemeinschaft von bestimmten politischen und gesellschaftlichen Konstellationen abhängig. [...]
> So wird die Vertrautheitsform der Hörerrolle in Briefen, öffentlichen Bekanntmachungen und in der Werbung immer großgeschrieben, sowohl im Singular (*Du, Dich, Dir*) als auch im Plural (*Ihr, Euch, Ihnen*). Diese Großschreibung der Anfangsbuchstaben gilt auch analog für die Possessiv-Artikel und Possessiv-Pronomina der Hörerrolle.[59]

Weinrich describes second-person *du* as a form of trust and collectivity, an element which is inherent in the distinction between formal and informal address. This social dimension adds implications also inherent in the second person; those, however, change over time. Hence, in many cases, the choice of pronoun reveals the period in which a text is written and the social codes of the time. Such an example we see in Butor and Perec where *vous* and *tu* are used reflecting different connotations and social codes.

59 | Harald Weinrich, *Textgrammatik der Französischen Sprache.* (Stuttgart: Klett, 1982) 104-107.

In French the (second person) pronoun is frequently employed in a reflexive way.[60] Here the formal diversity shows in the syntax as French has a rather complicated system. *Toi*, for instance, can be employed to serve different functions: as a subject like the expected *tu* when followed by an adjective and before the positioning and use of the *fable form (e.g. toi, malade et triste, tu étais brave);* when followed by a relative pronoun; when comparisons and distinctions are necessary (e.g. *moi par écrire et vous par réciter*); when answering a question without a verb; when the subject is addressed among others; when analysing the second-person plural (e.g. *Ton père, toi, tes enfants serez honorés*); with the infinitive or as part of a phrase acquiring a highly deictic sense (e.g. *c'est toi!*). Moreover, *toi* functions as an object in various cases: when coordinated with a noun or pronoun of the same function in the context; when responding without a verb or subject; after certain formulas like *ne...que* or in other syntactic variations.[61] Other functions of the second person designate the forms of *tu* as: "compléments circonstanciels, compléments d'agent du verbe passif, appositions, compléments déterminatifs, compléments de l'adjectif or mots mis en apostrophe."[62]

In French the second-person plural form designates the polite form of address. The French *vous* applies with greater frequency than the German *Sie* (social coding in French makes speaking in the tu-form rather intimate almost to the level of the vulgar). Hence German *Sie* and French *vous* do not share the same connotations of distance and relationship. In French we also come across a diverse use of the third person singular (subject pronoun) *on*. There are cases, too, when *on* is used to evoke a sense of empathy, the speaker's actual or emotional involvement or simply out of modesty. The

60 | "Le pronom personnel est dit réfléchi lorsque, comme complément désignant le même être ou la même chose que le sujet, il indique que l'action revient ou se réfléchir sur le sujet: 2e pers. te, vous." Grevisse (1936/1975), 455.

61 | Grevisse (1936/1975), 448-493.

62 | Grevisse (1936/1975), 449.

generic point of view, designated in English by the collective *you* and by the impersonal *man* in German, is expressed by *on*. *On* corresponds further to other equivalent forms like *chacun, nul, tel* or *personne*.

In English the second-person pronoun has undergone a profound transition, in which the old way of distinguishing persons gave way to a new simpler system, moving from the four older second-person forms (*thou, thee, ye, you*) to an exclusive use of *you*. The causes for this change are not to be found exclusively in the system of language but they have socio-political and other psychological origins that are not addressed in a grammatical overview of contemporary language usage.[63] In current usage, *you* covers a large range of communication needs and social circumstances even though the lack of formal distinction between number, gender or case creates ambiguity and confusion in conversation. As a result, the determining factors of the second-person pronoun in contemporary English turn out to be natural and notional rather than grammatical; they rely on the linguistic and perceptional competence of the interlocutors and the circumstances of the conversation. The morphology of the second-person pronoun in English is extremely minimal: in a text *you* can be generic, used to signal a polite form of address, in imperatives, in conditionals, or as part of the marketing rhetoric extensively employed in the world of advertising.

The second person is easier to note and analyse in languages that have grammatical systems richer in formal variation. The analytical and – to some extent – more symmetric syntactic and morphological diversity of German serves as a good example in which to observe such a typology of the second person. Here, the complications are different from those resulting from the single-form confusion in English grammar that was described above, as the available forms for case and number are so inextricably mixed up in nouns that dealing with them separately is almost impossible. Moreover, as for the polite form in German that is reflected in the third person,

63 | Jespersen (1962), 506.

understanding the pronoun's relationships and its signals allows interlocutors to use *du* or *Sie* occasionally to reflect politeness, intimacy or even lack of social discretion:

> Das Personalpronomen *du* ist als Bezeichnung für die **angesprochene Person** vor allem im intimen persönlichen Umfeld gebräuchlich: Man duzt sich in der Familie, zwischen Verwandten, Freunden, Jugendlichen; Erwachsene duzen Kinder. **Auch in Reden auf Beerdigung verwendet man doch *du*, wenn den Verstorbenen anredet, ebenso ist *du* die Anrede an heilige Personen, an Tiere, Dinge oder Abstrakta.** Daneben wird *du*, vor allem in der Umgangssprache, in kollektiver Bedeutung (anstelle von man) gebraucht. [...] Das Personalpronomen *ihr* wird wie *du* im vertrauten Kreise gebraucht, und zwar für mehrere Personen. Gelegentlich, vor allem in bestimmten Gegenden, wird es auch gegenüber Personen gebraucht, die man einzeln mit *Sie* anredet (etwa ein Geistlicher gegenüber seiner Gemeinde).[64]

In the Duden-excerpt above, Drosdowski states that the second person is used to **address** a person and if in the singular, it is for someone with whom the relationship is rather personal. However, he also mentions that the same concept of address is occasionally used at funerals for people who have passed away, or for holy persons, animals, things and even abstracts, paradoxically everything that is not a living person. What actually happens in this case is treated in rhetoric with the figure of *prosopopoeia* and consequently such entities take over the powers and roles of a person. This shows how important rhetoric is to the process of understanding second-person storytelling and it reveals one variant in the typology of the second-person narrative that contains referents and forms that could not legitimately be considered persons in a grammatical or literary sense.

In summary, the role of the addressee played by the second person takes on a broader sense (taken by persons and inanimate figures) and is rich in implications since it can also be expressed

64 | Drosdowski (1995), 330f.

in non-second person forms, especially with regard to aspired-to objectivity, indefinite meaning and ambiguity. Social codes and circumstances, relationships within social constraints and communication policies are determined by these grammatical attributes that are transmitted in the rhetoric of the second person. In the pages that follow, we will see how the essentials of the second person as a grammatical category and its expression in a pronoun are built into the second-person narrative mode and what rhetorical tropes and figures are brought into play when used in the narrative. Finally, based on texts, the discussion advances to a close reading of the narratives themselves, drawing important conclusions for the second-person narrative technique in each narrative as related to the language system in which it is written.

The Rhetoric of the Second Person

The technique of telling a story in the second person has been used since the time of the ancients. Homer used it in his epic poems, and he became the model for poets including Virgil who wrote epic poetry after him; the second person was used in psalms and prayers, in epistolary novels and in diaries. Telling a story in the second person was employed when transmitting philosophical dialogues into writing, appeared in guidebooks and instructions and was vital to hypnosis, reflecting a dramatisation of dialogue deriving from the theatre and plays. The narrative and communicational circumstances in which the second person appears reveal its richness and resilience; it establishes a narrative situation in which various implications and attributes can come into play. In prose, the second person gathers rhetorical elements and developments of different origins (poetry, drama) and applications, and forms a rich field of narratives in terms of thematic variation and poetic implication.

a. Apostrophe

Ἄνδρα μοι ἔννεπε, Μοῦσα, πολύτροπον, ὃς μάλα πολλὰ
πλάγχθη, ἐπεὶ Τροίης ἱερὸν πτολίεθρον ἔπερσε·
πολλῶν δ' ἀνθρώπων ἴδεν ἄστεα καὶ νόον ἔγνω,
πολλὰ δ' ὅ γ'ἐν πόντῳ πάθεν ἄλγεα ὃν κατὰ θυμόν,
ἀρνύμενος ἥν τε ψυχὴν καὶ νόστον ἑταίρων.
ἀλλ' οὐδ' ὧς ἑτάρους ἐρρύσατο, ἱέμενός περ·
αὐτῶν γὰρ σφετέρῃσιν ἀτασθαλίῃσιν ὄλοντο,
νήπιοι, οἳ κατὰ βοῦς Ὑπερίονος Ἠελίοιο
ἤσθιον· αὐτὰρ ὁ τοῖσιν ἀφείλετο νόστιμον ἦμαρ.
τῶν ἁμόθεν γε, θεά, θύγατερ Διός, εἰπὲ καὶ ἡμῖν.
ἔνθ' ἄλλοι μὲν πάντες, ὅσοι φύγον αἰπὺν ὄλεθρον,
οἴκοι ἔσαν, πόλεμόν τε πεφευγότες ἠδὲ θάλασσαν·
τὸν δ' οἶον, νόστου κεχρημένον ἠδὲ γυναικός,
νύμφη πότνι' ἔρυκε Καλυψώ, δῖα θεάων,
ἐν σπέεσι γλαφυροῖσι, λιλαιομένη πόσιν εἶναι.[65]
(Οδύσσεια, Α στ. 1-15)

---

65 | "O Muse, sing to me of the man full of resources, who wandered very much after he had destroyed the sacred city of Troy, and saw the cities of many men, and learned their manners. Many griefs also in his mind did he suffer on the sea, although seeking to preserve his own life, and the return of his companions; but not even thus, although anxious, did he extricate his companions; for they perished by their own infatuation, fools! Who devoured the oxen of the Sun who journeys on high; but he deprived them of their return. O goddess, daughter of Jove, relate to us also some of these things. Now all the others, as many as had escaped from utter destruction, were at home, having escaped both the war and the sea. But him alone anxious for a return [home], and for his wife, the venerable nymph Calypso, a divine one of the goddesses, detained in her hollow grot, desiring him to her husband." Homer and Theodore A. Buckley. *The Odyssey of Homer: With the Hymns, Epigrams, and Battle of the Frogs and Mice.* (London: Henry G. Bohn, 1853) I. 1-15, 1.

One striking rhetorical attribute associated with second-person narratives is that of *apostrophe* which has its origins in antiquity and which has since undergone an extensive development.

Μῆνιν ἄειδε θεὰ Πηληϊάδεω Ἀχιλος
ολομένην, ἣ μυρί' Ἀχαιος ἄλγε' θηκε,
πολλὰς δ' ἰφθίμους ψυχὰς Ἄϊδι προΐαψεν
ἡρώων, αὐτοὺς δὲ ἑλώρια τεῦχε κύνεσσιν[66]
(Ιλιάδα, Α στ. 1-4)

A primary instance of second-person *apostrophe* is Homer's invocation of the Muse in both his epic poems, *Iliad* and *Odyssey*; since then, almost every epic poet has followed his example. Similar invocations occur in Virgil's *Aeneid*, Dante Alighieri's *Divine Comedy* and John Milton's *Paradise Lost*; they all appeal to the Muse or a similar absent source of inspiration. Here the second person points to aspects of the generation of the poem.[67] Apart from epic poetry, other examples of second-person *apostrophe* in literature can be found in Shakespeare's sonnets in their direct address to a lady or a friend, or in Ezra Pound's *Coda*, "O my songs,/Why do you look so eagerly and

66 | "The wrath do thou sing, O goddess, of Peleus' son, Achilles, that baneful wrath which brought countless woes upon the Achaeans, and sent forth to Hades many valiant souls of warriors, and made themselves to be a spoil for dogs and all manner of birds;" Homer and Augustus T. Murray. *The Iliad*. (Cambridge: Harvard University Press, 1891) I. 1-4, 2.

67 | "Apostrophe: Traditionally, the Greek term apostrophe (Lat. aversio) has designated the rhetorical device that indicates the momentary interruption of discourse, in order to address – often in a vehement tone – a real or imaginary, present or absent, human or nonhuman, living or dead addressee of that discourse. This interruption is characterized linguistically by a change from one discursive type to another as when, for example, one inserts in an expositive-narrative modality, modalities associated with the expressive and appellative functions of language." Thomas O. Sloane, ed. *Encyclopedia of Rhetoric*. (Oxford: Oxford University Press, 2001) 29.

so curiously into people's faces,/Will you find your lost dead among them?,"[68] where poetry itself is addressed in an elaboration of the Muse/deity concept that links the employment of the second person with the *lyric you*, emphasising its self-reflexive character.[69]

The apostrophic employment of the second person is indicative of consistency in the development of the genre up to the post-modern and contemporary writings of our times. In the most recent texts, the second person is generally used apostrophically in the discourse to refer to absent (Günter Grass 1961, *Katz und Maus*) or dead (Oriana Fallaci 1979, *Un Uomo*) addressees. This is a rather interesting observation since it reveals the existence of some sort of hidden intertextuality, a connecting link between second-person forms that are spread over time and that appear to have nothing (else) in common, yet connect Homer and Virgil with authors like Butor and Perec.

Addressing absent or inaccessible beings through the second person enables narrators to coexist and interrelate with them, fulfilling a narrative convention for the discourse and allowing the generation of the story itself. This constructed present derives from the fact that the pronoun presupposes contextual synchrony and evokes a sense of contemporaneity that would otherwise be impossible. This allows narrators to start their stories again and again *in medias res* so as to stress this actual position and the notion of a synchronic episode. The narrative tactic of starting a story in the middle, appearing frequently in second person examples, strengthens the sense of intertextuality that second-person texts share with one another, since it implies their participating in a literary dialogue.

---

68 | Ezra Pound, *Lustra of Ezra Pound, with Earlier Poems.* (New York: Alfred A. Knopf, 1917) 43.

69 | T. V. F. Brogan and Alex Preminger, eds. *The New Princeton Encyclopedia of Poetry and Poetics.* (Princeton: Princeton University Press, 1993) 82.

Tu es assis, torse nu, vêtu seulement d'un pantalon de pyjama, dans ta chambre de bonne [...] Le soleil tape sur les feuilles de zinc de la toiture. En face de toi, à la hauteur de tes yeux, sure une étagère de bois blanc, il y a un bol de Nescafé à moitié vide, un peu sale, un paquet de sucre tirant sur sa fin, une cigarette qui se consume dans un cendrier publicitaire en fausse opaline blanchâtre.[70]

Though surprising and uncomfortable at first due to the lack of a specific point of reference, opening a narrative with an undefined *you* is not only a designation of the orientation of the text towards its reader and natural addressee but it also has a naturalising effect, supporting his/her familiarity with the narrative environment. Whereas the use of the second person challenges the reader with its inherent ambivalence and strikes him/her as a less common narrative mode, a detailed description of the environment serves as a familiarising factor that has a totally opposite effect and balances the surprise provoked by the second person.

Second-person narratives usually contain excerpts in which the experience of the surroundings through the senses is stressed, with visual and auditory elements, presented in so-called formal realism. The formal realism and the attention to the material detail that the narrative personae show to their environment *strengthen* the identification of the reader with the addressing *you* and evoke the sense of a situation of live communication. Invited to position and imagine himself or herself within the narrative world, the reader is confronted with a discourse that involves numerous deictical elements that have a heightened demonstrative force and that lend a notion of contemporaneity to the discourse.

Assis, vous étendez vos jambes de part et d'autre de celles de cet intellectuel qui a pris un air soulagé et qui arrête enfin le mouvement de ses doigts, vous déboutonnez votre épais manteau poilu à doublure de soie

70 | Georges Perec, *Un homme qui dort*. In *Romans et Récits*. 1967. (Paris: La Pochothèque (Le Livre de Poche), 2002) 223.

changeante, vous en écartez les pans, découvrant vos deux genoux dans leurs fourreaux de drap bleu marine, dont le pli, repassé d'hier pourtant, est déjà cassé, vous décroisez et déroulez avec votre main droite votre écharpe de laine grumeleuse, au tissage lâche, dont les nodosités jaune paille et nacre vous font penser à des œufs brouillés, vous la pliez négligemment en trois et vous la fourrez dans cette ample poche où se trouvent déjà un paquet de gauloises bleues, une boîte d'allumettes et naturellement des brins de tabac mêlés de poussière accumulés dans la couture.[71]

This also explains why in second-person narratives we normally see the establishment of the narrative mode at the start, highlighted at the opening of the text. This narrative strategy may cause some awkwardness initially as the reference of the addressee – the *you* – is not determined, but at the same time it offers an ambiguity that adds to the reading process. The second-person pronoun carries a double address, gesturing both towards the (literary) persona implied in the discourse yet at the same time forcing the reader to feel referred to and addressed.

This sense of ambiguity inherent in the employment of the second-person pronoun is associated with the classic use of *apostrophe* and the concept of the double audience (primary and secondary). For example, apart from deities, Homer's tales were addressing audiences with different kinds of attention. In the time of the epics, narratives were performed in which the apostrophe connected the speaker was turning away from the normal audience while pretending to address it. *Apostrophe* referred to the fact that in productions of Greek drama, the actors addressed some of their remarks not to other actors on stage but directly to the audience. This kind of constant "digression" reflects an elaboration of *apostrophe* called *parabasis* and aimed to activate the audience or, in our case, the reader of prose to an active involvement. It has since become a rhetorical term, used for the writer's tactic of occasionally addressing

71 | Michel Butor, *La Modification*. 1957. (Paris: Éditions de Minuit, 1980) 10f.

his or her readers directly, rather than concentrating on the narrative only.

However, it must be mentioned here that the reader was not always implied in the reference of the second person as a secondary hearer and addressee of the discourse. There have been narrative examples where the reader becomes explicitly mentioned in the text, for example in Calvino's *Se una notte d'inverno un viaggiatore*, or even earlier in the time of Mary Shelley when authors were employing the *dear reader* introduction to their texts, stressing the intriguing relationship between author, text and readership. *Frankenstein* (1818), for example, written in epistolary form but bringing the reader into play, uses the second-person address as a self-revealing and playful narrative trick that grabs the attention of readers, drawing them into a self-conscious constellation and establishing itself as a work of fiction at the same time.

In doing so, the author acknowledges and addresses the reading audience, moving his/her focus away from the fictional frame to that of the audience or at least to a perception of it, namely the implied reader. The same effect is frequently found in the performing arts such as in theatre or cinema (eg. in *Breathless*, where Jean-Paul Belmondo turns his face directly to the camera), but in literature it can function only through the second person that enables this interaction as part of a narrative convention. The temporal distance between the two available audiences (the one in the fictional frame and the one outside, at whom the work of art is actually aimed) and the author, not to mention the medium itself, prohibits an *apostrophe* in the classical sense of oratory but allows it on a cognitive level. This phenomenon is defined as *narrative apostrophe* by Irene Kacandes:

> [...] a technique I propose we call narrative apostrophe, borrowing from the rhetorical figure for turning from one's normal audience to address someone or something who, by reason of absence, death, inanimateness, and/or mere rhetorical convention, cannot answer back. [...] Texts written in this mode [...] constitute an obvious if complex form of talk fiction, since orientation toward exchange (Talk) is always based on a fiction: that the

"you" is inanimate and capable of response [...]; that the message is not for readers, when it is, since readers read the book; that a specific actual reader is being called by the narrating voice in the text, whereas any reader could feel called by it. Recognising both the vocative force of such discourse and the fictions on which it rests - that it is and is not for you - constitutes the Talk of narrative apostrophe.[72]

In attempting to define *narrative apostrophe* Kacandes introduces the term "talk fiction." It appears very often in second-person storytelling and underlines an orientation towards exchange and the dialogic sense that dominates the technique due to the usage of the pronoun; second-person fiction evokes a sense of conversation ("talk") in a certain contrivance ("fiction").[73] Formed in a dynamic way so that multiple agents can simultaneously be involved as potential addressees in the discourse, the shifting reference of the second person, expressed either in the pronoun or with the reader reference that assumes the same position, creates a sense of orality and of coexisting, synchronic instances that have active relationships constantly recreated and reproduced within the *talk*.

Whether referring to the reader as a literary persona, to the actual reader or to any other figure or person internal or external to the world of fiction, the second person potentially signals an emphatic apostrophic mechanism which is linked with narrative contemporaneity and sense of presence (not just grammatical). In turn, this feature of presence allows transgression and temporal transition by bringing conditions of the narrative into the same context.

b. Mise-en-scène

The sense of synchrony and of belonging to the same context inherent in the rhetoric of apostrophe, combined with the associated emphasis on contemporaneity and actuality, can be considered

72 | Kacandes (2001), 144f.

73 | Kacandes (2001), x.

a kind of staging, a *mise-en-scène*, however, that occurs not only rhetorically but suggests also a *poetic act*. Authors may employ the second-person address either in the form of a *dear reader* construction or in other forms such as the use of imperatives and adverbs (*here, there, now*) so as to create immediacy in the text, amplifying the conative function and encouraging coherence between non-compatible persons situated in different temporal and spatial circumstances (as authors and readers are). Hence the deictic element is associated with the second person as a designation of the addressee since it expresses the orientation of the discourse towards him/her and a condition of coexistence. Therefore, that type of formation not only functions as a rhetorical act that introduces the theme and conditions of the narrative, but also creates the grounds of the narrative and enables the generation of the story itself, on a poetic level.

The *dear reader* construction, for example, and the concept of addressing (pointing to) an actual human being within a fictional text can be seen as a self-revealing element that admits to the text being a fiction addressed to and made for the reader, and suggests the romantic transformation that occurred at the beginning of the 19th century from the epistolary circuit of the medieval period, transforming to a rhetorical formula without any signs of epistolary function. At the same time, it reveals the same aspiration to engage the reader in a more active reading, by forcing him/her to position himself/herself in the same context and *participate* more in the narrative.

> It must be confest, *Damon*, that you are the most importuning Man in the World. Your Billets have a hundred times demanded a *Discretion*, which you won of me; and tell me, you will not wait my Return, to be paid.[74]

Following a period of epistolary novels in which the interaction and synchrony were between fictional personae, we enter a later stage of the novel in which sentiments and the way they affect the reader

---

74 | Aphra Behn, *La Montre, or The Lover's Watch by Mrs. A. Behn*. (EEBO Editions ProQuest, 1686) 5.

are brought into focus. Since the second person reflects directness, intimacy and interaction, it can be used to express the idea of the reader as a recipient and vital component of the literary product, as we saw in the case of Shelley. Thus, the dominance of the second-person voice comes with an emphatic reference to the recipient of the text, that is its deictic centre, and the process of contemporaneity, the notion of *co-staging*, expands further in cases where the narrative *you*, the addressee, happens to be imaginary or absent but still represented or even actually present. In such narrative circumstances the *co-staging* is due to a narrative convention and another rhetorical figure, that of *prosopopoeia*.

c. Prosopopoeia

Verses 1-7, Unto thee, O Jehovah, do I lift up my soul.
2 O my God, in thee have I trusted,
Let me not be put to shame;
Let not mine enemies triumph over me.
3 Yea, none that wait for thee shall be put to shame:
They shall be put to shame who deal treacherously
without cause.
4 Show me thy ways, O Jehovah;
Teach me thy paths.
5 Guide me in thy truth, and teach me;
For thou art the God of my salvation;
For thee do I wait all the day.
6 Remember, O Jehovah, thy tender mercies and thy
lovingkindnesses;
For they have been of old.
7 Remember, not the sins of my youth, nor my
transgressions:
According to thy lovingkindness remember thou me,

For thy goodness' sake, O Jehovah.[75]

In most languages people address God by using the intimate and direct *you* in their prayer, availing themselves of the connotations of the second person to characterise their relationship to the divine: directness, intimacy and coexistence. God is a valid addressee, present in any context, for anyone uttering a prayer. This is what the use of *you* in prayer ultimately tells us: that the person uttering the prayer is in a relationship with God. It reflects a certain vivid and established relationship with Him, just by the fact that He can be and is being addressed, even though no dialogue takes place in terms of interchange. In terms of narrative, every time the second person is used in a prayer it occurs as a mechanism that makes God a narrative persona, hence it functions apart from the operation of *apostrophe* also as *prosopopoeia* in rhetorical terms.[76]

Prosopopoeia specifies physical entities by giving them the shape and properties of a literary persona the moment they are addressed. We see a liminal example of this figure in Aichinger's *Spiegelgeschichte*, which is one of the texts that will be analysed in detail in the second part of this book.

75 | James Burton Coffman and Thelma B. Coffman, eds. "Psalm 25[a], 1-7". In *Psalms 1-72. Vol. 1-1.* (Austin: Abilene Christian University, 1992) 188f.

76 | "Prosopopoeia. Under the term prosopopoeia (Lat. Fictio personae, sermocinatio), as can be inferred etymologically from the Greek and Latin appellations, authors use the device of introducing in discourse a feigned presentation of characters or personified things, that is, things feigned sub specie personae. The usual form of this presentation is through the attribution of human properties or qualities, especially those of speaking or of listening (the terms dialogismos and sermocinatio refer to this property). The device must be properly regulated by the literary norms of stylistic decorum." Sloane (2001), 637.

Wenn einer dein Bett aus dem Saal schiebt, wenn du siehst, daß der Himmel grün wird, und wenn du dem Vikar die Leichenrede ersparen willst, so ist es Zeit für dich, aufzustehen, leise, wie Kinder aufstehen, wenn am Morgen Licht durch die Läden schimmert, heimlich, daß es die Schwester nicht sieht - und schnell![77]

In Aichinger's narrative a dying woman is addressed by an enigmatic voice within an interrupted second-person narrative that recounts episodes of her life in reverse: it is a way of bringing her back to life, at least rhetorically. By addressing a dying person – a soon-to-be unavailable addressee – the rhetoric of the narrative specifies and determines her as a narrative persona (*prosopopoeia*) with the properties and function of a legitimate person, transgressing the limits of mortality and elaborating on the dynamic of language and its amplified potential.

Volventi mihi multa ac varia mecum diu, ac per multos dies sedulo quarenti memetipsum ac bonum meum, quidve mali evitandum esset, ait mihi subito sive ego ipse sive alius quis, [sive] extrinsecus sive intrinsecus, nescio: nam hoc ipsum est quod magnopere scire molior, ait mihi *Ratio:* Ecce, fact e invenisse aliquid: cui commendabis, ut pergas ad alia?[78]

---

77 | Ilse Aichinger, *Spiegelgeschichte. Erzählungen und Dialoge.* 1954. (Leipzig und Weimar: Kiepenheuer, 1979) 43.

78 | "Wie ich mich lange Zeit mit den verschiedensten Gedanken trug und viele Tage ernsthaft mich selber suchte und was für mich ein Gutes sei oder ein Übel, das es zu meiden gilt, da sagte plötzlich zu mir - vielleicht ich selber, vielleicht ein Zweiter, in mir oder außer mir (ich weiß es nicht, und doch möchte ich gerade dies es so gerne wissen...) - nun, da sagte zu mir die *Vernunft:* Merk auf! Nimm an, du hättest eine Entdeckung gemacht: wem willst du sie anvertrauen, um zu anderem weiterschreiten zu können?" Aurelius Augustinus, *Selbstgespräche. Von der Unsterblichkeit der Seele.* Ed. Harald Fuchs. (München und Zürich: Artemis Verlag, 1986) 7.

Augustine, for example, uses *prosopopoeia* to address Reason in his *Soliloquia [Selbstgespräche]*, an inner dialogue (textualised in the narrative as a dialogue between Reason and the Self) leading to self-knowledge. In the *Soliloquia* we are actually presented with a rather frequent theme of second-person storytelling, namely the journey towards self-discovery, also processed through a narrative representation. It shows the converting man at the very moment of his conversion benefitting from the actuality and sense of presence established by the dialogue (second person). This theme is linked to the process of creating a character within the narrative itself and will be discussed in more detail in connection with Butor's *Modification* as well as the other narrative examples. In terms of rhetoric this process of character development within the narrative is linked with *ethopoeia*, a figure that will be discussed next.

d. Ethopoeia

> Μένων: ἔχεις μοι εἰπεῖν, ὦ Σώκρατες, ἆρα διδακτὸν ἡ ἀρετή; ἢ οὐ διδακτὸν ἀλλ' ἀσκητόν; ἢ οὔτε ἀσκητὸν οὔτε μαθητόν, ἀλλὰ φύσει παραγίγνεται τοῖς ἀνθρώποις ἢ ἄλλῳ τινὶ τρόπῳ;
> **Σωκράτης:** ὦ Μένων, πρὸ τοῦ μὲν Θετταλοὶ εὐδόκιμοι ἦσαν ἐν τοῖς Ἕλλησιν καὶ ἐθαυμάζοντο ἐφ' ἱππικῇ τε καὶ πλούτῳ, [70b]νῦν δέ, ὡς ἐμοὶ δοκεῖ, καὶ ἐπὶ σοφίᾳ, καὶ οὐχ ἥκιστα οἱ τοῦ σοῦ ἑταίρου Ἀριστίππου πολῖται Λαρισαῖοι.[79]

79 | "MENO: Can you tell me, Socrates, whether virtue is teachable? Or is not teachable, but attainable by practice? Or is it attainable neither by practice nor by learning, and do people instead acquire by nature or in some other way?
SOCRATES: In the past, Meno, the Thessalians were renowned among the Greeks and admired for both horsemanship and wealth, but now, I think, they are admired for wisdom as well, and particularly the fellow-citizens of your friend Aristippus, the men of Larisa." Plato, "Meno". In *Meno and Plato.* Ed. David Sedley. Trans. Alex Long. (Cambridge: Cambridge University Press, 2011) 1.

Interesting for the understanding of the second person is that Plato, who is known to be a polemic of literature for its fictional, elusive character, delivered his philosophical dialogues in the original second-person form thus enriching his texts with vividness, authenticity and immediacy. Plato's dialogues can be described as dramatised narratives that resemble a theatrical performance. He focuses on the features of character, action and the relation of drama to the audience, and he (re-)creates literary figures resembling as closely as possible actual historical persons by using the rhetorical tropes of *dialogismos, sermocinatio*[80] and *ethopoeia.* Speaking characters

80 | "Sermocinatio. Die sermocinatio steht in einem gewissen Zusammenhang mit der evidentia, ohne ein notwendiger Teil der Figur der evidentia selbst zu sein. Die sermocinatio ist die der Charakterisierung natürlicher (historischer oder erfundener) Personen dienende Fingierung von Aussprüchen, Gesprächen und Selbstgesprächen oder ausgesprochenen gedanklichen Reflexionen der betreffenden Personen. [...] Inhaltlich braucht die sermocinatio nicht historisch wahr zu sein, sie muss nur wahrscheinlich sein, d.h. insbesondere dem Charakter der sprechenden Person entsprechen. [...] Die fictio personae ist die Einführung nichtpersonhafter Dinge als sprechende sowie zu sonstigem personhaften Verhalten befähigte Personen. Die fictio personae ist eine durch Übersteigerung der schöpferischen Phantasie erzeugte hochpathetische Figur. Die Unterscheidung zwischen fictio personae und sermocinatio wird von den meisten Theoretikern scharf aufrechterhalten, indem die Prosopopoiie auf die nicht personhaften Dinge (und die Toten) beschränkt wird, während die Ethopoiie die natürlichen Personen betrifft. [...] Außer den nichtpersonhaften Dingen können in der fictio personae auch Tote als redend und sich personhaft verhaltend eingeführt werden. [...] Die Erweiterung der Prosopopoiie auf die Toten führt bei einigen Theoretikern dazu, daß auch Phantasienpersonen, ja eine lebende, aber abwesende Person zugelassen wurden. [...] Die fictio personae durch Reden verleiht besonders gern Kollektiven (Vaterland, Städte usw.) Stimme." Heinrich Lausberg, *Handbuch der Literarischen Rhetorik. Eine Grundlegung der Literaturwissenschaft.* (München: Max Hueber Verlag, 1960) 407-412.

in a dialogic discourse contribute to an implicit and indirect characterisation through their words, hence these literary *personae* are developed within the narratives they belong to; the impression given in such cases is that their development into rounded characters is concurrent with the narration.

Die Abwendung des Redenden von sich selbst besteht in der sermocinatio (ethopoeia, ηθοποιία, μίμησις); der Redner legt, obwohl nur er selbst redet, seine Rede einer anderen Person in direkter Rede in den Mund und ahmt dabei auch deren charakteristische Redeweise (daher «Ethopoiie») nach (imitatio, μίμησις). Die sermocinatio (seltener in indirekter Rede) kommt vor: 1) als dialoglose Rede [...] 2) als Dialog [...] 3) als Selbstgespräch (Monolog) oder gedankliche Reflexion, die, wenn sie deliberierende Fragestellungen (quid faciam?) enthält, διαλογισμός heißt, ohne daß die deshalb als Frage-Antwort-Spiel ausgebaut sein muß.[81]

The dramatisation offered by the second-person perspective and the making of literary *personae* concurrent with the progress of the narrative are features we can observe in numerous examples in the history of literature, for example in the French *nouveaux romans* that will be discussed in detail in the second part of this project. However, much earlier, the same rhetorical technique had been applied in one of the key texts of the world and of second-person literature: Augustine's *Confessions*.

[N]umquid semper tacebis? et nunc erues de hoc inmanissimo profundo quaerentem te animam et sitientem delectationes tuas, et cuius cor dicit tibi: quaesivi vultum tuum; vultum tuum, domine, requiram: nam longe a vultu tuo in affectu tenebroso. non enim pedibus aut spatiis locorum itur abs te aut reditur ad te, aut vero filius ille tuus equos aut currus vel naves

81 | Heinrich Lausberg, *Elemente der Literarischen Rhetorik*. 1963. (München: Max Hueber Verlag, 1990) 142f.

quaesivit aut avolavit pinna visibili aut moto poplite iter egit, ut in longinqua regione vivens prodige dissiparet quod dederas.[82]

Augustine thematised his strong relationship with God and composed his autobiographical *Confessions* in the form of a prayer. His *Confessions* are spoken in the present tense, showing him in a continuous dialogue with God, an invisible interlocutor whose unheard words are subtly perceived in the interior of his soul. In this ongoing inner dialogue with God, Augustine's confessions and the narrative itself are constantly recreated, evoking a sense of a text in progress and a persona re-created and represented gradually within the words spoken. As readers are caught up in the fervour and intimacy of Augustine's address to God, the imitation of a voice speaking in the present engages our feelings; the prayer incorporates dramatic qualities that make the narrative dynamic.

As a dramatised version of the present, the *confessing* (and the writing) reveals that Augustine – the narrator and writer – is not in full control of his material or of the movements of his thoughts but rather is in an active relationship with God, whose presence is total, forming them and his character at the same time. Confession is described more as an exercise in self-awareness.

82 | "But wilt thou be silent for ever? Even now thou wilt draw out of this horrible pit, that soul that seeks after thee, and that thirsts after thy pleasures: whose heart saith unto thee, have sought thy face, and thy face. Lord, will I seek. For I had straggled far away from thy countenance in the mistiness of my affections. For we neither go nor return, from, or to thee, upon our feet, or by distance of spaces: nor did that younger brother seek post-horses, or waggons, or ships, or fly away with visible wings, or take his journey by the motion of his hams, that living in a Luke far country he might prodigally waste that portion, which thou hadst given him at his departure." Aurelius Augustinus, *St. Augustine's Confessions: with an English translation*. Eds. William Watts and W. H. D. Rouse. Trans. William Watts (London: W. Heinemann; Cambridge: Harvard University Press, 1950) 52f.

It is interesting to note that in the *Confessions* the self-awareness narrative is occurring after the actions that have challenged the narrator's knowledge of self, whereas the *Soliloquia* reflect the truly continuous and concurrent process of a self-awareness dialogue, parallel to the narrative. From the medieval examples of *Confessions* and *Soliloquia* to the contemporary cases of *Kindheitsmuster, Un homme qui dort* and *La Modification*, the theme of reconciling oneself with the self – the first-person authority – appears as a common *topos* in the second-person narratives. The same variation between self-awareness narratives from a superior temporal point (Wolf) or concurrent to the narration (Butor) strengthens the sense of intertextuality in second-person narratives.

Ethopoeia and self-discovery are traced in Butor's *La Modification* when Léon is developed as a concrete character while the narrator narrates to him his own thoughts and experiences; in Perec's *Un homme qui dort* within the narrative of an experiment in self-detachment narrated to a de-personalised student who acquires his identity gradually in the (second-person) story; and in various other contemporary examples that use the self-talk second-person narrative mode to express the problem of identifying with the *I* and a character in development.

The problems in the relationship to first-person authority and the objectivity that is inherent in the second person explain the popularity of the technique in autobiographies. Composing second-person autobiographies is related to a process of exposing the first person to the second, described as transcendence in the previous section on pronouns, the concept of the *Other* and Benveniste's study. This technique reflects a form of *prosopopoeia* of the first person to the exposed second, and a transit from the situation of an acquired self-authority to a process of acquiring self-awareness through an outer perspective on the self, a situation perfectly dramatised by Sartre in his play *Huis Clos*, as mentioned earlier.

Second-person autobiographies reflect the making of the self as a narrative persona; this persona would have concrete and specific characteristics that are recognised and explored by the narrating subject who is different from the experiencing persona – maybe not physically but certainly cognitively, for various reasons. Not only did Plato write his autobiographical 7th *Letter* in epistolary form, hence in the second person, and Augustine compose his autobiography in the form of a prayer addressed to God; traditional forms of fictional autobiography continue to appear in this form: the most recent being Paul Auster's *Winter Journal.* Auster confronted his past by using the second-person technique in his autobiographical *memoir,* describing his life blow by blow.

You think it will never happen to you, that it cannot happen to you, that you are the only person in the world to whom none of these things will ever happen, and then, one by one, they all begin to happen to you, in the same way they happen to everyone else.[83]

Published only recently in 2012, his memoir (as he calls it) received ambivalent comments regarding its style. Criticised for its taint of artificiality, the immediacy of its prose is nonetheless effective and draws the reader in as an accomplice. In one of his interviews following the publication of his book, the author speaks of the depersonalising (distancing) role that the second-person narrative voice has in his text. The use of the second person's generalising and objectifying sense helped in making the autobiographical text as impersonal as possible and more the story of an everyday man. For Auster, there couldn't be a purely autobiographical novel based on *true* memories without fictional elements, because memory and remembering are always unreliable. Hence Auster has defined this work as a "literary composition composed of autobiographical fragments."

It was an instinctive decision. I started it that way without a lot of reflection. But then, as I got into the writing of the book, I understood there was

83 | Paul Auster, *Winter Journal.* (New York: Henry Holt and Company, 2012) 1.

a reason for this, and number one, again, goes towards answering your question about this memoir issue: because I see myself as anybody, as everybody; I'm not just telling the story of my life to give the reader a picture of who I am. No, I wanted to do something different. Therefore, the first person I thought would have been too exclusionary. It would have said me, me, me, me, me. I, I, I, I, I. As if I were pushing away my experiences from the experiences of others. Because basically what I was trying to do was show our commonality.
I mean to say, in the very ordinariness of what I recount I think perhaps the reader will find resonances with his or her own life. And so the second person seemed ideal because it conveys a certain intimacy and yet a certain kind of separation between writer and subject. In a sense I am able to interrogate myself, address myself from that slight distance and enter a kind of dialogical relationship with myself. Because I'm saying, "Look, these are things that have happened to me, but how odd they are or how ordinary they are [is up to the reader to decide]." So second person seemed perfect. There's this sense that, as a reader when you're reading a book in the second person, you do feel addressed, and more implicated in what's going on than you would if you read it in the first or third. I think. This is my intuition about this.[84]

e. Voice-over[85]

In 1835 Nathaniel Hawthorne wrote *The Haunted Mind*, an in-between narrative of a half-asleep hero, connecting the second-person narrative technique for the first time with the (non-fiction) narrative format of the process of hypnosis.

84 | Paul Auster interview – "Winter Journal" preview. (n.d.). Date accessed 23 September 2017. http://www.timeout.com/london/books/paul-auster-interview.

85 | The "voice-over" narrator reflects a term used in films to reflect a narrator who is only present in the story *acoustically*. Stanzel also mentions "voice-over" in reference to screen-adapted novels to express a narrator who is absent from the stage. "[...] einfach einem auktorialen "voice over"-

WHAT a singular moment is the first one, when you have hardly begun to recollect yourself, after starting from midnight slumber! By unclosing your eyes so suddenly, you seem to have surprised the personages of your dream in full convocation round your bed, and catch one broad glance at them before they can flit into obscurity. [...]
Hitherto you have lain perfectly still, because the slightest motion would dissipate the fragments of your slumber. Now, being irrevocably awake, you peep through the half drawn window curtain, and observe that the glass is ornamented with fanciful devices in frost work, and that each pane presents something like a frozen dream.[86]

The rhetoric of voice-over enjoys numerous applications in contemporary texts that derive mainly from the cinema. We see it, for example, in Lars von Trier's *Zentropa/Europa* opening scene, where a voice-over opens the movie, instructing the protagonist regarding what he will be confronted with in the movie.[87] The same rhetoric

Kommentar, das ist die kommentierende Stimme einer Person, die nicht auf der Filmleinwand sichtbar ist." Stanzel (1979/2001), 118.
In prose the term reflects an absent narrator who is present in the story only as a voice narrating the events and who hence remains *offstage*, which in literature means out of the world of fiction.

86 | Nathaniel Hawthorne, "The Haunted Mind". In *Twice-Told Tales.* (Ohio, Ohio State University Press: 1974) 304f.

87 | "You will now listen to my voice. My voice will help you and guide you still deeper into Europa. Every time you hear my voice, with every word and every number, you will enter into a still deeper layer, open, relaxed and receptive. I shall now count from one to ten. On the count of ten, you will be in Europa. I say: one. And as your focus and attention are entirely on my voice, you will slowly begin to relax. Two, your hands and your fingers are getting warmer and heavier. Three, the warmth is spreading through your arms, to your shoulders and your neck. Four, your feet and your legs get heavier. Five, the warmth is spreading to the whole of your body. On six, I want you to go deeper. I say: six. And the whole of your relaxed body is slowly beginning to sink. Seven, you go deeper and deeper and deeper. Eight, on is found in Beckett's narrative of imperatives *Imagination Dead Imagine*[88] and in Jay McInerney's *Bright Lights, Big City:*

> Monday arrives on schedule. You sleep through the first ten hours. God only knows what happened to Sunday.
> At the subway station you wait fifteen minutes on the platform of the train. Finally a local, enervated by graffiti, shuffles into the station. You get a seat and hoist a copy of the New York Post. The Post is the most shameful of your several addictions.[89]

Bright Lights, Big City was published in New York in 1984. It is Jay McInerney's first novel, set in New York City. The protagonist, a 24-year-old aspiring writer who remains nameless throughout the novel finds himself in a crisis. He is bored of his job at a prestigious New York magazine, his wife has left him and he suffers from writer's block. To distract himself from his problems he has developed a cocaine habit and spends every night out in the bars and clubs of New York. The narrative recounts a second-person self-talk he performs every night, one that presents and develops the character indirectly within the confines of the narrative.

The same voice-over construction is found in Perec's *Un homme qui dort.*

---

every breath you take, you go deeper. Nine, you are floating. On the mental count of ten, you will be in Europa. Be there at ten. I say: ten." *Zentropa/ Europa*. Dir. Lars von Trier. (Nordisk Film Biografdistribution, 1991) Opening scene.

88 | "No trace anywhere of life, you say, pah, no difficulty there, imagination not dead yet, yes, dead, good, imagination dead imagine. Islands, waters, azure, verdure, one glimpse and vanished, endlessly, omit. Till all white in the whiteness the rotunda. No way in, go in, measure." Samuel Beckett, *Imagination Dead Imagine*. 1965. Trans. Samuel Beckett. (London: Calder and Boyars Ltd. 1967) 7.

89 | Jay McInerney, *Bright Lights, Big City*. (London: Bloomsbury, 1984) 10.

Tu as tout à apprendre, tout ce qui ne s'apprend pas: la solitude, l'indifférence, la patience, le silence. Tu dois te déshabituer de tout: d'aller à la rencontre de ceux que si longtemps tu as côtoyés, de prendre tes repas, tes cafés à la place que chaque jour d'autres ont retenue pour toi, ont parfois défendue pour toi, de traîner dans la complicité fade des amitiés qui n'en finissent pas de se survivre, dans la rancœur opportuniste et lâche des liaisons qui s'effilochent.[90]

Surveying this tradition and coming to more recent employments of the technique, one sees that the voice-over rhetoric dominates. Almost one hundred years after the publication of *The Haunted Mind,* one of the most bizarre fiction books ever written appeared. It was unconventional not only in structure and form but also in premise. Rex Stout's *How Like a God,* published in 1929, is the first second-person text of the modern period and more of a book of fiction than a novel. It consists of chapters that are interwoven with segments of a seemingly unrelated short story, with the threads uniting only in the terrifying conclusion. Stout's story, printed entirely in italics but otherwise told in conventional third-person narration, is divided into segments lettered A through Q. These reveal the thoughts of one Mr Lewis as he ascends a staircase with a pistol in his coat pocket, intending to kill someone in an upstairs room. Lewis's sense of impending doom raises the possibility that perhaps his intent is not murder but suicide, or perhaps both.

You fool, to stand here on the edge of hell and listen to dead voices, to her dead voice. You did so stop on those stairs, though, that night in Cleveland many years ago, and Lucy Crofts did call down to you as you stood hesitating whether to bother to go back and turn on the lights of the car.[91]

---

90 | Perec (1967/2002), 247.

91 | Rex Stout, *How Like a God.* 1929. (New York: Pyramid Books, 1963) 56.

Alternating with these brief cliff hanger segments are the long chapters I through XVI of a novel written in second-person narration. As MacIntyre in his entry in "FandSF" in the column "Curiosities" describes: "*You* – in narrative – is and you (the reader) are William Barton Sidney. Your entire existence, from childhood through sexual awakening into prosperous middle age, is recounted in these pages. (Your) life is respectable, normal, and prosaic. Yet nobody suspects that you are aware of multiple personalities within your body and that your head is full of voices. The final segment, Q, is a chilling climax that reveals Lewis's intended prey (human in visage only), the true relationship between Lewis and Sidney and the full significance of the novel's title, which is a quotation from Hamlet (intertextual reference)."[92]

We see the same narrative model in *Moon Deluxe,* written in 1983, a collection of short stories most of which appeared first in the *New Yorker* magazine. In *Moon Deluxe* Barthelme gives a wonderful portrait of contemporary life in the American landscape.

> You're stuck in traffic on the way home from work, counting blue cars, and when a blue-metallic Jetta pulls alongside, you count it - twenty-eight. You've seen the driver on other evenings; she looks strikingly like a young man - big, with dark, almost red hair clipped tight around her head.[93]

It is the first of Barthelme's minimalist books in which the writer attempts to come to terms with the real world in a way meta-fiction never could. Introducing his character by using the second-person narrative technique recalls McInerney: "You are not the kind of guy who would be at a place like this at this time of the morning. But

92 | Gwynplaine F MacIntyre, "How Like A God, by Rex Stout (1929)." In *Fantasy and Science Fiction - Curiosities.* January 2008, Date accessed 21 September 2017. SF Site spot art, www.sfsite.com/fsf/2008/cur0801.htm.

93 | Frederick Barthelme, *Moon Deluxe. Stories.* (Harrisonburg: Penguin Books, 1983) 61.

here you are, and you cannot say that the terrain is entirely unfamiliar, although the details are fuzzy. You are at a nightclub talking to a girl with a shaved head."[94]

In both cases the narrative convention of a *voice-over narrator* is established right from the beginning as a neutraliser that introduces readers to the stories. To that extent, it is interesting also to mention that we can witness a further expansion and elaboration of the second-person rhetoric of voice-over narrators in narratives that resemble the process of hypnosis or even guidebooks.

> Begin to wonder what you do write about. Or if you have anything to say. Or even if there is such a thing as a thing to say. Limit these thoughts to no more than ten minutes a day; like sit-ups, they can make you thin.[95]

Lorrie Moore's *Self- Help* (1985) is a highly transgressive and metatextual short story collection including several second-person narrations such as "How to Be an Other Woman," "How", "How to Talk to your Mother" and "How to Become a Writer". The titles of the passages determine right from the start that they are to be read as instruction manuals announcing their relationship to pseudo-guidebooks, the "How To" literature that is fictional, trivial and very popular. In such texts, the authorial *I* appears to be so instructive and omniscient that it corresponds more closely to a superior concept of the *ego (I)*, a super-human *instance* able to solve problems that ordinary people cannot. Subsequently, second-person address here depicts an objectified protagonist who stands as a representative of a particular society or social group facing a particular situation.

One could argue that when resembling guidebooks, second-person storytelling makes use of a certain concept of classifying the audience (readers) into different groups depending on some striking characteristics they might share. In doing so, Moore, for

94 | McInerney (1984), 1.

95 | Lorrie Moore, *Self-Help*. (London: Faber and Faber, 1985) 124.

example, not only undermines this generalising approach of books that promise to be guidebooks for life (elaborating on the traditional speciality guidebooks, e.g. travel) but also highlights that storytelling is a process designed by the author for a certain audience.

Up to this point these pages have proved the resilience and richness of the second-person technique, its appearance in different eras, genres and periods and have strengthened the argument articulated at the outset of this project that theorising attempts regarding the second-person technique can only be unsuccessful in so far as such an approach would be contradictory to the shifting nature and ambiguity of the pronoun, given the existence of different second-person texts in different genres, and then it would reduce and limit the potential of the rhetoric of the second person for a narrative.

The present project, by selecting four masterpieces of world literature – Christa Wolf's *Kindheitsmuster,* Michel Butor's *La Modification,* Georges Perec's *Un homme qui dort* and Ilse Aichinger's *Spiegelgeschichte* –, will aim to clarify and discuss in depth the rhetorical and thematic richness of each novel by emphasising the effects of the second-person technique and the radical intertextuality and affinity that these texts share with other texts that are also written in the second person but not analysed here. It will also aspire to show the validity of generalising some aspects of the second-person technique in a certain typology in order to elaborate on the case studies and provide the grounds of a preliminary classification that is not limiting the versatility of the second-person texts but still highlights their implicit or explicit affinities.

Part 2
Close Reading

2.1 Christa Wolf's *Kindheitsmuster*

Learning to Say "I"

> "Je forme une entreprise qui n'eut jamais d'exemple et dont l'exécution n'aura point d'imitateur. Je veux montrer à mes semblables un homme dans toute la vérité de la nature ; et cet homme, ce sera moi."
> (Rousseau, *Confessions*, Livre 1)

Born in 1929, Christa Wolf grew up under the Third Reich. In 1976 she published *Kindheitsmuster [Patterns of Childhood]*, a novel about growing up in Nazi Germany in an ordinary middle-class family. Her text presents a childhood during the years of National Socialism from the perspective of the survivors who were not among the victims of the Nazis, and also the challenge of preserving the memory of it for future generations. Elaborating on a common theme among the German writers of her generation, Christa Wolf composed *Kindheitsmuster* by employing a remarkable technique of narrative layers with multiple voices which investigate the making of a generation within the making of a book and aspire to express events and experiences long silenced.

Kindheitsmuster is a novel *about* autobiography rather than an autobiography as such. Though the book does contain autobiographical traces, it focuses more on autobiographical writing as a theme, elaborating and challenging the genre from within, and it is characterised by formal experimentation and radical reflexivity. The text highlights how individuals create themselves over time and through processes of representation such as writing. Featuring a highly self-reflexive storytelling mode, the book reveals aspects of and thematises the writing process while describing the challenges and problems inherent in (autobiographical) writing especially in cases when authors are dealing with a controversial or polemical past such as the Nazi period.

Kindheitsmuster therefore will be regarded as an exceptional example of post-war literature not because of its theme (the experience of the War and its aftermath) but mainly because of the way it reflects on it, structurally, formally and thematically, adopting the perspective of an autobiographer who has experienced the events from the position of the survivors. *Kindheitsmuster* is a post-war text about post-war literature and is striking also for its uncommon genre classification. The novel invents a unique narrative form and presents an alternative writing strategy for coping with the sensitive topic of a childhood under National Socialism, challenging and contesting the genre of autobiography from within.[96]

Within a project that focuses on the understanding of second-person storytelling, Wolf's novel might appear a poor fit at first sight since only one part is narrated in the second person and it is not entirely written from the second-person perspective. However, it does contribute significantly to the theme of this thesis and so will be discussed first in the close-reading part. *Kindheitsmuster* does contain a solid second-person narrative level which blends with the main third-person narrative and offers grounds for being examined in comparison to the more frequent, and expected, third- and first-person (singular) narrative perspectives (the latter missing for reasons that will be analysed further in this part). Such a comparative study of the second-person narrative perspective in fiction provides an ideal starting point for the project itself before it brings the focus deeper in the understanding of the phenomenon.

---

96 | Gretchen E Wiesehan, *A Dubious Heritage: Questioning Identity in German Autobiographical Novels of the Postwar Generation.* (New York: Peter Lang, 1997) 108.

Moreover, the narrative layering witnessed in *Kindheitsmuster* suggests a rich example for observing the functionality and broader use of pronouns in a narrative that addresses the theme of self-discovery, which appears to be one of the key themes in second-person fiction. In Wolf's case the second-person narrative perspective is employed to elucidate aspects of (autobiographical) writing, reflecting a self-control mechanism used by the narrator while performing her cross-examination. Here, second person designates (an aspiration for) authenticity and is linked with major issues addressed within the narrative mode such as self and self-awareness, reflexivity and representation.

The Main Narrative Components

The story centres on the continuous struggle of an anonymous female "Erzählfigur," an unconventional narrator (Christa Wolf's *fictional persona*) who chronicles her attempt to narrate her childhood under the Third Reich in the third person, after several failed attempts to do so from a first-person perspective which is more common and traditional on such narrative occasions.

Ein erneuter Versuch, dich zu verschanzen. Allmählich, über Monate hin, stellte sich das Dilemma heraus: sprachlos bleiben oder in der dritten Person leben, das scheint zur Wahl zu stehen.[97]

The story of the narrator, who is also the central character of the book (therefore *Erzählfigur*), evolves within a self-addressing dialogue written in the second person, which describes and comments on the writing process and its stimuli. The most important of these is the protagonist's recent trip to her birthplace in Poland, to which she reluctantly agreed and which she undertook with her husband H.,

97 | Christa Wolf, *Kindheitsmuster.* 1976. (Berlin und Weimar: Aufbau Verlag, 1987) 9.

her daughter Lenka, and her younger brother Lutz in the summer of 1971. This trip triggers her memory and offers grounds for evaluating what she remembers; it stands as a bridge between her and the events she tries to narrate, described in detail as a distinct sub-narrative. Complementing these narrative levels are generic comments and intertextual allusions that add a metatextual narrative level of generic and universal character.

Das Vergangene ist nicht tot; es ist nicht einmal vergangen. Wir trennen es von uns ab und stellen uns fremd.
[...] In die Erinnerung drängt sich die Gegenwart ein, und der heutige Tag ist schon der letzte Tag der Vergangenheit. So würden wir uns unaufhaltsam fremd werden ohne unser Gedächtnis an das, was wir getan haben, an das, was uns zugestoßen ist. Ohne unser Gedächtnis an uns selbst.[98] [...]
Wer gäbe nicht viel um eine glückliche Kindheit? Wer Hand an seine Kindheit legt, sollte nicht hoffen, zügig voranzukommen.[99]

These comments and generic statements are articulated in the first person plural or are embedded in the narrative through an impersonal syntax spread in the text, and they attempt to respond to the question which appears throughout the text as a motif and which also provides a title for the ninth chapter of the novel: "Wie sind wir so geworden, wie wir heute sind?"

This question appears repeatedly, at key points in the narrative to highlight its central theme and the narrator's aspiration to understand the evolvement of a generation and a person through time and to bridge the distance between the past and the current self, which prevents a sense of continuity and the use of the first person for the whole period. Dealing with an alienated past, the *Erzählfigur* reflects on every aspect of the writing process and her memories. This reflection is realised mostly at a second-person narrative level

98 | Wolf (1976/1987), 9f.
99 | Wolf (1976/1987), 37.

that enables the process of bringing the two levels together, examining them and involving numerous self-reflective parts.

For example, in the part quoted below, she describes the process of finding the appropriate title for the book. She then argues that the title should address the process of recalling the past rather than that of remembering it. Trying out several words such as "Grundmuster" or "Verhaltensmuster," she agrees with her husband's proposal of *Kindheitsmuster.* "Kindheitsmuster," a noun consisting of two words full of semantic potential, announces the theme and structure of the book. It primarily declares that the narrative will cover a childhood story and also that the narrated childhood reflects a pattern.[100]

> Ein Nachruf. Nach-Ruf könnte im Titel vorkommen. Gedächtnis nicht. Titelproben, beim Einkaufsweg mit H. In den Geschäften dieses Jahr immer noch die großen Apfelsinen, "Navelfrüchte". Einkreisung des unbekannten Wortes, das unter einer hauchdünnen Schicht zu stecken scheint, aber von den Such-Organen des Gehirns nicht zu fassen ist. Grund-Muster. Verhaltens-Muster.
>
> Kindheitsmuster, sagte H. beiläufig, es war vor der Apotheke, Ecke Thälmannstrasse. Damit war das geregelt.
>
> "Muster" kommt vom lateinischen "monstrum", was ursprünglich "Probestück" geheißen hat und dir nur recht sein kann.[101]

Wolf's *Erzählfigur* discusses the term "Muster" commenting on its origin and connotations. She seems to favour the first meaning of the word as it appears in the Etymological Dictionary of the GDR, communicating however erroneously its origin.[102] By adding the

100 | Therese Hörnigk, *Christa Wolf.* (Göttingen: Steidl, 1989) 169.

101 | Wolf (1976/1987), 52.

102 | "Muster n. "Probe(stück), Modell, Vorbild, Vorlage, Verziehung", entlehnt aus ital. *mostra* "das Zeigen, Schaustellung, Ausstellung," das auf vlat. *mostra* beruht, zu vlat. *mostrare*, lat. *monstrare*, zeigen, (hin)weisen" Wolfgang Pfeifer and Wilhelm Braun, *Etymologisches Wörterbuch des Deutschen*. (Berlin: Akademie-Verlag, 1989) 1142.

meaning "Probestück," additional implications enrich and deepen its meaning such as draft, exemplar and ideal. The title hence suggests a text in progress, a story which may be set in the past, but by designating it as a *probe* it also has a component that takes place and evolves in the present and extends into the future, an element of universality and continuity. By choosing to name the childhood story *Muster,* Wolf (through her persona) generalises the content of the story effect that comes as a result of adding a collective, thus, universal character to the text. She makes it less *autobiographical* by reducing to a pattern the sense of subjectivity and individuality that is inherent in autobiography and succeeds to *de-personalise* a personal story.

Der Titel "Kindheitsmuster" bezeichnet zugleich Thema und Struktur des Textes, von dem hier aus den ersten hundert Seiten ein kleiner Ausschnitt gegeben wird. Eine Gedächtnisprüfung findet statt. Die Kindheit der **Erzählfigur** soll erschlossen werden, geprägt in der Zeit des Faschismus, in einer östlichen Stadt, die heute zu Polen gehört.[103]

The title calls attention to some frequent and apparently acquired patterns of behaviour and shifts the emphasis from the individual to the collective, more precisely to Germans of the same generation. Consequently, it entails an additional shift in the historical focus from the debate about personal responsibility and participation in Nazi governance to the factors that shaped that generation's (and Wolf's) character and their attitude towards history. Hence it reveals and explains the approach and perspective that the author has towards the past involving references to the actual historical incidents as well, adding a metatextual and thus authentic element to the novel.

103 | Christa Wolf, "Kindheitsmuster." In *Text + Kritik,* 46. (München, 1980) 1.

Die später so genannte "Kristallnacht" wurde vom 8. zum 9. November durchgeführt. 177 Synagogen, 7500 jüdische Geschäfte wurden im Reichsgebiet zerstört.[104]

Consistent with her choice of title, Christa Wolf also warns readers even before the text proper begins that potential similarities with real people dead or alive should not be seriously considered, explaining that they are an inevitable outcome of the fact that the period narrated cultivated certain patterns of behaviour:

Alle Figuren in diesem Buch sind Erfindungen der Erzählerin. Keine ist identisch mit einer lebenden oder toten Person. Ebensowenig decken sich beschriebene Episoden mit tatsächlichen Vorgängen.
Wer Ähnlichkeiten zwischen einem Charakter der Erzählung und sich selbst oder ihm bekannten Menschen zu erkennen glaubt, sei auf den merkwürdigen Mangel an Eigentümlichkeit verwiesen, der dem Verhalten vieler Zeitgenossen anhaftet. Man müßte die Verhältnisse beschuldigen, weil sie Verhaltensweisen hervorbringen, die man wiedererkennt.[105]

Interesting also is the fact that Wolf refused to classify her text as pure autobiography while still conforming to an autobiographical narrative mode. She drew a line confirming the fictional aspect of it (implying that the same applies for every autobiographical text) by stressing the fictional origin of the names used, keeping the narrator anonymous and choosing another name for the experiencing subject.

[...] ich meine, ich kaschiere an keiner Stelle, daß es sich sozusagen um Autobiographisches handelt; das wird nicht verschwiegen. Wobei dieses "sozusagen" wichtig ist, es ist nämlich keine Identität da. Aber es gibt doch – das ist eine Eigentümlichkeit meiner Biographie, aber vielleicht

104 | Wolf (1976/1987), 209.
105 | Wolf (1976/1987), 6.

geht es andern in meinem Alter auch so - ein **Fremdheitsgefühl** gegenüber dieser Zeit.[106]

Although Wolf complicates the process of categorising her text as a specific genre by adding that it is *somehow* autobiographical, there are several elements which make this quotation more of a disclaimer than a statement. While the author states that her text is not a conventional autobiography and prevents the book from being read as such, the fact that the text does involve numerous autobiographical references contradicts its being pure fiction in the traditional sense. However, by including fictional elements, *Kindheitsmuster* questions and challenges the norms of autobiography and it presents a way of dealing with the limitations of the genre and its inherent problems. For this reason it cannot be simply classified as autobiography. As it combines facets of both autobiography and fiction it can be regarded as a unique narrative example which addresses and experiments with autobiography and reveals how it is generated. The text admits the unreliability of memory and remembering and adds fictional aspects to complete the story that the narrator (and fictional author) is unable to write purely based on her memories.

Gedächtnis. Im heutigen Sinn: "Bewahren des früher Erfahrenen und die Fähigkeit dazu." Kein Organ also, sondern eine Tätigkeit und die Voraussetzung, sie auszuüben, in einem Wort. Ein ungeübtes Gedächtnis geht verloren, ist nicht mehr vorhanden, löst sich in nichts auf, eine alarmierende Vorstellung. Zu entwickeln wäre also die Fähigkeit des Bewahrens, des Sich-Erinnerns.[107]

The activity of remembering as the author describes it above presupposes constant activation in order not to fade away; with this state-

---

106 | Wolf in Caroline Schaumann, *Memory Matters. Generational Responses to Germany's Nazi Past in Recent Women's Literature.* (Berlin: Walter de Gruyter, 2008) 92.

107 | Wolf (1976/1987), 18.

ment Wolf explains the *narrator* wilfully exercising some control over her memories, the process of cross-examination narrated in the second person which designates the key element of the plot and the generation of the story. It will be analysed in more detail later.

Very important before we proceed to the analysis of the book but also for this thesis is Wolf's choice of an "Erzählfigur" (see previous excerpt) instead of an "Erzähler(in)." The term – difficult to translate into English – implies the ambiguous nature of the *narrator* in Wolf's text: she is both the generator of the story and the subject of the narrated action and belongs to the discourse that she chronicles, hence she is not a conventional narrator ("Erzählerin") but the persona of a fictional narrator ("Figur"), a fact that justifies the use of the German term "Erzählfigur" or using the English *narrator* in italics for this chapter. This duality is worked into the form of the text itself and will be discussed in more detail in the pages relating to the pronominal use in *Kindheitsmuster.*

The passage quoted earlier contains one more key term that needs to be taken into account for the reception and understanding of the text: "Fremdheitsgefühl." Estrangement, self-alienation and the notion of an abandoned and dead childhood are fundamental themes in the narrative. Those notions stem from a poem by Pablo Neruda, which is cited prior to the main narrative:

Wo ist das Kind, das ich gewesen,
ist es noch in mir oder fort?

Weiß es, daß ich es niemals mochte
und es mich auch nicht leiden konnte?

Warum sind wir so lange Zeit
gewachsen, um uns dann zu trennen?

Warum starben wir denn nicht beide,
damals, als meine Kindheit starb?

Und wenn die Seele mir verging,
warum bleibt mein Skelett mir treu?

[...]

Wann liest der Falter, was auf seinen
Flügeln im Flug geschriebenen steht?[108]

Agreeing with the poem and echoing the same problematic regarding the past and its reception, the opening sentence of the text paraphrases the opening sentence of Faulkner's *Requiem for a Nun*, as Caroline Schaumann notices.[109] In Wolf's narrative, too, the past is viewed as an integral, living part of the present.[110] This approach reflects the subject's agonising search for reconnection with a deliberately forgotten past and an abandoned childhood, but it also emphasises the notion of a pattern, which leaves the *narrator* and *Erzählfigur* no other choice but to individualise her past self as another person. The childhood pattern described in the third person evolves into the present adulthood of the *narrator* (and, apparently, Wolf and all her contemporaries) told in the second person. This transition is what she tries to access as a continuous process, making the autonomous past an integral part of the present, without an appropriation process but in its most authentic form.

Das Vergangene ist nicht tot; es ist nicht einmal vergangen. Wir trennen es von uns ab und stellen uns fremd.[111]

---

108 | Pablo Neruda, *Buch der Fragen*. Trans. Erich Arendt. In: Wolf (1976/1987), 7.

109 | "The past is never dead. It's not even past." William Faulkner, *Requiem for a Nun*. (London: Chatto and Windus, 1919) 85.

110 | Schaumann (2008), 69.

111 | Wolf (1976/1987), 9.

Narrative Levels: Nelly Jordan

As mentioned above, the structure of the book in layers consists of a third-person narrative for the experiences of Nelly Jordan during the years 1932-1947 as well as a second-person narrative for the writing struggle of the adult *narrator*. This narrative is divided into two subplots: one which describes the process of autobiographical writing starting in 1972 and finishing in 1975, and the other chronicling the trip to Poland during the summer of 1971 that stimulated the writing process. An additional metatextual level is spread across the narrative's universal comments, common truths, intertexts and intertextual references. These phrases and comments fill the main narrative by enriching and commenting on scenes described, and they signal the central figure's and narrator's tendency to clarify, comment and reflect on what is remembered and written.

Es handelt sich ja nicht um eine Geschichte, die notwendig zu einem bestimmten Ende führen muß. Oder welches wäre der gedachte Punkt, bis zu dem sie vorgetrieben werden müßte? Im Krankenhaus, ohne Arbeitslust, unter den ersten, noch unverstandenen Anfällen von Angst, glaubst du klar zu sehen: Der Endpunkt wäre erreicht, wenn zweite und dritte Person wieder in der ersten zusammenträfen, mehr noch: zusammenfielen. Wo nicht mehr "du" und "sie" – wo unverhohlen "ich" gesagt werden müßte. Es kam dir sehr fraglich vor, ob du diesen Punkt erreichen könntest, ob der Weg, den du eingeschlagen hast, überhaupt dorthin führt. Es schien dir immerhin nicht wünschenswert, vorher aus der Welt zu gehen – wovon übrigens keine Rede sein konnte. Heimliche Rechnungen, die nur in Zeiten von Unglauben aufkommen: Unglauben an die Unerschöpflichkeit gewisser Fähigkeiten oder Antriebe. Oder Zwänge.

[...]

Steckt denn in der Frage "Wer bist du?" noch irgendein Sinn? Ist sie nicht hoffnungslos veraltet, überholt von der Verhörfrage: "Was hast du getan?", die in dir selbst auf die schwache Gegenfrage stößt: Was hat man mich tun lassen?[112]

Dann aber saßest du plötzlich - nicht du: Nelly, das Kind im Elternhaus, in dem schmalen Durchgang zwischen elektrischer Rolle und Laden auf einem Zuckersack, und Schnäuzchen-Oma, erblindet, stand neben Nelly und stützte sich ungebührlich schwer auf ihre Schulter. Von dem Druck bist du erwacht. Du konntest diesen Druck nicht abschütteln.[113]

Kindheitsmuster is a text in which all pronouns are used for different narratives, coexisting in the same story and thus revealing their narrative functions and rhetorical properties. The third-person voice employed in the story of Nelly, though detached from the personal life and memories of the *narrator*, does not evolve independently of the other narratives. The central figure of the novel reflects diverse *narrators* – the inquisitor, the one remembering the trip to Poland, the other chronicling Nelly's story and the impersonal one offering generalising comments – that reflect on each other continually. The one performing the composition of the autobiography admits that writing is destined to improve her self-awareness, re-establish her connection to the past and resolve the problem of self-continuity. A successful ending would restore the broken relationship with the past and allow her to use again the first-person narrative voice for all parts of her life.

Das Kind selbst aber, das nun zu erscheinen hätte? Kein Bild. Hier würde die Fälschung beginnen. Das Gedächtnis hat in diesem Kind gehockt und hat es überdauert.[114]

Nelly Jordan stands for the *narrator's* former self and re-experiences the incidents of the narrated childhood from 1932 to 1947 in a process of integrating a hidden non-articulated past into the present. She is a

112 | Wolf (1976/1987), 453.
113 | Wolf (1976/1987), 170.
114 | Wolf (1976/1987), 12.

figure created and named by her to fill the gaps in her memory and create a restored sense of autobiographical continuity of self.

Aus dem Wohnzimmerfenster hätte die Mutter nun das Kind zum Abendbrot zu rufen, wobei sein Name, der hier gelten soll, zum erstenmal genannt wird: Nelly! (Und so, nebenbei, auch der Taufakt vollzogen wäre, ohne Hinweis auf die langwierigen Mühen bei der Suche nach passenden Namen.)[115]

Her story covers the larger part of the text and is narrated purely from the third-person point of view of the adult *narrator* who narrates the story from an emotionally distant perspective and who can re-assess the past with the knowledge of how things turned out. Nelly Jordan, the imagined child, becomes an object of observation, a case study that brings the *narrator* closer to her own past by simulating it. At this narrative level, she may have a temporal superiority to the experiences narrated but she is still challenged by the limitations of memory and the reliability of her sources. She chooses to position herself outside the world of the narrative by being intentionally heterodiegetic and aims to evaluate the prompting testimony and to deal with the fundamental problem of authenticity in conventional homodiegetic autobiographies in order to be able to produce the most authentic version of her own autobiography whilst admitting that it includes fictional elements.

Das Kind - Nelly - erscheint dir allerdings hilfsbedürftig, und du hast es, man kann wohl sagen: vorsätzlich, in diese Lage gebracht. Nun kannst du sie schon mit keinem anderen Namen mehr anreden: Dabei ist es dein Wunsch und Wille gewesen, sie so und nicht anders zu nennen. Je näher sie dir in der Zeit rückt, um so fremder wird sie dir. Und das nennst du merkwürdig? [...]
Oder glaubst du, man könnte den verstehen, dessen man sich schämt? Den in Schutz nehmen, den man mißbraucht, um sich selber zu verteidigen?[116]

115 | Wolf (1976/1987), 13.
116 | Wolf (1976/1987), 277f.

[...]
Das Kind, das in mir verkrochen war – ist es hervorgekommen? Oder hat es sich, aufgescheucht, ein tieferes, unzugänglicheres Versteck gesucht? Hat das Gedächtnis seine Schuldigkeit getan? Oder hat es sich dazu hergeben, durch Irreführung zu beweisen, daß es unmöglich ist, der Todsünde dieser Zeit zu entgehen, die da heißt: sich nicht kennenlernen wollen?[117]

Nelly Jordan is portrayed as an ordinary girl of her time and generation; the focus on ordinary people applies also to her parents Charlotte and Bruno Jordan. The Jordans appear to be apolitical "Kleinbürger" whose main concern is their family business and children, and they represent an example of the German lower middle class of the time. They may not promote fascist ideals but they have also no objection to Nelly participating in local youth organisations. In fact, the entire order of the Jordan family is founded on silence and secrecy, which is a common phenomenon of childhood that the narrative attempts to break. Nelly seems to keep silent so as to fulfil her parents' wishes and the social values and virtues of the time. Similarly sensitive issues like marital conflict, sexuality and alcoholism are banished from discussion or acknowledged in the same way as Nazi actions are.[118]

Was ich nicht weiß, macht mich nicht heiß.
Was sie nicht wussten, machte sie lau. Übrigens hatten sie Glück. Keine jüdische oder kommunistische Verwandt- und Freundschaft, keine Erb- und Geisteskranken in der Familie (auf Tante Jette, Lucie Menzels Schwester, kommen wir noch), keine Auslandsbeziehungen, keine nennenswerten Kenntnisse in irgendeiner Fremdsprache, überhaupt keinen Hang zu zersetzenden Gedanken oder gar zu entarteter und anderer Kunst. [...]

---

117 | Wolf (1976/1987), 530.

118 | Elizabeth Snyder Hook, *Family Secrets and the Contemporary German Novel: Literary Explorations in the Aftermath of the Third Reich.* (Rochester: Camden House, 2001) 26.

Überhören, übersehen, vernachlässigen, verleugnen, verlernen, verschwitzen, vergessen.[119]

Charlotte Jordan appears to be the only person to express reservations about Nazi policies, however this happens just after these have affected her family, and all her objections are silenced by her husband Bruno. Charlotte, a mother who decided to stay behind and be separated from her children in 1945 when Germans were exiled and left as refugees, is presented as a dynamic person who had a significant impact on Nelly as she grew up and even after her death remained an influence on the adult *narrator*:

Plötzlich ein Schreck bis in die Haarspitzen: Auf dem Tisch im großen Zimmer das Manuskript, auf dessen erster Seite in großen Buchstaben nur das Wort "Mutter" steht. Sie wird es lesen, wird deinen Plan vollständig erraten und sich verletzt fühlen ...[120]

Interestingly enough the *narrator* calls her *Charlotte* rather than *mother*. This indicates the emotional and psychological distance necessary to assess their relationship more honestly. The *narrator* does not openly express feelings of guilt or pain towards her, and we, as readers, are only able to track their relationship indirectly through incidents in the narrative. The daughter-mother relationship becomes a central theme of the text as it is not limited to the bond between Nelly and Charlotte but expands to the *narrator*'s relationship with her daughter Lenka, implying that history repeats itself and that a broader approach to the topic is needed.

Lenka personifies the younger generation to which the *narrator* wishes to relate Germany's Nazi past. This purpose is confirmed by the fact that at the very beginning Christa Wolf dedicates the book to her real daughters Annette and Tinka. During the trip to the *narrator*'s birthplace in 1971 Lenka is the same age as Nelly was in 1945.

119 | Wolf (1976/1987), 197.

120 | Wolf (1976/1987), 19.

But in certain ways the two characters are very different. Unlike Nelly, Lenka dares to express her protest or dissent; she criticises and refuses to accept the ideologies of the GDR authorities and their politics as well as the Nazi ideology and questions its impact on the everyday life of the common people who lived in that era.

Lenka does not show any interest in hearing Nelly's story or hearing about her worldview. In fact she seems to be reluctant to accept the distance from her mother when disguised as Nelly Jordan. She even has difficulty understanding her and her mother Charlotte. Her attitude reflects some of the reasons that caused the *narrator*'s former (narrative) silence and inability to write her autobiography. However, despite these challenges, the experience of the Nazi past is communicated in an authentic way from one generation to the next by supporting memory with real facts while Lenka, as a representative of the younger generation, personifies hope and continuity as she dares to criticise, comment on and examine history in constant pursuit of the historical past.[121]

Set in the period of the Third Reich, Nelly's story offers a glimpse into the circumstances and incidents that created the generation of Christa Wolf's contemporaries. Everyday incidents, ordinary events and random moments, which in Nelly's eyes had minimal significance, are described in such a way as to show how influential they actually were or how decisive they were to the evolution of the story. They helped to shape Nelly's personality within complex familial relations and values that served to facilitate the transmission of Fascist ideology. Thus Nelly Jordan can be read as a symbol of her time, with whom readers – especially contemporaries of Christa Wolf – can identify, confirming the appropriateness of the word "Muster" in the title and offering the author a means to present typical patterns of a childhood during the Third Reich.[122]

121 | Schaumann (2008), 73.

122 | "Eine Kindheit wird intensive betrachtet, "gemustert" - nicht nur, um diesen Erinnerungsbereich möglichst vollständig zu erfassen, sondern mit dem Ziel, Wurzeln für heutiges Verhalten, prägende Einflüsse zu finden."

The use of a third-person *narrator* in this part of the story serves a self-protecting function, which makes questioning and evaluating the past possible. It makes the disclosure of sensitive, upsetting information safer and more bearable as they are assigned to another person rather than being treated as personal. However, the gesture of putting the elaborated autobiographical part in third-person syntax may be judged as ambiguous: on the one hand the distance from Nelly eases self-criticism while on the other hand it suggests a further source of guilt as the denial of the past constitutes a moral lapse.[123] The *narrator*'s choice to disguise her childhood behind Nelly's fictional persona enables her to adopt a more objective perspective on events as well as serving authenticity. At the same time, though, the alienation of what is narrated and the fictionality of the third-person narrative make it hard to distinguish between the fictional and the factual and to arrive at any safe conclusions regarding Christa Wolf's true past or that of the narrator.

> Weil es nämlich unerträglich ist, bei dem Wort "Auschwitz" das kleine Wort "ich" mitdenken zu müssen: "Ich" im Konjunktiv Imperfekt: Ich hätte. Ich könnte. Ich würde. Getan haben. Gehorcht haben.[124]

The above quote clarifies one of the reasons why the *narrator* does prefer the third person for her autobiographical memoir. The issues here are not just related to temporal distance and forgetfulness but also involve a moral distance as the memories of the past relate to a shameful period. When she acknowledges the degree of shame and pain involved in the narrative with powerful examples such as putting the word "ich" next to "Auschwitz" she proves that employing the third person is not a narrative trick to avoid responsibility but a narrative form that helps her writing to achieve authenticity.

Christine Schaper, *Christa Wolf: "Kindheitsmuster". Epische Struktur und Gehalt* (Doctoral Dissertation Halle, 1980) 163.

123 | Wiesehan (1997), 111.

124 | Wolf (1976/1987), 303.

Christa Wolf confirmed as much during a public discussion when she explained that employing the third person in this part of the text provided her and her *Erzählfigur* with an emotional safeguard and also resulted from her estrangement from the past. The author maintained that during the composition of *Kindheitsmuster* her detachment from her past was so strong that it would have been impossible and self-deceiving to use the first person; it would apply to any person having the same experience as, for example, the *narrator*'s persona.[125]

Schließlich kann man ein Spiel mit sich um sich beginnen. Ein Spiel in und mit der zweiten und dritten Person, zum Zwecke ihrer Vereinigung.
Zwei Brände beschließen dieses Kapitel, einander so ungleich wie Brände es nur sein können, in Nellys Erinnerung aber unlösbar miteinander verkoppelt: In solchen Dingen kann man sich nicht helfen.[126]

Apparently the attempt to explore and re-experience the past is connected to that of arranging grammatical conditions in the right order again. The text can succeed only if at the end the *narrator* manages to re-establish first-person authority and connect with the child she once was, thereby restoring the past in an accurate way. However, in

125 | "Ich habe vorhin gesagt, daß ich mehrere Anfänge habe, und davon sind die meisten in der Ich-Form. Und gerade das hat sich aus Gründen, die mir damals nicht einleuchten wollten, die ich auch gar nicht richtig verstand, immer wieder als Hindernis erwiesen, wirklich an die Sache heranzugehen [...] Aber es gibt doch – daß ist eine der Eigentümlichkeiten meiner Biographie, aber vielleicht geht es anderen in meinem Alter auch so – ein Fremdheitsgefühl gegenüber dieser Zeit. Seit einem nicht auf den Tag genau, aber doch auf eine Zeitspanne genau anzugebenden Moment ist man nicht mehr diese Person, habe ich nicht mehr das Gefühl, das ich das war, die das gedacht, gesagt oder getan hat. Und das wollte ich mit der dritten Person ausdrücken, das heißt, ich mußte es, weil sich anders das Material mir nicht öffnete, wie ich durch Versuche erfuhr." Wolf in Schaumann (2008), 92.

126 | Wolf (1976/1987), 209.

the third-person environment personified by Nelly, there is only one moment when the adult *narrator* identifies her own *I* with Nelly's – but this happens during sleep and therefore at a sub- or unconscious level.

Taking into account all the above, it seems as if the narrative took the form of a "Bildungsroman" that shows how the character learns to claim the first person again. Such a learning may involve stages and parts of the text that are told in other non-first-person narratives but the ability to say *I* remains the principal goal and aspiration of the entire narrative attempt. And indeed, at the end of the narrative, the *narrator* adopts a first-person perspective. This, however, is presented more as a necessity and compulsory convention than a successful outcome of the lasting struggle to restore and establish the continuity of her own self and of integrating her past into her present.

Und die Vergangenheit, die noch Sprachregelungen verfügen, die erste Person in eine zweite und dritte spalten konnte – ist ihre Vormacht gebrochen? Werden die Stimmen sich beruhigen? Ich weiß es nicht.[127]

Narrative Levels: The *Narrator*

The second-person *narrator* records the process of writing her autobiography starting on 3 November 1972 and finishing on 2 May 1975:

Was du heute, an diesem trüben 3. November des Jahres 1972, beginnst, indem du Packen provisorisch beschriebenen Papiers beiseite legend, einen neuen Bogen einspannst, noch einmal mit der Kapitelzahl I. anfängst.[128]

Within this narrative territory she discusses the difficulties of writing, admits to the limitations of memory and gestures towards

127 | Wolf (1976/1987), 530.

128 | Wolf (1976/1987), 9.

the perplexities of self-representation. Acknowledging the reasons that doomed previous writing to failure, she confesses her inability to respond directly to questions about her past, a phenomenon that may also apply to her contemporaries. The part of the narration that covers her efforts to write her autobiography is written in present tense and it suggests a simultaneous narration, giving the impression that it is happening now and is synchronised with the writing act as it evolves through the second-person self-reflexive dialogue which the author likens to a *cross-examination* process. Person and time align towards the production of the text:

Im Kreuzverhör mit dir selbst zeigt sich der wirkliche Grund der Sprachstörung: Zwischen dem Selbstgespräch und der Anrede findet eine bestürzende **Lautverschiebung** statt, eine fatale Veränderung der grammatischen Bezüge. Ich, du, sie, in Gedanken ineinanderschwimmend, sollen im ausgesprochenen Satz einander entfremdet werden. Der Brust-Ton, den die Sprache anzustreben scheint, verdorrt unter der erlernten Technik der Stimmbänder. **Sprach-Ekel**. Ihm gegenüber der fast unzähmbare Hang zum Gebetsmühlenklapper: in der gleichen Person.[129]

At the centre of *Kindheitsmuster* is the notion of personal and civic obligation and the relationship between history and writing as a moral activity in which remembering is analysed, assessed and reflected upon "im Kreuzverhör mit dir selbst."[130] Within this investigation, the *narrator* aspires to identifying the reasons for her inability to use language in a grammatically correct way and also for her attempt to deal with this problem through employing the second person. She announces that she is experiencing an annoying "Lautverschiebung," a term used rather incorrectly to reflect a violent change of grammatical conditions which affects her writing. Being somewhat blocked between a hybrid internal monologue and apostrophe, she discusses the problem profoundly affecting her self-au-

129 | Wolf (1976/1987), 9.
130 | Wolf (1976/1987), 9.

thority at the level of language as well. Though referring to the same person, "ich," "du," 'sie" are mixed but need to be separated into different voices. The child self and the adult self cannot be referred to as identical; self-schism and self-discontinuity provoke a "sprach-Ekel," which, while additionally challenged by the weaknesses of memory, generates the writing.

Memory forms one of the central patterns under investigation in the book. The *narrator* maintains that without memory we would be estranged from the things that have happened to us and thus from ourselves. In times when memory is universally lost, she argues that the present should be built on a vividly and properly remembered past.

> Im Zeitalter universalen Erinnerungsverlustes (Ein Satz, der vorgestern mit der Post kam) haben wir zu realisieren, daß volle Geistesgegenwart nur auf dem Boden einer lebendigen Vergangenheit möglich ist.[131]
> Es ist der Mensch, der sich erinnert – nicht das Gedächtnis.
> Der Mensch, der es gelernt hat, sich selber nicht als ein Ich, sondern als ein Du zu nehmen. Ein Stilelement wie dieses kann nicht Willkür oder Zufall sein. Der Sprung von der dritten Person in die zweite (die nur scheinbar der ersten nähersteht) am Morgen nach einem lebhaften Traum.[132]

Aware of the limitations inherent in the process of remembering and the unreliability of memory as a mechanism, the *narrator* employs several techniques so as to filter and legitimate it. One of the devices employed is cross-examination, as she calls the dialogue she performs with herself while writing. This process means that what she remembers from the past is double-checked before being incorporated into the story itself. Within this process she then manages to stimulate and make the writing genuine, as the second-person voice enables the division of the self into two sub-selves: one testifying, the other evaluating the testimony. Should she appropriate another

131 | Wolf (1976/1987), 202.
132 | Wolf (1976/1987), 157.

voice or narrative form for this part, this memory filtering could never take place.

Another device employed to support her memory is the trip to her birthplace L. in Poland to which the *narrator* had reluctantly agreed. The place that she had left as a refugee in January 1945 became travel destination G. with another name, language and currency, and it constitutes a narrative bridge enabling the transitions between Nelly's story and the *narrator*'s. Detached from any emotional involvement the *narrator* mentions that the reason for the trip should correspond to its true purpose and argues that she would call it "Arbeitsreise" or "Gedächtnisüberprüfung" if this would not sound odd and strange to the authorities.

> Damals, im Sommer 1971, gab es den Vorschlag, doch endlich nach L., heute G., zu fahren, und du stimmtest zu. Obwohl du dir wiederholtest, daß es nicht nötig wäre. Aber sie sollten ihren Willen haben. Der Tourismus in alte Heimaten blühte.[133]
>
> [...]
>
> Zutreffende Angaben wie "Arbeitsreise" oder "Gedächtnisüberprüfung" hätten Befremden erregt. (Besichtigung der sogenannten Vaterstadt!) Die neuen Passfotos fandet ihr - im Gegensatz zu den Angestellten der Volkspolizeimeldestelle - euch unähnlich, eigentlich abscheulich, weil sie dem Bild, das ihr von euch hattet, um den entscheidenden nächsten Altersschritt voraus waren. Lenka war, wie immer, gut getroffen, nach eurer Meinung. Sie selbst verdrehte die Augen, um sich zu ihren Fotos nicht äussern zu müssen.
>
> Während die Anträge auf Ausreise und bei der Industrie- und Handelsbank die Gesuche um Geldumtausch liefen, bestellte Bruder Lutz in der Stadt, die in deinen Formularen zweisprachig, unter verschiedenen Namen auftauchte, als "Geburtsort" L. und als "Reiseziel" G., vorsichthalber telegrafisch Hotelzimmer, denn ihr kennt in deiner Heimatstadt keine Menschenseele, bei der ihr hättet übernachten können.[134]

133 | Wolf (1976/1987), 10.

134 | Wolf (1976/1987), 10f.

The trip to the actual location of the memories filters remembering and past reflections as either correct, false, or modified. Due to its temporal and cognitive proximity to the narrative in which the character is writing her autobiography, the account of it is also composed in the second person. It prompts the *narrator* to re-evaluate her childhood, not only by re-examining her memories in terms of their authenticity but by uncovering new and unexpected ones.[135] During this trip the reader witnesses not only her past reflections but also the memories and the comments of her fellow travellers. H., her husband, appears mainly in the narrative of the trip, and he is described through his reactions and brief comments. He seems to be a vital contributor to the writing process. Similarly Lutz, her brother, represents a realistic and laconic fellow-traveller during the trip to Poland, yet he remains almost unmentioned during the narrative at Nelly's level, thus stressing her very young age and her inability to comprehend the past when it happened. The trip, which is undertaken by a group, is narrated in the second-person plural, stressing its dynamic and the sense of collectivity and echoing the respective experience of each person ("denn ihr kennt in deiner Heimatstadt").[136]

While remembering the trip the *narrator* compares her approach to the narrative that is taking place in the past with a "Krebsgang," signalling a sideways and backward movement rather than a linear backward one. *Crabwalk*, defined by Günter Grass as "scuttling backward to move forward,"[137] refers both to the necessary as well as to other events, some of them occurring at the same time, the same events that would lead to disaster eventually. Crabwalk might also imply a more abstract backward glance at history so as to allow

135 | Schaumann (2008), 71.

136 | Wolf (1976/1987), 11.

137 | "Ob ich der Zeit eher schrägläufig in die Quere kommen muß, etwa nach Art der Krebse, die den Rückwärtsgang seitlich ausscherend vortäuschen, doch ziemlich schnell vorankommen." Günter Grass, *Im Krebsgang*. (München: Steidl, 2002) 8f.

people to move forward. A crabwalk approach to the past allows the *narrator* actually to reflect on her experiences while shifting back and forth between past and present and provides multiple perspectives (narrative voices) on the narrated events. By doing this and by involving a gnomic statement, she highlights the importance of knowing one's past as a firm basis for future decisions while the sideways movement enables seemingly disconnected levels to be linked.[138]

> Frühere Entwürfe fingen anders an: mit der Flucht - als das Kind fast sechzehn war - oder mit dem Versuch, die Arbeit des Gedächtnisses zu beschreiben, als Krebsgang, als mühsame rückwärts gerichtete Bewegung, als Fallen in einen Zeitschacht, auf dessen Grund das Kind in aller Unschuld auf einer Steinstufe sitzt und zum erstenmal in seinem Leben in Gedanken zu sich selbst ICH sagt. Ja: am häufigsten hast du damit angefangen, diesen Augenblick zu beschreiben, der, wie du dich durch Nachfragen überzeugen konntest, so selten erinnert wird. Du aber hast eine wenn auch abgegriffene Original-Erinnerung zu bieten, denn es ist mehr als unwahrscheinlich, daß ein Außenstehender dem Kind zugesehen und ihm später berichtet haben soll, wie es da vor seines Vaters Ladentür saß und in Gedanken das neue Wort ausprobierte, ICH ICH ICH ICH ICH jedesmal mit einem lustvollen Schrecken, von dem es niemandem sprechen durfte. Das war ihm gleich gewiß.[139]

In the same gnomic statement, she comments on the unreliability of memory and reveals as a starting point for her autobiographical narration the moment when her past self is consciously articulated as the *I* for the first time. Showing that the claiming of the first-person pronoun is an outcome of a process of learning and experimenting which does not occur automatically as one grows older, she then implies that for the needs of her text this procedure should be

138 | Schaumann (2008), 71f.

139 | Wolf (1976/1987), 11f.

reversed. The *narrator* needs to *un-learn* the use of the first person and employ the second person instead, so as to *learn* to use it again.

As Snyder Hook highlights, Nelly's first awareness of *I* is accompanied by shock, excitement and a fierce awareness of self. Later in the story we find Nelly alienated from her initial sense of autonomy and forced to change her feelings and behaviour out of obedience and for self-preservation conforming to social norms and parental wishes.[140] While assessing patterns of childhood and perception, Wolf also explores the act of remembering supporting the process with additional, authentic material. This is the third device employed for filtering and controlling memory and supporting the credibility of what is being chronicled. By involving such material and mentioning actual historical events, Wolf's text connects to reality showing the development of collective history in tandem with her personal history.

Erinnerungshilfen. Die Namenlisten, die Stadtskizzen, die Zettel mit mundartlichen Ausdrücken, mit Redewendungen im Familienjargon (die übrigens nie benutzt wurden), mit Sprichwörtern, von Mutter oder Großmutter gebraucht, mit Lied anfangen. Du begannst Fotos zu sichten, die nur spärlich zur Verfügung stehen, denn das dicke braune Familienalbum wurde wahrscheinlich von den späteren Bewohnern des Hauses an der Soldiner Straße verbrannt. [...] Wie es nicht umsonst sein mag, gleichzeitig den Blick für das, was wir "Gegenwart" nennen, zu schärfen. "Massive Bombenangriffe der USA-Luftwaffe auf Nordvietnam." Auch das könnte ins Vergessen sinken.[141]

[...]

Wie so oft in den letzten eineinhalb Jahren, in denen du lernen mußtest: die Schwierigkeiten haben noch gar nicht angefangen. Wer sich unterfangen hätte, sie dir der Wahrheit nach anzukündigen, den hättest du, wie immer,

140 | Snyder Hook (2001), 3.

141 | Wolf (1976/1987), 15f.

links liegenlassen. Als könnte ein Fremder, einer, der außen steht, dir die Rede abschneiden.[142]

Other Narrative Levels

Welche Grenzen also? Halblaut: Zum Beispiel Grenzen dessen, was man mit Lenka bespricht. Und in welcher Weise. Man kann Kinder auch überfordern. Man kann ihnen auch zuviel zumuten - Du fragst: Und uns? Als wir Kinder waren? Und man uns immer nur diese halben Sätze zumutete? Unverständliche Blicke, an uns vorbei? Geschlossene Türen? Und diese mörderischen Szenen?[143]

As mentioned earlier, the *narrator* frequently offers to the core story additional – detailed – information or commentary in the first-person plural voice. The first-person plural narrative level refers to the people of her generation in the GDR. It comes in terms of the *we* mentioned in the question motif "Wie sind wir so geworden, wie wir heute sind?," enquiring about the evolution of her generation and also emphasises the collective nature of the narrated events while it immerses the reader in a joint or common experience with her and the events and experiences narrated.[144]

The implied or articulated *we* includes the first-person singular, the *I*, which is never employed in a narrative spanning more than five hundred pages. The authority of the first person is disguised in a comfortable collective identity, a need already evident in childhood, when Nelly's estranged *I* seeks to be included in a collective *we* and is illustrated as a process of losing self-identity within the group and self-consciousness during the oppressive Nazi period. This problematic search for the self encompasses the things that Nelly suppressed in her enthusiasm for National Socialism, an identity

142 | Wolf (1976/1987), 9.

143 | Wolf (1976/1987), 241.

144 | Hörnigk (1989), 174.

later confused by post-war GDR policy. During that time the blame for Nazism was shifted onto the West, away from *us* onto *them*.[145]

Similar to the use and function of the first-person plural is the impersonal ("man") or the passive voice as an alternative way to express generic thoughts and ideas so that they sound broader and more universal and less limited to the German context. By choosing impersonal or passive syntax (voice) the *narrator* avoids the difficult task of ascribing responsibilities to individuals, children and common people and concentrates instead on the events themselves and on how they are treated today by her contemporaries.

Fragen muß man sich, ob sich wirklich in derartig extremen Lagen zwangsläufig und zwingend herausstellt, was einem das Wichtigste ist: durch das, was man tut. Wenn aber der Betreffende nicht vollzählig die Informationen hätte, die ihm erlaubten, seine Entscheidung genau den Umständen anzupassen?[146]

The dilemma the text seeks to resolve reflects a historical paradox: human beings were physically present during the Third Reich though, at the same time, oddly absent. Wolf's text attempts to find an appropriate voice to narrate a period that was silenced, acknowledging the historic circumstances and investigating the formation of a generation without intending self-excuse or self-accusation:

Frühere Leute erinnerten sich leichter: eine Vermutung, eine höchstens halbrichtige Behauptung.

[...]

Zwischenbescheide geben, Behauptungen scheuen, Wahrnehmungen an die Stelle der Schwüre setzen: ein Verfahren, dem Riß, der durch die Zeit geht, die Achtung zu zollen, die er verdient.

In die Erinnerung drängt sich die Gegenwart ein, und der heutige Tag ist schon der letzte Tag der Vergangenheit. So würden wir uns unaufhaltsam

145 | Snyder Hook (2001), 23.

146 | Wolf (1976/1987), 38.

fremd werden ohne unser Gedächtnis an das, was wir getan haben, an das, was uns zugestoßen ist. Ohne unser Gedächtnis an uns selbst.
Und die Stimme, die es unternimmt, davon zu sprechen.[147]

Christa Wolf (and her *Erzählfigur*) acknowledges that what is experienced and what is narrated ideally should be identical. Admitting that such an aspiration cannot succeed and given the fact that there is no technique that could provide preciseness, the *narrator* in her text needs multiple narrative voices to describe the events from different perspectives and memory filters to objectify her writing and support its authenticity. In that sense one could argue that the book is a unique work of narrative art that reproduces at an autobiographical level historical and personal details of the past and tests the childhood world against authorial fantasies and perceptions in a work of fiction.[148]

Im Idealfall sollten die Strukturen des Erlebens sich mit den Strukturen des Erzählens decken. Dies wäre, was angestrebt wird: phantastische Genauigkeit. Aber es gibt die Technik nicht, die es gestatten würde, ein unglaublich verfilztes Geflecht, dessen Fäden nach den strengsten Gesetzen ineinandergeschlungen sind, in die lineare Sprache zu übertragen, ohne es ernstlich zu verletzen. Von einander überlagernden Schichten zu sprechen – "Erzählebenen" – heißt auf ungenaue Benennungen ausweichen und den wirklichen Vorgang verfälschen. Der wirkliche Vorgang, "das Leben", ist immer schon weitergegangen; es auf seinem letzten Stand zu ertappen bleibt ein unstillbares, vielleicht unerlaubtes Verlangen[149].

Success would consist in managing to do so in accordance with the actual historical events, which are implied or briefly mentioned in the main text and which match the character's persona as credible. By motivating the process of remembering through use of docu-

147 | Wolf (1976/1987), 9f.
148 | Snyder Hook (2001), 20.
149 | Wolf (1976/1987), 354.

mentary material, the *narrator* may slip into genre confusion, but she succeeds in composing a personal narrative of what she calls *subjective authenticity*. Wolf developed this practice to reconcile the demands of Socialist Realism and authenticity with a subjectivity associated with eccentricity and aberrance from the collective.

Kindheitsmuster involves a complex mixture of personal memories, critical comments and self-reflections alongside historical facts and observations on the nature of memory. In contrast to the narrator of a conventional autobiography, the *narrator* of *Kindheitsmuster* is not projected as a self-knowing subject; rather, as the veracity of the *narrator* is being established within the narrative itself in which she performs, she portrays a subject caught up in a process of growing self-awareness. Wolf's life story introduces the notion of "phantastische Genauigkeit," accepting the subjective perception of reality and consequently the narrative necessity of constructing a fictional character along with his or her memories within the autobiographical process.[150]

> Weggefegt ist der Rauchvorhang vor dem Gewimmel der erdichteten Gefühle. Einsicht herrscht, Nüchternheit und Kenntnis bei gesteigerter Sensibilität: Realismus. Nicht Dürre der Konstruktion oder Naturalismus, aber auch der Überschwang erhitzter Empfindungen nicht.
> Sondern: phantastische Genauigkeit.
> [...] Ihnen mag es leichter fallen als den Schreiben, zu definieren, woran sie arbeiten – sie wollen herausfinden, aus welchem Material die Welt besteht; aber merkwürdigerweise brauchen sie – je kleiner die Teilchen werden, mit denen sie es zu tun haben, je schwieriger exakte Messungen – eingestandenermaßen eine unmeßbare Größe: die schöpferische Phantasie.[151]

150 | Renate Rechtien, "From Vergangenheitsbewältigung to Living with Ghosts: Christa Wolf's *Kindheitsmuster* and Leibhaftig." In *The Self in Transition. East German Autobiographical Writings Before and After Unification*. Eds. David Clarke and Axel Goodbody. (New York: Rodopi, 2012) 126.

151 | Christa Wolf, *Lesen und Schreiben: Neue Sammlung*. (Darmstadt: Luchterhand, 1980) 33.

The author avoids the instructive character of Socialist Realism and describes an alternative. She does not describe what is supposed to be *real* in terms of her past or even Nelly's past admitting the unreliability of memory and confirming the fact that what is historically projected as real, also in autobiographies, might not be. Nelly's persona experiences the real events but in a non-realised way, not really being in a position to perceive the incidents as they are; as readers we therefore read an experience-based text without speculations and assumptions about the past, taking into account the situation of the experiencing subject and the distance from the one narrating it. At the same time, Wolf rejects the charge that her writing is *subjectivistic* as she attempts to produce a narrative as close to the real as she is able to, as close as possible to the unattainable goal of total accuracy.[152]

Dies ist eine durchaus "eingreifende" Schreibweise, nicht "subjektivistische". Allerdings setzt sie ein hohes Maß an Subjektivität voraus, ein Subjekt, das bereit ist, sich seinem Stoff rückhaltlos ... zu stellen, das Spannungsverhältnis auf sich zu nehmen, das dann unvermeidlich wird, auf die Verwandlungen neugierig zu sein, die Stoff und Autor dann erfahren. Man sieht eine andere Realität als zuvor ... Die Suche nach einer Methode, dieser Realität schreibend gerecht zu werden, möchte ich vorläufig "subjektive Authentizität" nennen - und ich kann nur hoffen, deutlich gemacht zu haben, daß sie die Existenz der objektiven Realität nicht nur nicht bestreitet, sondern gerade eine Bemühung darstellt, sich mit ihr produktiv auseinanderzusetzen.[153]

152 | Wiesehan (1997), 107.

153 | Wolf (1980) in *Lesen und Schreiben*, 75.

Conclusion

Das Letzte zu sagen: Die Wirklichkeit dieses Jahrhunderts selbst wendet sich gegen die Prosaschreiber. Sie ist phantastischer als jedes Phantasieprodukt. Ihre Grausamkeit und ihre Wunderbarkeit sind durch Erfindung nicht zu übertreffen. Wer also "die Wahrheit" lassen will, das heißt: wie es wirklich gewesen ist, der greift zu Tatsachenberichten, Biographien, Dokumentensammlungen, Tagebüchern, Memoiren.
Der Kuchen "Wirklichkeit", von dem Prosaschreiber sich früher in aller Seelenruhe Stück für Stück abschnitt, ist aufgeteilt.[154]

Wolf suggests that recalling the past, no matter by what process we do so, can never lead to fiction or autobiography only. For her, restoring the reality of the past is a mixing of fictional/invented memories with pieces of truth, provided by memoirs, diaries and real documents. Containing different layers and involving complex social structures and schemes, *Kindheitsmuster* shows how even when the attempts of an authorial *I* fail, painful memories can be still expressed.

Vielleicht sollte es dir um Verluste, die Nelly erlitt - unwiderruflich erlitt, wie du heute weißt -, doch leid tun. Vielleicht sollte es dir leid tun, um das Kind, das sich damals verabschiedete: von niemandem gekannt und als derjenige geliebt, der es hätte sein können. Das sein Geheimnis mitnahm: das Geheimnis von den Wänden, in die es eingeschlossen war, die es abtastete, um jene Lücke zu finden, die ihm etwas weniger Angst machte als die anderen - aber doch auch noch Angst genug.
Eine Angst, die sich damals in einem durchdringenden, andauernden Gefühl von Selbstfremdheit zu erkennen gab und deren Spur eben darin besteht, daß sie die Spuren löschte: Einem Menschen, der nicht auffallen will, fällt bald nichts mehr auf. Der entsetzliche Wille zur Selbstaufgabe läßt das Selbst nicht aufkommen.[155]

154 | Wolf (1980) in *Lesen und Schreiben*, 17.
155 | Wolf (1976/1987), 305.

Writing (and reading) appears in *Kindheitsmuster* as the essence of life. Writing gives the *narrator* a skeleton on which to hang memories and thoughts and making them more understandable; whereas the second-person self-cross-examination works as a mechanism by which to distinguish invented memories from actual ones thus adding validity to the statements and memories. The act of writing supports the work of associating the *narrator*'s multiple selves by integrating its past and present into a single, unified, diachronic sense of self.

Kindheitsmuster is defined by the unattainable *I* and is narrated using all narrative voices except for the first person singular while reflecting on their use and function. The multiple narrative voices employed correspond to different perspectives, and they constitute a narrative palimpsest of a broader range of narrative voices and rhetoric. Wolf manages herewith to show the circumstances and processes which shaped her generation, and she communicates her findings and thoughts as authentically as she can by revealing to the younger generation and her contemporaries as well as admitting to herself the various doubts, problems and insecurities she feels while writing.

In this process, a first-person level coexists of course, but that is only implicit because of the suspension and omission of the first person in every utterance of the novel. Readers can never decide whether the first person is just silenced or missing. Whether singular or plural (including her company on the trip), even when the narration is realised in the second person exclusively, the first person is not eliminated as a possibility but remains the unarticulated outcome of a sort of speech disorder or aphasia, emphasising the problem of self-continuity and disconnection from the past.

The implicit first person designates an unattainable possibility that highlights its being unavailable for the *narrator* and justifies the selection of the third person in Nelly's part reflecting the radical alienation from the past, and the second person in the self-reflexive part serving as a carrier of objectivity and enabling the cross-examination that she performs to generate the text. Thus the narrative, though reflecting a personal story, is deprived of every subjectivity, alienated in the sphere of a third-person territory – narrated as a story of Nelly's – and examined externally by the narrative "du."

By dramatising the past and present disruption with the employment of the second person, Wolf is creating a sort of second self to double the first. The "du" is not only a device for the self-talk that generates Nelly's story but also refers to the reader within a narrative space which acts as a mirror and includes him/her in the purpose of her book which is to understand her own generation. At the same time this narrative "du" qualifies as an essential part of the writing process, orienting its content towards its recipients.

First-person discontinuity as detected here is a problem inherent in autobiographical writing. Most frequently, essential factors such as the distance between the narrating and the experiencing self, youth or even (deliberate) ignorance obscure the process by which the past can be narrated by the autobiographer with full authority and reliability. Wolf deals with this problem openly, using Nelly Jordan as the past self of her *narrator* to experience the chronicled childhood and to evolve into her adulthood while composing her autobiography. Dealing with the problem of a person's development and the pronouns to use, Michel Butor proposes the second person as an appropriate narrative form in such cases.

Si le personnage connaissait entièrement sa propre histoire; s'il n'avait pas d'objection à la raconter ou se raconter, la première personne s'imposerait: il donnerait son témoignage. Mais il s'agit de le lui arracher, soit parce qu'il ment, nous cache ou se cache quelque chose, soit parce qu'il n'a pas tous les éléments, ou même, s'il les a, qu'il est incapable de les relier convenablement. Les paroles prononcées par le témoin se présenteront comme des îlots à la première personne à l'intérieur d'un récit fait à la seconde, qui provoque leur émersion.[156]

156 | Michel Butor, *Répertoire II.* (Paris: Éditions de Minuit, 1964) 66f.

Butor claims that using the second person rather than the first enables the narrator to speak the truth; it broadens his/her perspective and gives the narrative a sense of testimony. This dialogic form of narrative, made possible by the use of the second-person agent, addresses the division of the self into sub-selves marked by different pronouns as distinct instances and reveals the temporality of the self as a sum of individual synchronic instances and not as a single, continuous diachronic unit.

The existence of second-person autobiographies already in antiquity proves the intriguing relationship between the second and the first person as interchangeable in certain narrative cases and supports the above argument. The employment of the second person in autobiography enables the author to bridge the temporal distance between narrated time and narrating time, corresponding to different versions of the self and enabling her to make them part of the narrative. Furthermore, the dialogic dimension of second-person narrative adds to its perceived reliability and authenticity, even though it is of course purely subjective, as we discussed earlier and in greater detail.

Paul Eakin defines autobiographical writing "as a ceaseless process of identity formation in which new versions of the past evolve to meet the constantly changing requirements of the self in each successive present."[157] This definition reflects the inner need of the autobiographer to express the ongoing struggle of experiencing the self in textual terms and treats the process of autobiographical writing as a work in progress, thematising the relationship between past and present and their continuity. Hence appropriating the use of a pronoun that can express the contemporaneity is legitimised as well as the dominance of the present tense. Seeing the past as an integral part of the present is crucial to understanding the self as a diachronic continuous unit and justifies its being the primary aspiration of the notion of autobiography that Wolf writes about.

157 | Paul John Eakin, *Fictions in Autobiography: Studies in the Art of Self-Invention.* (Princeton: Princeton University Press, 1985) 36.

In Wolf, however, we identify a major difference from and exception to what Butor and other theorists imply. In *Kindheitsmuster* the past self and the present self are separated not only by a chronological but also by a moral distance. Experiencing events of shame, guilt and historical importance, the past self is represented by a non-personal alienated third-person agent, whereas the second-person voice dictating the story appears within the writing itself in a dialogue that the *narrator* performs with herself. To put things more simply the events are narrated to the *narrator* in a second-person narrative and not to Nelly, as she and the *narrator* are different. The *narrator* is the one to whom Nelly's story should be narrated in a form that is more understandable as Nelly does not exist anymore. To this extent, the second-person entity represents the inherent but constant transformation of the writing *I* to the narrated *I*, expressed in the third person due to this recorded alienation and in the second person in the part reflecting the investigation that the *narrator* performs and the aspiration of objectifying and authenticating what is narrated.

Weil es schwerfällt, zuzugeben, daß jenes Kind da – dreijährig, schutzlos, allein – dir unerreichbar ist. Nicht nur trennen dich von ihm die vierzig Jahre; nicht nur behindert dich die Unzuverlässigkeit deines Gedächtnisses, das nach dem Inselprinzip arbeitet und dessen Auftrag lautet: Vergessen! Verfälschen! Das Kind ist ja auch von dir verlassen worden. Zuerst von den anderen, gut.[158]

In other words, whereas the third person represents the voice of alienation and enables the observation of a narrative persona different from the *narrator* which functions as an object of narration, the second-person voice suggests the device for inquiry and investigation and is a vital part of the writing process. It orientates the narrative towards its addressee (reader, contemporaries, the *narrator,* Christa Wolf, future generations), examines and controls that which is narrated and reflects the self-reflective relationship between the

158 | Wolf (1976/1987), 14.

writing and the narrated *I*, which is actually the main theme of the novel. This transcendence appears in the narrative with the cross-examination that the *narrator* performs and reflects the constant transformation of the composing *I* to a reflected *you*, which stimulates the writing and functions as a self-awareness mechanism.

In addressing this problem of autobiographical narratives, namely the reliability or unreliability of her *narrator*, Wolf introduces the term "phantastische Genauigkeit" (see previous excerpt) which describes the form and technique of her book and summarises the balance between fictional and autobiographical elements in the narrative: fictional events coexist with historical ones and make the text as genuine as it can be, even while acknowledging its subjectivity, reflecting a person's past and emotions.

Structured in layers and narrated by different narrative agents at different points, *Kindheitsmuster* offers a palimpsest of narrative forms revealing and thematising its own nature. It thus provides the basis for modelling and mapping second-person narrators in other texts written exclusively from the second-person point of view. Wolf, using different pronouns to narrate different versions of the same person, echoing periods or variations of the self, reveals a more depersonalising aspect of the pronominal use as it brings ambiguity to the character and identity to different persons or personae of the same person. However, it would be reductive to claim that the use of the pronoun is just a narrative trick and wrong to examine it only as a grammatical form because it actually designates the exact opposite, a manifestation of the versatility and resilience of the persona. An assumption that we may make about Wolf's text is that through a process of depersonalisation, provoked by the dominance of the second-person pronoun, it makes the narrative more impersonal even though it addresses a personal theme and opens up an additional field for experimentation and elaboration on some complicated themes and self-constructions, related to authenticity, reception and representation.

Having started with the genre of autobiography and focussing on self-referring and self-reflecting texts, the next example of second-person storytelling to be examined is Michel Butor's *La Modification*, presenting a pure second-person text, written almost entirely as "vous" and thematising a self-awareness story, this time entirely at the level of the adult self.

2.2 Michel Butor's *La Modification*

Addressing the Unknown

"L'œuvre d'art, comme le monde, est une forme vivante: elle est, elle n'a pas besoin de justification."
(Alain Robbe-Grillet, *Pour Un Nouveau Roman*)

[...] le terme de *Nouveau Roman,* ce n'est pas pour désigner une école, ni même un groupe défini et constitué d'écrivains qui travailleraient dans le même sens; il n'y a là qu'une appellation commode englobant tous ceux qui cherchent de nouvelles formes romanesques, capables d'exprimer (ou de créer) de nouvelles relations entre l'homme et le monde, tous ceux qui sont décidés à inventer le roman, c'est-à-dire à inventer l'homme.[159]

La Modification, published in 1957 and winner of the Renaudot prize that year, is Michel Butor's third novel and his best-known book. Emerging out of the *nouveau roman* period, the novel contains two fundamental features of the movement – formal experimentation and self-reflexivity – and contributes to the evolution of the genre by contesting it from within. The *nouveau roman,* as Robbe-Grillet describes it in the quotation above, is characterised by the writers' tendency towards formal and structural innovation in their literary work, rather than constituting a homogenous literary school with specific features.

159 | Alain Robbe-Grillet, *Pour un Nouveau Roman.* 1963. (Paris: Les Éditions de Minuit, 2013) 10.

The movement established itself in France in the fifties, during the period of French structuralism (1950-1975) that had its primary origin in the theories of Ferdinand de Saussure and signalled a shift from an emphasis on content to formal realism. Hence initially, the *nouveau roman* was seen more as a challenge to traditional realism and what was vaguely called the Balzacian novel. It developed in a time during which literature and linguistics fertilised each other and blossomed. Roman Jakobson's early formalism, Roland Barthes's study of semiology and semiotics, Claude Lévi-Strauss's application of de Saussure's structural linguistics to anthropology and Émile Benveniste's published works expanding de Saussure's linguistic paradigm at the end of the 1960s and the beginning of the 1970s are all major inputs in theory and criticism that influenced the writers of the time. The *nouveaux romanciers* experienced a generally active period in other arts as well; between 1950 and 1960 photography, theatre and most importantly cinema (*Nouvelle Vague*) enjoyed a significant development echoing the needs of the time and positioning the *new human* in the post-war world.[160]

Among the ideas that were embraced by the *nouveaux romanciers* and that can be identified in Butor's *La Modification* is the recognition that description is potentially infinite in the sense that any scene could be broken into ever-smaller units, with more and more detail supplied. For the *nouveaux romanciers* there could never be a definite or definitive transcription of reality and so they endeavoured to expose the selectivity and non-objectivity of traditional realist description. In the works of the *nouveau roman* and in the particular example of *La Modification,* the description of reality is so detailed and authentic that it includes what could also be considered unnecessary detail, thus making the ordinary into a source of fascination in fiction.

160 | For a historical account of French structuralism, see Hans Bertens, *Literary Theory: The Basics.* (London and New York: Taylor and Francis Group, 2nd ed., 2008)

Moreover, writers of the *nouveau roman* rejected the traditional view of language as an unproblematic vehicle for the representation of reality. The objection concerned the distance between experience and writing, a distance that can never be closed in real time as new events are happening during the composition. These events multiply relentlessly the number of data points to be taken into account. The *nouveaux romanciers* rejected the concept of reducing literature to a medium for the propagation of messages to the world and argued that formal experimentation could actually make the reader see the world anew.[161] *La Modification* is the first purely second-person narrative to be examined in the project, and it will be analysed as was *Kindheitsmuster* by focussing on its narrative perspective and structure. As with all narrative examples discussed here, the focus lies on the impact of the second-person pronoun and its use and function in the narrative.

It is also important to point out that with *La Modification* and the second-person employment in the narrative Michel Butor contributes significantly to the theme of self-discovery as a key topic of second-person fiction and the fundamental question as to whether pronouns should be regarded more as a grammatical phenomenon or as related to the person, designating above all personal reference.

THE NOVEL

Michel Butor, born in 1926, was a student of literature and philosophy before becoming a prolific writer. With *La Modification* he presented in 1957 the common story of a love-triangle though narrated from the less common second-person perspective (with some rare exceptions). Avoiding any ethical messages, he depicts both the adventures of his main character and the adventure of writing. *La Modification* chronicles the story of an intended life change which,

161 | Jean H Duffy, *Butor: La Modification*. (London: Grant and Cutler Ltd, 1990) 14-16.

however, is never realised. The plot details a sequence of minor modifications which result in a major modification of the hero's perspective on life rather than the big life change that is (ironically) implied in the title.

The book enjoyed popularity and praise from its contemporaries and was a milestone of the *nouveau roman* period: it blends the traditional format of a specific framed plot and character with a postmodern self-reflexive dimension while inscribing many of the ideas of the *nouveau roman* as briefly described in the introductory passage above.[162]

> Vous avez mis le pied gauche sur la rainure de cuivre, et de votre épaule droite vous essayez en vain de pousser un peu plus le panneau coulissant. Vous vous introduisez par l'étroite ouverture en vous frottant contre ses bords, puis, votre valise couverte de granuleux cuir sombre couleur d'épaisse bouteille [...][163]

The narrative starts *in medias res*, opening with a striking "vous" and a detailed description of the protagonist's movements and surroundings. Information is limited to what the protagonist witnesses visually in his environment: a train carriage. The narrative evolves based on observations and associations, without revealing any of the character's inner thoughts or emotions. The plot and the main character's situation are gradually revealed as the narrative develops along with the journey that is about to begin. The narrator offers access only to the senses of the character and lets readers witness his experience through his eyes, without any direct characterisation but introducing the character through his thoughts and actions gradually proceeding on his journey towards self-awareness (*ethopoeia*):

162 | Duffy (1990), 96.

163 | Butor (1957/1980), 7.

par moments la pensée du voyager (qui n'est alors qu'un pur regard) se porte sur les endroits représentés par les photos publicitaires dont sont garnies les cloisons du compartiment.[164]

The story begins one morning when Léon Delmont – the main character of the book, a middle-aged man in 1950s Paris, France, who is married with children – boards a train to Rome in Paris. He is about to leave his wife for his mistress, whom he meets every time he visits the Italian capital on business as chief representative of Scabelli, an Italian firm of typewriter manufacturers. This time he is travelling to Rome for purely personal reasons and, contrary to his business habits, travels third class. He wishes to tell his mistress Cécile that he has found a job for her in Paris and that they can start a new life together there as he has decided to divorce his wife Henriette.

During the journey all manner of associations and memories overcome Léon and blend with his desires and hopes. The narrative constantly shifts between different periods of Léon's life as fragments of former journeys are evoked again and again, constantly interrupting the narration of the current trip. In the linear development of the train journey, these minor narratives involving the past or even the future appear as intermissions with a random associative order in a non-linear sequence as they are triggered by ordinary incidents and external stimuli, without any specific justification. Flashbacks of the past and daydreams of the future exceed the time frame of the twenty-four-hour journey, yet they become integral parts of the present, influencing how it is perceived. Léon is assailed by these memories and dreams and the upset they cause. As a result he is increasingly tortured by self-doubt as he approaches his destination, and the firmness of his purpose gradually erodes.[165]

164 | Michel Leiris, Afterword: "Le réalisme mythologique de Michel Butor." 1958. In Michel Butor, *La Modification*. 1957. (Paris: Edition Minuit, 1980) 293f.

165 | Mary Lydon, *Perpetuum Mobile: A Study of the Novels and Aesthetics of Michel Butor*. (Edmonton: Alberta University Press, 1980) 101.

Before finally arriving in Rome, Léon's plan has definitively altered; he has come to realise that his love for Cécile is actually connected with his love of Rome and that her moving to Paris would deprive him of having Rome as a rejuvenating getaway. Therefore, by the end of the novel and by the time the train finally reaches the Italian capital, Léon has reversed his decision: he intends to spend his days alone without seeing Cécile, revisit Rome with his wife in the form of a second honeymoon at some point in the future and record his experience in a book. In the final part of *La Modification*, Léon states his wish to keep the conditions of his life the same as before and the distance between the two cities unchanged. His adventure, however, is not diminished by the fact that his initial intention is not realised: when Léon steps off the train at the end, the need to recreate the adventure in a book is declared, implying the beginning of a new adventure, namely that of writing.

Léon's Adventure

La Modification is a book that involves two different adventures, that of its central character and that of writing. Both of them are subject to modifications and are narrated from a second-person perspective. The choice of a common narrative mode/voice for both adventures and this style of unspecified address add coherence to the narrative which appears unified although it inscribes two distinct narrative levels.

The first level, depicting Léon's adventure and train experience, involves a thematic modification and reflects the gradual reversal of his decision. The modification of Léon's determination, culminating in his final decision not to leave his wife, is presented and reasoned gradually in three different stages corresponding to three simultaneous narratives of the journey. These three narrative stages are reflected in the structure of the book, which is divided into three parts each of which is subdivided into untitled, numbered chapters.

Each of the chapters begins with Léon Delmont entering a train compartment and ends with him leaving it, marking his seat always with a book he bought at the station in Paris and which remains unread until the end. The chapters, numbered with Roman numerals, are subdivided into smaller units of varying length, and there is the same variation in the length of the sentences, which are most often long and complicated, with minimal punctuation and frequent repetitions. Similarly, paragraphs often start with non-capitalised words or phrases, thus seeming to have been picked up from a previous utterance in verse-like form.[166] This writing style reflects the obsessive attention to detail that *nouveaux romanciers* favoured in their writings; it also aligns the narrating process with the movement of the train. Flashes of views through the window of the compartment interrupt its duration and undifferentiated repetitiveness, just as the narrative about Léon's decision to change his life involves memories, daydreaming and other sub-narrative interruptions.

Part A: A Life-Changing Plan

The first part of the novel is about Léon looking forward to a new life of freedom and romance with Cécile, lingering over memories of their first encounter and hopes for their future together.

Ce voyage devrait être une libération, un rajeunissement, un grand nettoyage de votre corps et de votre tête; ne devriez-vous pas en ressentir déjà les bienfaits et l'exaltation?[167]

Written in the present tense exclusively, this part chronicles the actual trip from Paris to Rome that Léon Delmont takes and defines the main narrative conditions of the text:

166 | Laurent Le Sage, *The French New Novel: An Introduction and a Sampler.* (Pennsylvania State University Press, 1962) 72.
167 | Butor (1957/1980), 23.

> Le train s'arrête et tout le monde en même temps lève les yeux, laissant sa lecture dans l'immobilité soudaine et le silence.[168]

Within these first ninety pages, the narrator describes the train environment and reveals Léon's thoughts which involve visions of Rome and Paris as well as episodes with the two women in his life, Henriette and Cécile. The thoughts in this part show his dissatisfaction with Henriette while emphasising the pleasures of being with Cécile, and they implicitly move towards Léon's decision. We can feel Léon's euphoria and eagerness for the future as the narrative is enriched with imagined future moments of his life with Cécile in Paris.

> Maintenant Cécile allait venir à Paris et vous demeureriez ensemble. Il n'y aurait pas de divorce, pas d'esclandre, de cela vous étiez, vous êtes bien certain; tout se passerait fort calmement, la pauvre Henriette se tairait, les enfants, vous iriez les voir une fois par semaine à peu près; et vous étiez certain aussi non seulement de l'accord, mais de la triomphante joie de Cécile qui vous avait tant taquiné sur votre bourgeoise hypocrisie.[169]

Léon describes his current life situation as a menacing "asphyxie"[170] from which he strives to escape; confident about his decision and reassured that his intention to continue his life with another woman will save him from this menace, he keeps observing other passengers and makes up stories about their lives. Subconsciously, his perception of the future changes slightly under the influence both of invented stories and memories. Léon comments on his decision repeatedly and his tone gradually changes from a secure voice to a reassuring one:

168 | Butor (1957/1980), 46.
169 | Butor (1957/1980), 36.
170 | Butor (1957/1980), 36.

Mais maintenant ça y est, c'est fait, vous voilà libre. Il y aura encore bien des détails à régler certes, et la situation ne pourra se stabiliser avant quelques mois, mais le seuil est franchi.[171]

By the end of the first part the train is already at Dijon and Léon needs a walk to stretch his legs as he is probably tired from the confinement of his third-class seat; the professor who was travelling with him leaves the train and Léon pushes the book towards his seat, laying claim to more space and showing some irritation. The fatigue these last actions show offers a first hint at Léon's negativity and defeatism, more of which is to come, and it opens a space for Léon to have second thoughts.

Les rails et les fils se multiplient; on aperçoit les premières maisons de Dijon. Vous avez envie de vous dégourdir les jambes. Le roman que vous avez acheté sur le quai de la gare de Lyon et que vous n'avez pas encore ouvert est toujours sur la banquette à gauche de la place où vous étiez assis; vous le poussez pour qu'il la marque.[172]

Part B: Modifying the Plan

The second part of the narrative covers almost exactly the same number of pages as the first. This transitional section shows the gradual modification of Léon's perceptions that will justify his eventual abandonment of his own plan in the third and final part. At the beginning of the second part Léon is still confident about his decision:

A présent, par votre décision, par votre voyage pour elle seule, vous lui aurez bien montré que vous avez rompu ce genre de chaînes, et par conséquent

171 | Butor (1957/1980), 84.
172 | Butor (1957/1980), 90.

ces images et ces statues ne devraient plus représenter pour elle un obstacle à tourner pour vous atteindre [...][173]

As the narrative develops, Léon Delmont imagines various projections of his return to Paris, which involve connotations different from his previous thoughts. Moments of tension and disharmony with Cécile are brought to light and Léon's state of mind is challenged by doubts which confuse him. These scenes intervene unexpectedly; they amplify Léon's stress and raise doubts as to whether Cécile could indeed be Léon's salvation from his social *asphyxia*:

"Alors, quand reviendras-tu?" et à qui vous avez répété ce qu'elle savait déjà, ce que vous lui aviez déjà dit vingt fois au cours de ce séjour: "Hélas, pas avant les derniers jours de décembre", ce qui est devenu faux maintenant[174]

This part, written mainly in the future tense, describes Léon's anticipated confrontations both with his wife and his mistress upon the announcement of his decision. Images of future conversations with his wife Henriette proliferate:

Mardi prochain, lorsque harassé par votre voyage en troisième classe vous aurez ouvert avec votre clé la porte de l'appartement, quinze place du Panthéon, vous trouverez Henriette en train de coudre à vous attendre, qui vous demandera comment s'est passé ce séjour, et vous lui répondrez: "Comme tous les autres."[175]

Through these imagined future conversations the conviction of his decision and, most importantly, the anticipation of his idealised life with Cécile wane. The narrator, in the form of a voice-over, narrates this progress in reverse in a sequence of future scenes in which Léon lies about his real travel purposes and his relationship with

173 | Butor (1957/1980), 96.
174 | Butor (1957/1980), 98f.
175 | Butor (1957/1980), 160.

Cécile until his final non-realised confession. As the modification is already taking place, the future tense of the narrated scenes becomes a future of the past, proving in linguistic terms that it doesn't belong to the present anymore.[176]

> Mardi prochain, lorsque vous entrerez dans sa chambre, en effet vous lui raconterez tout ce voyage et vous lui direz: "J'étais allé à Rome pour prouver à Cécile que je la choisissais contre toi, j'y étais allé dans l'intention de lui demander de venir vivre avec moi définitivement à Paris..."[177]

Meanwhile, memories of past visits to Rome, projections into the future of the arrival in Rome and the return to Paris along with museum visits and other associations are all fused in the narrative present. Before the end of the second part, the opposition between the two women, which dominates the narrative until that moment, is relativised. Léon remembers the meeting of the two women in Paris which made him feel uncomfortable and uneasy as he witnessed their similarities:

> Quelle blessure, lorsque toute détendue Henriette sur le palier a supplié Cécile de revenir trois jours plus tard et que celle-ci a accepté avec une chaleur, hélas, indubitablement sincère, quoi qu'elle en ait cru elle-même! Mais vous ne pouviez pas lui crier: "N'accepte pas, je ne veux pas que tu reviennes!"[178]

At the end of the second part, Léon appears very irritated by a lack of sleep, a consequence of the inconvenience of his third-class seat and of his subconscious mental challenges. As in the other narrative parts, at the end of the second part he leaves the train compartment

176 | Lois Oppenheim, *Intentionality and Intersubjectivity: A Phenomenological Study of Butor's "La Modification"*. (Kentucky: Lexington, 1980) 150.

177 | Butor (1957/1980), 162.

178 | Butor (1957/1980), 188.

with the book on his seat to hold his place. The section ends with a general sense of doubt and negativity and prepares the ground for the definitive reversal of his plan.

Part C: Life Has Modified the Plan

The final part of the novel forms a correspondence to the first, again covering almost the exact number of pages and giving the novel a triple symmetry. This part reflects Léon's current mental state and it frequently reaches into the past in search of balance as well as to strengthen the perceived consistency of his life decisions:

> Considérer le problème de votre voyage, de la décision que vous aviez prise, du sort de Cécile, de ce qu'il faudra dire à Henriette, maintenant que vous êtes rassasié, reposé raisonnablement, et non plus dans cette espèce de désarroi qui vous avait envahi, aveuglé, égaré loin de la route que vous aviez choisie, dans les ténèbres froides et honteuses, dépouillant de son sens tout votre être présent, le fait que vous étiez ici à cette place marquée par le livre non lu, [...][179]

The imagined journey depicts the protagonist's future life after the reversal of his initial decision. The pages describe a new perspective on the days to follow now that Léon has changed his initial plans and reveal how he has started to associate his experience with his unread book. The relationship with Cécile has become a thing of the past rather than of the future; unpleasant memories of her occupy more and more space while his honeymoon with Henriette is recounted. Narrated in the future perfect ("futur antérieur/futur II") in the form of free indirect speech, part three shows the fears and hesitations that made Léon change his mind and describes Léon's reconciliation with his present life.

While the change of perspective is profound, the modification is also reflected in the sequences of the phantom of the Grand Veneur's

---

179 | Butor (1957/1980), 195.

obsessive questioning which develop in the course of Léon's reflections throughout the novel. The phantom appears sporadically in the text as an intertextual and historical reference to France in medieval times, an appearance that shows how reading, writing and living interact with and reflect one another, following the same modification scheme. His continuous questioning mirrors Léon's doubts and functions as a leitmotif, one that adds to the tension of the text and invites the reader not only to witness but also to *participate* in the interrogation that is taking place in the world of the narrative.

Whereas in the previous part the phantom's questions "M'entendez-vous?" on page 114 and later "Qu'attendez-vous?" on page 135 prompted Léon's plans to bring Cécile to Paris, the question "Où êtes-vous?" on page 151 actually reflects the protagonist's growing confusion. Before the end of the second part the confusion increases and the Grand Veneur asks of Léon on page 183: "Êtes-vous fou?" This question comes on Léon and Henriette's return to Paris after their disastrous second honeymoon in Rome, which they had undertaken by car rather than by train. In the third part, by page 220, the Grand Veneur's initial question has been taken up by a female in Léon's dream, and the inquiry "Qu'attendez-vous?" is now combined with the question "Qui êtes-vous?" echoing Léon's agonising search for self-awareness and determination. The voice is trying to persuade Léon to make a final decision and thereby be saved:

> "Je suis venu pour vous mener sur l'autre rive. Je vois bien que vous êtes mort; n'ayez crainte de chavirer, le bateau ne s'enfoncera pas sous votre poids."[180]

The transformations of the motif of questions reflect those of Léon's perceptions.[181] When Léon visualises his unrealised life the phantom's questions become more pointed: "Où êtes-vous, que fait-

180 | Butor (1957/1980), 220.

181 | Duffy (1990), 33f.

es-vous, que voulez-vous?"[182] What he finally comes to realise is that he cannot do without Rome ("À Rome, nous serons libres"[183] – "Tu ne pourras plus jamais revenir"[184]) and that his love affair with Cécile is bound up with his feelings for the city.

Vous vous dites: que s'est-il passé depuis ce mercredi soir, depuis ce dernier départ normal pour Rome? Comment se fait-il que tout soit changé, que j'en sois venu là?[185]
[...]
Vous dites: il faudrait montrer dans ce livre le rôle que peut jouer Rome dans la vie d'un homme à Paris [...][186]

By the end of the narrative, Léon remembers his promise to his wife:

Vous dites: je te le promets, Henriette, dès que nous le pourrons, nous reviendrons ensemble à Rome, dès que les ondes de cette perturbation se seront calmées, dès que tu m'auras pardonné; nous ne serons pas si vieux.[187]

Before stepping off the train he states categorically that the two cities should keep their geographical distance, implying that there will not be any major change in his life. His ultimate aim has changed: he plans to revive in the form of a book the experience of his mental journey and decision-making, recounting the change of perspective and the final modification. The book he decides to write is actually the book we, the readers, have in hand.

182 | Butor (1957/1980), 230.
183 | Butor (1957/1980), 213.
184 | Butor (1957/1980), 225.
185 | Butor (1957/1980), 278.
186 | Butor (1957/1980), 280.
187 | Butor (1957/1980), 285.

Vous vous levez, remettez votre manteau, prenez votre valise, ramassez votre livre. Le mieux, sans doute, serait de conserver à ces deux villes leurs relations géographiques réelles et de tenter de faire revivre sur le mode de la lecture cet épisode crucial de votre aventure, le mouvement qui s'est produit dans votre esprit accompagnant le déplacement de votre corps d'une gare à l'autre à travers tous les paysages intermédiaires, vers ce livre futur et nécessaire dont vous tenez la forme dans votre main. Le couloir est vide. Vous regardez la foule sur le quai. Vous quittez le compartiment.[188]

As a title, *La Modification* reflects both the plot of the novel structured in narrative levels that reflect the stages of the decision-making, but also their relationship, coherence and interrelation as a sequence. In addition it reflects the writing as a process involving modifications and showing its development within these changes. The latter modification is applied to the plot in the way the story is transformed from experience to verbal act, while the experience of travelling is adapted in written form. The adaptation in writing inevitably brings about changes and modifications in the way the journey is evolving and is thus represented rather than chronicled. What we actually read is not the (non-) modification of Léon's life but the modification of a real experience into a narrative act and the representation of life in fiction. This narrative can reach out from the level of fiction to that of the real world of real author and real reader and is therefore encapsulated – by the train timetable Léon holds during the journey for example – within the frame of reality so as to be credible and verifiable.

The fictional space and time within which Léon's adventure takes place is compatible with the space and time of a real Paris to Rome train journey at the time. The train timetable that Léon holds during the journey has this function. The allusion to real life echoes ideas of the *nouveau roman* about formal realism and implies that the ordinary can be the source of fictional representation even for something extraordinary. The real-time effect is also emphasised by

188 | Butor (1957/1980), 285f.

the tenses of the verbs ("present" or "passé composé") that evoke a sense of concurrence with reality as well as the use of various deictic pronouns ("cet," "cette") that foster a sense of immediacy in the visual apprehension of the fictional world.

> [C]ette serviette noire bourrée de dossiers dont vous apercevez quelques coins colorés qui s'insinuent par une couture défaite, et de livres sans doute ennuyeux, reliés, au-dessus de lui comme un emblème, comme une légende qui n'en est pas moins explicative, ou énigmatique, pour être une chose, une possession et non un mot, posée sur le filet de métal aux trous carrés, et appuyée sur la paroi du corridor, cet homme vous dévisage, agacé par votre immobilité, debout, ses pieds gênés par vos pieds: il voudrait vous demander de vous asseoir, mais les mots n'atteignent même pas ses lèvres timides, et il se détourne vers le carreau, écartant de son index le rideau bleu dans lequel est tissé le sigle SNCF.[189]

The structure of the narrative corresponds to the protagonist's thinking, and it evolves as the train progresses to its final destination, thus reflecting a mind in flux with – oftentimes – contradictory associations. The action of the book lasts as long as the journey from Paris to Rome, consequently somewhat less than twenty-four hours. The perspective of the text is framed according to what a person could see and perceive within such a timespan; the *Zeitdeckung* (engl. in 'real time', *erzählte Zeit = Erzählzeit*) – a technique frequently used in *Nouvelle Vague* films – strengthens the link between fiction and reality. This real-time effect links the fictional world with the external world in which both the real author and the reader are located and adds to a sense of credibility and verifiability.

189 | Butor (1957/1980), 8f.

The Adventure of Writing

Mais ce livre qui, pour l'auteur supposé, est un fragment d'autobiographie et, pour l'auteur réel, une fiction dont l'*authenticité* (à défaut de sa véracité) ne saurait être mise en doute et qui doit donc plus ou moins retracer (en termes transposés) l'expérience qui conduisit à son élaboration, ce livre auquel l'auteur réel comme l'auteur supposé ont abouti, et qui n'a pu que les aider - l'un comme l'autre - à savoir qui ils sont, est un pas fait vers une réponse et une solution.[190]

By the end of the novel, readers recognise writing as the second narrative level of *La Modification*. The written representation of Léon's adventure suggests a recreation of the plot, namely that which readers actually read in *La Modification*. Léon's adventure offers the core plot, which is the basis upon which the specific version that we actually have in hand is narrated, hence it provides the grounds for the generation of the second narrative level, the written representation.

This duplicity and mirroring of the two levels is reflected in the two books that are mentioned within the story: the train timetable and Léon's book that he bought at the Paris train station to read during the journey, though he never does. This book is a material representation of the one Léon announces he will write at the end of *La Modification*; the same book we have in hand, completing a perfect narrative circle.

[...] ce livre qu'on peut dire *parfait* en ce sens qu'il se referme sur lui-même et qu'il n'est pas autre chose que le récit de sa propre genèse, le résumé aussi schématique qu'il soit de ce qu'on pourrait nommer son contenu manifeste montre d'emblée qu'il joue sur plusieurs plans.[191]

190 | Leiris (1958), 312.
191 | Leiris (1958), 292.

Butor inscribes both levels in his novel, that of happening (the plot) and that of narrating/writing, and he presents the story of a fictional author narrating the adventures of Léon shortly after his journey of self-discovery. His aspiration to be authentic is reflected in the narrative convention according to which he is writing the story, though taking the reader's perspective, as if he was unaware of its final outcome. Hence the story is presented as if it was concurrent with the process of narration. Hints of this narrative level are difficult to locate in the text: Butor's elevated style, the sense of contemporaneity and the homogenous use of the second-person pronoun to designate both levels make it hard to separate them. It is only through certain allusions that readers feel the narrative might reflect another narrative after all (before the end of the text when this reflection is made explicit). An example is the way fellow travellers are described in the book, implying the possibility that the narrator is in the middle of a composition process.

> Si vous êtes entré dans ce compartiment, c'est que le coin couloir face à la marche à votre gauche est libre [...]. Un homme à votre droite, son visage à la hauteur de votre coude, assis en face de cette place où vous allez vous installer pour ce voyage.[192]

All the stories that Léon makes up about their lives are part of the narration and imply that the fictional author is exploring his imagination not distractedly but instrumentally: that is, for his writing exercise. Also, when the writing style of school essays is recalled in the passage below, yet another allusion to the writing process is made, this time as a hint about the writing method the fictional author might have chosen. Like *Kindheitsmuster* the narrator reveals parts of the writing process adding a self-reflective character in the narrative:

---

192 | Butor (1957/1980), 8.

Des livres de classe peut-être s'il est professeur dans un collège, s'il va y rentrer déjeuner dans quelques instants [...] des analyses "A rapporter avec la signature de vos parents", des narrations "vous écrivez une lettre à vos amis pour lui raconter vos vacances", [...] "Imaginez que vous êtes monsieur Léon Delmont et que vous écrivez à votre maîtresse Cécile Darcella pour lui annoncer que vous avez trouvé pour elle une situation à Paris", "On voit bien que vous n'avez jamais été amoureux"; et lui, que sait-il de cela?[193]

La Modification is a story of self-discovery: for its hero Léon Delmont it reflects his journey towards certainty while for the fictional author it mirrors the journey towards knowing the unknown. Léon, who is the addressee of his own story, moves from stability to doubt and back to stability. The fictional author addressing the story to his narrative hero shows the creation of a narrative persona and, to that extent, the making of a person. Léon is a narrative persona created and defined within the narrative, in a sense within the recreation of his own story. As a character he emerges through the way his actions are presented and through his own process of self-confrontation. Consequently, the narrative is composed partly in the form of questions that highlight these reflections and the way in which Léon tarries before a major change in his life:

Alors terrorisée s'élève en vous votre propre voix qui se plaint: ah, non, cette décision que j'avais eu tant de mal à prendre, il ne faut pas la laisser se défaire ainsi; ne suis-je donc pas dans ce train, en route vers Cécile merveilleuse?

The questions of the narrative offer their answers in the narrative itself, resembling a dialogue performed while travelling:

Mais il n'est plus temps maintenant, leurs chaînes solidement affermies par ce voyage se déroulent avec le sûr mouvement même du train, et malgré tous vos efforts pour vous en dégager, pour tourner votre attention ailleurs,

193 | Butor (1957/1980), 114f

vers cette décision que vous sentez vous échapper, les voici qui vous entraînent dans leurs engrenages.[194]

The adventure of writing suggests a parallel narrative level that the reader can recognise only at the end of reading the main story. It belongs to the narrative itself, being part of the fiction as in Wolf's *Kindheitsmuster*, and reveals elements of its process of generation – even in a fictional disguise – that reflect on a *real* meta-fictional level which concerns writing and reading as a narrative theme but also as a mechanism for self-awareness. Like the narrator in Wolf's novel, Léon is created within the narrative, reflecting the making of a person and the journey of self-discovery involved, and realised within writing and narrating.

The Narrative Perspective

The use of the second-person pronoun instead of the traditional and more usual first and third still requires discussion. Why is Léon's story not narrated using the *je* nor the *il*, and what are the reasons for and functions of *that* poetic modification that Michel Butor seems to have prioritised? The author discusses the topic in one of his essays published after the novel.

C'est ici qu'intervient l'emploi de la seconde personne, que l'on peut caractériser ainsi dans le roman: celui à qui l'on raconte sa propre histoire.[195]
C'est parce qu'il y a quelqu'un à qui l'on raconte sa propre histoire, quelque chose de lui qu'il connaît pas, ou du moins pas encore au niveau du langage, qu'il peut y avoir un récit à la seconde personne, qui sera par conséquent toujours un récit «didactique».
Si le personnage connaissait entièrement sa propre histoire, s'il n'avait pas d'objection à la raconter ou se la raconter, la première personne s'impose-

194 | Butor (1957/1980), 162.
195 | Butor (1964), 66.

rait: il donnerait son témoigne. Mais il s'agit de lui arracher, soit parce qu'il ment, nous cache ou se cache quelque chose, soit parce qu'il n'a pas tous les éléments, ou même, s'il les a, qu'il est incapable de les relier convenablement. Les paroles prononcées par le témoin se présenteront comme des îlots à la première personne à l'intérieur d'un récit à la seconde, qui provoque leur émersion.[196]

For Butor the choice of the second-person plural form is dictated by the fact that the main character is unaware of his own story, hence by the aspiration for self-awareness, Léon's narrative persona is created the moment the story is generated. Léon Delmont suffers from a lack of self-awareness and determination, and he is challenged by a difficult life decision that challenges his self-reception and understanding and connects not with a new self but with a new self-perception. The purpose of the narrative is not to chronicle what has happened but to help Léon understand the process and to experience what he is going through. As a result his adventures are narrated and addressed to him in the second-person by the fictional author in order to restore Léon's authority over them, aspiring to transform the adventures into a conscious choice and to make his personality more solid and determined.

As discussed in connection with the narrator in *Kindheitsmuster,* Léon finds it difficult to tell his own story from the first-person perspective as he in not fully aware of it yet. His situation is different to that of the narrator in *Kindheitsmuster* who ended up using the third person and inventing Nelly Jordan, due to a problematic relationship with the past. Léon's difficulty with saying the *I* comes from the fact that his *I* is being formed within the narrative and it has no association with feelings of historical guilt or an estranged childhood; it is linked with the process of creating a person. In his case stimuli and associations that are investigated align with his state of mind and chart his progress from uncertainty to stability and determination.

196 | Butor (1964), 66f.

The alienating third-person perspective is therefore unnecessary, but as the self-discovery is in progress and the first person is not available to Léon, the second person is the only valid choice to reflect his consciousness and the transitional state in which he finds himself. It reflects the two narrative levels that coexist in the book: that of the central protagonist story and that of writing. Léon's situation resembles the self-cross-examining narrator that we have encountered in Wolf but expresses different narrative needs and circumstances. These are performed in a more implicit though extended form through rhetorical questions and interplay with the Grand Veneur, and oriented more towards the present and future rather than towards the past and an attempt at autobiographical writing. The second person qualifies as a functional device in the rhetoric of self-discovery, designating the perspective of the unknown and reflecting a troubled consciousness by showing the distance between thinking and acting. It mirrors the notion of contemporaneity and highlights the making of a person (and a book) as a continuous, live "happening-now" process.

If *La Modification* were written in the first person, the narrative would also require a temporal displacement from the experience, and its crystallisation as the modification would have had to occur before the recounting of it. In that case it would not be possible to distinguish the level of action from that of writing as they would be identical; this, however, would run counter to the *nouveaux romanciers'* idea of realism. The first person, an indication for determination, can be employed only once a decision is made and so would not work to reflect Léon's changing his mind and his evolving journey towards self-awareness.

Therefore we rarely see any first-person excerpts in the novel, and whenever instability and the overwhelming power of the imagination take over, the second person returns and the tone becomes that of an indictment through interrogation. When the narrative is not centred on Léon dealing with his uncertainty and mental challenges or when it drifts from the core plot, the second-person voice that stimulates the modification can be and is temporarily suspended. It is definitively abandoned only towards the end of the novel, when Léon Delmont announces his project to transform the experience of the modification into writing. Then we see the first person being preferred, signalling that Léon might have reached the level of certainty and self-awareness associated with the first person. In this way, the fictional author indicates that Léon Delmont's narrative persona is now (by the end of the novel) completely shaped and created.

Je ne puis espérer me sauver seul. Tout le sang, tout le sable de mes jours s'épuiserait en vain dans cet effort pour me consolider.
Mais pourquoi restez-vous debout dans l'embrasure à vous balancer selon le mouvement qui se poursuit, votre épaule heurtant le montant de bois presque sans que vous vous en rendiez compte?[197]

The third person, too, is used only rarely in *La Modification* although more frequently than the first person. It appears as a manifestation of the unconscious, for example in Léon's dreams. The dream sequences offer access to a realm in which repressed thoughts and censored desires may appear, and they highlight Léon's difficulty in understanding and verbalising his thoughts and recognising his mental state. Most importantly, the third-person pronoun is used when the experience of the modification is projected onto the hero of the unread book, that is when the episode of Léon Delmont's life is fictionalised as if it belonged to another, revealing his being as a version of his self.

[...] dans ce livre que vous aviez acheté [...] il doit bien se trouver quelque part [...] un homme en difficulté qui voudrait se sauver, qui fait un trajet et qui s'aperçoit que le chemin qu'il a pris ne mène pas là où il croyait, comme s'il était perdu dans un désert, ou une brousse, ou une forêt se refermant

197 | Butor (1957/1980), 196.

en quelque sorte derrière lui sans qu'il arrive même à retrouver quel est le chemin qui l'a conduit là.[198]

Butor's novel could not generally be narrated in the third person as this would estrange Léon radically from his own adventures and destroy the immediacy of the experience narrated. Léon may suffer from finding it difficult to say *I* as he is challenged by uncertainty and self-awareness but, nevertheless, he recognises the narration as his personal experience which is valuable enough to merit being transmitted in written form. Neither would the third-person perspective work for the fictional author as it would not reflect the attempt to create a character within writing. As with the first person, the third-person perspective would fail to reflect a mind in flux and the simultaneity of the narration as it would convey in a definite form an adventure already over and understood.

Donc préparer, permettre, par exemple au moyen d'un livre, à cette liberté future hors de notre portée, lui permettre, dans une mesure si intime soit-elle de se constituer, de s'établir.[199]

In summary the second person is the only narrative perspective that can merge both narrative levels – the one of the plot and that of narrating – efficiently and coherently into one while respecting their distance and differences. It reflects the elevated style of the book and the remarkable narrative artefact that Butor created with *La Modification*.

Il fallait absolument que le récit soit fait du point de vue d'un personnage. Comme il s'agissait d'une prise de conscience, il ne fallait pas que le personnage dise *je*. Il me fallait un monologue intérieur en-dessous du niveau du langage du personnage lui-même, dans une forme intermédiaire entre la

198 | Butor (1957/1980), 197f.

199 | Butor (1957/1980), 276.

première personne et la troisième. Ce *vous* me permet de décrire la situation du personnage et la façon dont le langage naît en lui.[200]

The second-person voice indicates a voice-over narrator narrating to Léon what he actually experiences. Butor himself comments on the absence of a first-person narrator as an outcome of the fact that his novel reflects "une prise de conscience." He explains that his goal was to find a form in which to depict a monologue, one that would evolve beyond the level of language in an intermediate form between the first and the third person. As Butor states above, the use of *vous* enabled him to capture in a genuine form the situation in which language is born within a person.

In fact, the second-person perspective partly involves the first- and partly the third-person perspective, in the sense that it reflects neither total authority nor total estrangement; it bridges the author with the narrator and the hero and offers a way of dealing with thoughts as yet unarticulated, thus mirroring the subconscious. Hence, *vous* as the voice of the subconscious stands as a bridge communicating between the two levels, that of plot (happening) and that of narration (narrating), reflecting the intermediate space (the middle-distance as described in the first chapter, based on Grimsley's observations) and shifting its status from thinking to acting.

The second-person plural form includes an *il* and a *je* and presupposes their interaction. Only seldom is the use of *vous* a plural reference, for example for both Léon and Cécile. Most often it addresses Léon according to the French social code of politeness and refers to him as a single male person. To understand the poetic and semantic value of *vous* better it is instructive to compare the translations of the novel into other languages. The significance of *vous* instead of the singular *tu* becomes more obvious when we look at the English translation of the book, for example, where there is only the one form *you* to reflect all second-person variations:

200 | Butor (1957/1980), 290.

Standing with your left foot on the grooved brass sill, you try in vain with your right shoulder to push the sliding door a little wider open. You edge your way in through the narrow opening, then you lift up your suitcase of bottle-green grained leather [...][201]

In the English version the narration is necessarily in the only *you*-form available, without any contextual sign of the form of the second person intended. However, as we read on in the English translation, we find several pronouns and phrases that are not translated. They reveal the problem as they offer evidence for the lack of a legitimate equivalence between the French *vous* and the English *you* and stress the significance of the choice of pronoun in terms of form and meaning for the narrative.

Before your next trip, you had written to let her know you were coming – the first letter you had ever written to her, very different from today's letters, for since then "Dear Madam" has given place to "Dear Cécile" and now to lovers' pet names, **vous** has become **tu,** and polite formulas have been replaced by kisses. [202]

You won't want to laugh. You won't have the least temptation to say **tu** to me, I'm sure of that. For all your directorship you're just a boy, at least when you're with me, and that's why I love you, because I want to make a man of you, which she has been unable to do in spite of appearances.[203]

Crossing through the woods of Fontainebleau, where the Great Huntsman called out to you, "Êtes-vous fou? Are you mad?" how you longed to be back in Paris at last, in your own room, in your bed! And when you were stretched out there together she murmured, "I'm very grateful to you, but I'm so weary, that journey was so long!"[204]

---

201 | Michel Butor, *A Change of Heart.* 1958. Trans. Jean Stewart. (New York: Simon and Schuster, 1959) 1.

202 | Butor Trans. Jean Stewart (1958/1959), 100.

203 | Butor Trans. Jean Stewart (1958/1959), 152.

204 | Butor Trans. Jean Stewart (1958/1959), 156.

The translator has to use the French *vous* or *tu*, to define the development of the relationship from a distant correspondence between strangers to an intimate love affair. This also happens in the Grand Veneur's questions. Léon Delmont doesn't address himself in the second person in the form of an intimate self-inquisition to which the reader is allowed access, as is the case in Christa Wolf. Butor chooses the second person plural/polite form to show – also in narrative form – the progress Léon makes, the alienation of his choices and self, and his ultimate self-determination. The voice narrating his life and actions reflects second thoughts, hesitations and inner fears, those witnessed when the perspective of the *Other* is employed via the narrative *vous*; it articulates and expresses what he cannot, designated by the proper French *vous* instead of an intimate and more personal *tu* that would sound inappropriate for Léon Delmont, before he reaches the state of self-awareness and can take over a more proximate (*personal*) perspective on himself and his decisions.

Conclusion

In addition to the thematic and formal modification, *La Modification* presents a meta-fictional one rich in theoretical and philosophical implications. The third modification deserving discussion refers to the reader and the reader's relationship with the world of fiction and the author himself. The fact that the second-person perspective is by definition an invitation to the reader to feel addressed and referred to raises questions for the reader's identification with the narrative *vous* and his/her involvement in the text.

Butor's *vous* doesn't urge the reader to identify with Léon, nor does it imply a generalisation of the experience or the attempt to build a pattern of collective identity as in Wolf's *Kindheitsmuster*. Léon's name, the detailed state of his life and the clearly male perspective adopted prove that the aim of the narrative is the development of *his* persona and *his* self-discovery without aspiring to create a sort of canonical text, a model novel, but rather a unique story of that character. That it is, however, a representation, a version of *his* story, both de-personalises it and makes it more impersonal, and hence more inviting for the reader in that sense.

The reader may not be offered space to participate in any way in the textual activity but is encouraged to feel invited and familiar with the narrative through the dominance of the second-person pronoun and is given some beneficial insights into his or her own life in the form and echo of a guideline about life decisions and self-understanding. Butor's continuous references to visual perception have the following effects: firstly the achievement of formal realism and the visual perception of the narrative world enable the reader to participate in the experience of the book, catching the attention of the audience and making the narrative more attractive and engaging; and secondly it offers a genuine conception of the narrative world that adds to the realistic effect.

In addition to this, the narrative perspective of the text creates an inherent didacticism, resembling a sort of *how to* basic narrative category which has blossomed in the contemporary literary production, presenting patterns of happiness or success and self-help manuals. The novel can be read as an encouragement by Butor to the reader to see the world anew and to assess it in different ways and expressive modes, like that which is presented within his writing as well as the writing itself. In his "Réalisme mythologique de Michel Butor" Michel Leiris comments on the use of the second-person plural form and its didactic meaning as well:

L'usage de la deuxième personne du pluriel dans l'ensemble d'un récit qui, envisagé sous cet angle, apparaît comme un immense énoncé de dissertation ou un canevas détaillé pour méditation ou examen de conscience semble donc se présenter – quels que soient les motifs d'ordre compositionnel qui ont déterminé ce choix – comme une façon de renvoyer sur vous (sur ce *vous* anonyme qui pourrait se dire *tous*) l'interrogation dont il est l'annonce ou le rappel tout au long de ces pages où, de l'impressionniste au didactique, tant de genres s'enchevêtrent à partir d'une anecdote si commune qu'on est tenté d'y voir un attrape-nigauds à mesure que, scrutant le livre avec plus d'attention, on le découvre plus riche en arrière-plans.[205]

According to Leiris the didacticism of *La Modification* is not limited to an ethical treatise on love affairs, social conventions and so on. Echoing the ideas of the time, the novel encourages readers to narrate their reality and reconcile it with their routine. What emerges from *La Modification* is that sometimes the social asphyxia that we often suffer from can be resolved by way of introspection and by seeing things anew rather than by a radical change. Readers are encouraged to reconcile themselves with their *vie quotidienne* implying that, should they undergo any process of self-discovery and re-evaluate their lives, they might value things and circumstances differently. In short, they are instructed as to how to find peace and a balance between desires and aspirations, idealism and routine.

Committed to the idea of literature as research,[206] Butor's *La Modification* is a fine example of the tension between story and experiment, one that characterised much of the literature of the fifties.[207] *La Modification* shows the profound influence of other art forms such as film and photography as well as disciplines such as linguistics. These influences manifest themselves in terms of techniques such as the voice-over narrative mode and the obsessive attention to the visual. They show in aesthetic ideas such as the focus on form as part of the meaning of language and in literary themes such as the journey (of self-discovery), the genesis of a book and the making of an author.

It is intriguing that although Michel Butor was not the first to publish a second-person narrative – Ilse Aichinger, for example, had already done so in 1949 with the prize-winning *Spiegelgeschichte* – it was his novel that triggered a lively discussion among theorists about

205 | Leiris (1958), 313.

206 | "Le Nouveau Roman n'est pas une théorie, c'est une recherche." Robbe-Grillet (1963/2013), 144.

207 | Duffy (1990), 11.

second-person narrative as a distinct narrative phenomenon that needed to be analysed in detail autonomously rather than as an elaboration of, or exception to, another narrative form. The reasons why *La Modification* signalled the beginning of this long-lasting debate are easy enough to guess. The first might be linked to the author's popularity and productivity. Butor's strong presence on the literary scene of his time through essays and literary works certainly invited special attention. Another reason may be its time and place of publication in France during the fifties which had a very lively literary scene. Moreover, his book is among the few examples of pure second-person narrative in a longer work (Aichinger's *Spiegelgeschichte* is a short story).

In this thesis, the analysis of *La Modification* follows Christa Wolf's *Kindheitsmuster.* This sequence runs counter to the chronological order in which the two books appeared but serves the purpose of highlighting the second-person perspective in both texts. Both Wolf and Butor use the second-person perspective as a means of dealing with the difficulty of saying *I;* Wolf, however, employed all possible pronouns in her narrative and specified the use of the second person *du* as depicting aspects of the writing process. In *Kindheitsmuster, du* refers to the self-examination of an *Erzählfigur,* applied to childhood memories and her own reflections, a process undertaken while she is writing her childhood autobiography under the name of Nelly Jordan in the third person. Wolf uses the second-person perspective partly to reflect the process of becoming *I* and also to reveal aspects of the generation and writing of the book in the moment of the present.

Butor also employs the second-person perspective to deal with the difficulty of saying *I,* but he does so throughout the whole text. In his case the second-person polite/plural form *vous* is used throughout the narrative; that is, unlike in *Kindheitsmuster* it is created at both narrative levels, strengthening the link rather than distinguishing between them. Butor uses the polite/plural *vous* to weave a more complex narrative that benefits from the ambiguity of the pronoun. Moreover, in his text *vous* is not a self-controlling mechanism but reflects the apostrophe towards an unknown addressee who refers to the uncertainty of his own status at the level of character and refers to a semi-developed narrative figure at the level of the fictional author.

Seen as part of the writing process and echoing the dynamic sense of representation, the narrative (in the second person) leads the narrating persona to a conscious choice (certainty) and towards acquiring a defined identity while aspects of the writing process are revealed. The postmodernist self-reflexive dimension of the narrative of *La Modification* reflects encouragement to readers to undergo a modification of their own by becoming authors themselves, inventing further versions of Léon(-like) stories. Readers are thus invited to familiarise themselves with narrating and writing as an effective means of self-confrontation and self-discovery; they are even given tips about writing such as the following reference to the writing method for a school essay:

> Vous à qui, par le truchement de ce roman, aura été passé le mot, parvenez à ce qui sera *votre* livre (sans être nécessairement un livre) et se révélera peut-être fort différent de ce que, primitivement, vous aurez cru chercher, car pour vous l'itinéraire peut se modifier comme il s'est modifié pour le personnage [...][208]

The text to be discussed next, though written during the same period as *La Modification*, evokes a different era. When ten years later in 1967 Georges Perec published *Un homme qui dort*, he elaborated the phenomenon of second-person narrative further, using the singular and more intimate form *tu* for his narrative and chronicling a much shorter episode of life in terms of space and time. The use of *tu* instead of *vous* in Perec's case reflects the time in which the book appeared.

In the France of the fifties, *vous* was not only regarded as a form that indicated distance, alienation and politeness appropriate to

208 | Leiris (1958), 314.

formal situations; at the time Butor was composing *La Modification*, *vous* was also frequently used for closer relationships such as that between children and parents, as well as at school, and therefore not only when talking to a stranger. While Butor chose to narrate *La Modification* in the most appropriate form according to the French cultural context of the time and simultaneously succeeded in referring to the unknown and showing the making of a person within the narrative, Perec could not use the same form ten years later without expressing formality and alienation.

In Perec's case the use of *tu* is an intertextual allusion to Franz Kafka and a reference to a personal, intimate story: his second-person journey of self-discovery is not a manifesto of life's possibilities and mental infinity as in Butor but instead shows the dead ends of consciousness and the limits of the human mind. With Perec we move from the limited space of a train compartment to the limited space of a student room in a dorm. From the positivity of Michel Butor we shift to a comparatively more obscure and pessimistic attitude towards reality and the absurd, one elaborated in an even more limited setting.

Perec introduces an experimental text not just in terms of its narrative form and agent, but also in terms of its structure and content. In his text *tu* is the main narrative figure. With *Un homme qui dort* we reach a part of this thesis where the use of the second person is closely linked to metatextual properties expanding the discussion of second-person storytelling further onto a metatextual level focussing on more liminal texts.

2.3 George Perec's *Un homme qui dort*

A Jigsaw Puzzle of Literary Pieces

Having discussed the employment of the second-person narrative perspective in Christa Wolf's *Kindheitsmuster* and Michel Butor's *La Modification*, the thesis will now focus on two highly experimental and liminal second-person examples: Georges Perec's *Un homme qui dort* and Ilse Aichinger's *Spiegelgeschichte*. Both texts elaborate on the use of the second-person narrative perspective by inaugurating the pronoun as their main narrative figure. By providing striking examples, they both show the expansion of the second person's rhetoric and poetic properties and reveal its dynamic and resilience at its most extreme, experimenting with the limits of language and representation.

Georges Perec's *Un homme qui dort* was written in 1966 and published a year later to little public acclaim. It was Perec's second novel, shorter but more lyrical than his earlier prize-winning *Les Choses*, and had been described by the author as "l'envers de ce que j'ai écrit," "un antidote," "[...] le "refus" des choses, le refus du monde." [209] Perec's novel centres, like the texts examined earlier, on a self-awareness and self-discovery story in a narrative that mimics the form of the *Bildungsroman* but does so in a non-heroic and unconventional mode. *Un homme qui dort* chronicles an experiment in social detachment and indifference, reflected in a striking reduction of plot and characters, that a student performs in order to gain his missing identity.

---

209 | Perec (1967/2002), 212.

Tu dois oublier d'espérer, d'entreprendre, de réussir, de persévérer.[210] [...] Tu apprends à rester assis, à rester couché, à rester debout. Tu apprends à mastiquer chaque bouchée, à trouver le même goût atone à chaque parcelle de nourriture que tu portes à ta bouche.[211]

The narrator of the story remains anonymous until the end; he narrates the experiment to a 25-year-old student who is the only character in the text and performs it by guiding him throughout the project of indifference in an intimate tone (established by the choice of the second-person singular form *tu*) and with the affirmative voice of an omniscient, controlling narrator who stands off-scene (*voice-over narrator*). *Un homme qui dort* mirrors other narrative heroes and texts that deal with the same effacement thus creating a palimpsest of literary variations on the same theme, sometimes implicitly, other times explicitly, coexisting in the narrative. The striking intertextuality of the novel is so intense, appearing almost in every sentence and utterance, that it justifies the characterisation of *Un homme qui dort* as a jigsaw puzzle of literary pieces in the title of this chapter. Perec's novel, a liminal and unique case of second-person fiction, invites such a ludic and thus concentrated approach analysing and examining its components.

The Novel

The story of *Un homme qui dort* begins the moment the experiment starts and lasts until its conclusion, finishing with passages that imply a shift towards re-socialisation and re-integration. Focussing solely on this experiment that is an episode in the student's life, the narrative reveals no other information about him. Perec isolates the story as a life fragment and employs, like Butor, an *in medias res* opening. In Perec's example, however, the technique illustrates

210 | Perec (1967/2002), 248.

211 | Perec (1967/2002), 248.

even more forcefully the notion of isolation which is key to the whole novel and the reduction in plot elaborating on the concept of a life (or story) fragment reaching its representational limits.

Naturally the end of the novel coincides with the end of the experiment. What is stressed throughout the pages is the student's experience and performance, reflected in the rhetoric of the text and in terms of content, and how the experiment, with its aspiration to fundamental disengagement from life's normal activities, collapses under the weight of its own purposelessness. To cut a long story short, *Un homme qui dort* ends with the rejection of the experiment and echoes the positivity of a new start in the student's life as he exits from this episode able to re-integrate into his normal life.[212]

Perec wrote this story one year before he joined the Oulipo movement in France in 1967. Of course, *Un homme qui dort* incorporates some of the ideas and characteristics of that movement – for example emphatic intertextuality – but it also signals the further developments in Perec's writing career. In 1978 the author confirmed the key role that intertextuality played in his text and described it as a "texte pré-oulipien. Un livre sur la rhétorique classique. J'ai construit un récit, puis j'y ai repéré toutes les figures dont je m'étais servi, dans un index à la fin du livre. C'est à la suite de ça que je suis entré à Oulipo."[213]

The reading of *Un homme qui dort* plunges readers into a network of textual relations. To interpret and understand the sentences of the novel one needs to undertake a parallel reading, moving between intertexts and tracing them. As revealed in the above statement, Perec in employing the second person to reflect his hero's experiment in social detachment is actually addressing all the narrative figures that influenced his novel, and he responds to them with his version of the indifferent hero.

212 | David Gascoigne, *The Games of Fiction. Georges Perec and Modern French Ludic Narrative.* (Bern: Peter Lang, 2006) 132f.

213 | Georges Perec, *Entretiens et Conférences I: 1965-1978.* Eds. Dominique Bertelli and Mireille Ribière. (Nantes: Joseph K, 2003) 242.

Un homme qui dort straddles Perec's juvenilia and his sociological writings of the early 1970s. However, the autobiographical dimension of the text (portraying the author and his friends) is impersonal, neither individual nor collective, as we have seen, for example, in Wolf's *Kindheitsmuster.*[214] In the text we read, all protagonists mentioned or implied remain anonymous until the end; even the central figure of the student lacks a specific identity. The sense of impersonality – emphasised by the theme of indifference and social detachment – is also strengthened by the selection of the ambiguous second-person pronoun as a narrative voice, depersonalising the tone with its inherent ambiguity and suspending the notion of a definite reference to a person. In addition the richness in intertextuality that characterises *Un homme qui dort* benefits from the ability of the pronoun to shift reference to different heroes of the absurd and prevents any reading of the story as a personal one.

The indefinite sense of the pronoun enables Perec to experiment with the limits of intertextuality, expanding on the notion of addressing the uncertain as we have seen in Butor and pushing the technique to its limit. In Perec's text it is not just the uncertain and unknown addressed through the indefinite *tu*, it is the not-yet shaped character of the student who is addressed, composed of all the heroes projected in his experiment. Given the shifting quality and the ambiguity of the *tu*-form, Perec was able to address each figure individually without challenging the coherence of his narrative. He introduced a *tu* that can actually be divided into multiple *tu*-s according to the intertextual references that can be traced in the novel. The key role that intertextuality plays in Perec's novel not only shows a liminal self-reflexive text of experimental character, but it also adds to the experiment around which the plot revolves, the interpretation of a reading. We not only read the evolution of an experiment and how a hero develops; by reading *Un homme qui dort* we complete a reading of all its intertexts.

214 | Michael Sheringham, *Everyday Life: Theories and Practices from Surrealism to the Present.* (Oxford: Oxford University Press, 2006) 253.

In 1974 Perec decided to adapt the story for the screen. Working in collaboration with the author, Bernard Queysanne directed the film version which lasted 78 minutes and won the Prix Jean Vigo.[215] While the film adaptation follows the script, structure and rhythm of the literary text, it is less obscure (partly due to the change in medium) and easier to follow. Consequently, the film may facilitate the reception of the text, especially regarding some points of critical debate and disagreement, but it lacks the uniqueness of the original text.

For example, the relationship between the narrator and the student is an issue that has prompted many questions and found various interpretations over the years. In the film, the narrator's voice is that of Ludmila Mikaël, and Jacques Spiesser speaks the part of the student. Choosing a female narrator for the film supports the argument that the voice narrating and dominating the discourse is dissociated from the student and prevents any reading of the text as internal monologue.

In contrast to the original novel, what is most strikingly missing from the film is the vital importance of intertextuality. Though the quotations and intertextual references are also present in the film, even foregrounded in close-ups of books and pictures of authors, the dominance of the visual element over the literary undermines and fails to reflect the significance of intertextuality. By presenting the same story in another medium, the references and allusions to other texts undermine the notion of intertextuality *per se,* that is the composition of a *polyphonic* novel and its dialogic nature by which it addresses other narratives. In the film version, the references to other narrative heroes suggest a transfer to another medium, and in doing so intertextuality loses its directness and immersive character that normally would impact on the actual narrative and generate it in the process. In the film adaptation, intertextuality reflects only

---

215 | *Un homme qui dort.* Dir. Georges Perec and Bernard Queysanne. (Dovidis/ Satpec: 1974), Film.

the origin of the story while depriving it of its dynamic and sense of current dialogue that occurs in the text-form.

With the employment of a second-person narrative agent, Perec may not have taken the readers of his time as much by surprise as Butor did with the publication of *La Modification* in 1957, nor did he manage to do so with the theme itself; after all the narrative implies his awareness of earlier texts that addressed the same theme. But he did surprise his audience in the way he used intertextuality in his text, making it fundamental to its structure and composing it with references, implications, hints and traces that are all listed in an index at the end of the book. In *Un homme qui dort* he thus reflects the idea that literary works are not purely original but rather are the result of a continuous literary interaction and interrelation between authors and texts and are part of an ongoing literary dialogue that transcends time and place.

Perec's novel will be analysed taking into account its fundamental duplicity and structural dualism, first as a text dealing with indifference and, second, as a palimpsest of other texts and literary influences. The aim of this chapter is to analyse and define the impact and various functions of the second-person employment in Perec's novel and expand the assumptions and conclusions of this study towards other themes and properties that could be key to second-person storytelling. With *Un homme qui dort,* the thesis offers the grounds to pursue yet again a story of self-discovery but this time studying the making of a person not just within the narrative, but influenced and shaped by other narratives as well. This chapter aims to elucidate second-person storytelling as related to intertextuality and suggests some deeper understanding of the technique based on a unique, experimental example.

The Script of the Experiment

Tu n'as envie de voir personne, ni de parler, ni de penser, ni de sortir, ni de bouger.
C'est un jour comme celui-ci, un peu plus tard, un peu plus tôt, que tu découvres sans surprise que quelque chose ne va pas, que, pour parler sans précautions, tu ne sais pas vivre, que tu ne sauras jamais.[216]

As briefly mentioned before, *Un homme qui dort* centres on an episode in the life of a 25-year-old sociology student who one day puts down his copy of Raymond Aron's *Leçons sur la société industrielle* and stops attending his classes at the university. Feeling connected to the world no longer and wishing to escape the preordained roles available to him, the student is shown to suffer from a lack of meaning in his life. A hero of the absurd, he doesn't attempt to ameliorate his situation; influenced by his reading as well as by several literary heroes dealing with the same problem, he intensifies his social alienation instead by deliberately trying to become "celui sur qui l'histoire n'a plus de prise."[217] Aspiring to find meaning in life and to reach a state of pure freedom, he starts in effect an experiment in indifference and social detachment, the one that constitutes the narrative.

Composed of a large number of short self-contained passages ranging in length from a few words to about four pages, the novel progresses from one unnumbered passage to the next, with no explicit sense of narrative logic. The 112 passages are each signalled by the start of a new page, forming sixteen chapters in total. To meet the requirements of the present thesis, the text is divided into three parts according to their thematic content thus corresponding to the experiment's stages of progress from decisiveness to doubt and, finally, to negation and failure. In each part the thematic develop-

216 | Perec (1967/2002), 225.
217 | Perec (1967/2002), 273.

ment is reflected in the narrative style, with different verbal forms, tones and rhetoric.

> Ce n'est pas un geste prémédité, ce n'est pas un geste, d'ailleurs, mais une absence de geste, un geste que tu ne fais pas, des gestes que tu évites de faire.[218] [...]
> Tu ne finiras pas ta licence, tu ne commenceras jamais de diplôme. Tu ne feras plus d'études.[219]

The narrative starts with a passage of reverie that connotes a numb reaction to the external environment. It thus implies the state of its main character and prepares from the very beginning the grounds for what is going to be narrated next in the text, the story of an experiment on social detachment and indifference.

> Dès que tu fermes les yeux, l'aventure du sommeil commence. À la pénombre connue de la chambre, volume obscure coupé par des détails, où ta mémoire identifie sans peine les chemins que tu as mille fois parcourus, les retraçant à partir du carré opaque de la fenêtre [...][220]

Immediately afterwards, the narrative continues with a detailed description of the adventure of sleep, communicating that the student suffers from a sleeping disorder. It also contains an extended reference to perception, introducing the existential and philosophical character of the text. The first part chronicles the experiment in indifference from the moment it has been decided upon until it reaches its peak, in a continuously affirmative tone reflecting security and determination.

Once the student has decided to be detached socially, he is pictured cloistered in his room during daytime and walking around the streets of Paris by night. The narrative takes place either in his

218 | Perec (1967/2002), 224.
219 | Perec (1967/2002), 225.
220 | Perec (1967/2002), 219.

small dormitory room or in random streets of the French capital, and it shows the process of increasingly complete isolation from any social encounter or commitment, emphasising the student's committed aspiration towards indifference.

Tu restes dans ta chambre, sans manger, sans lire, presque sans bouger. [...] Tu n'as pas envie de te souvenir d'autre chose, ni de ta famille, ni de tes études, ni de tes amours, ni de tes amis, ni de tes vacances, ni de tes projets. [...] Tu ne revois pas tes amis. Tu n'ouvres pas ta porte. Tu ne descends pas chercher ton courrier. Tu ne rends pas les livres que tu as empruntés à la Bibliothèque de l'Institut pédagogique. [...] Tu ne sors qu'à la nuit tombée, comme les rats, les chats et les monstres.[221]

The only time the action shifts away from Paris is at the end of the fourth chapter when the student visits his parents' house near Auxerre and spends some months there with them. Totally absorbed by indifference, even there he never shows any tendency to socialise or any desire to connect with them. The student's attitude in this episode emphasises the aspired-to social detachment as realised and makes the lack of human interaction even more evident. The student who hardly talks to his parents ("Tu parles à peine à tes parents. Tu ne les vois guère qu'aux heures des repas"[222]) spends most of his time alone and shows interest mainly in inanimate things that do not require any mutual interaction:

C'est à cause de cela que l'arbre te fascine, ou t'étonne, ou te repose, à cause de cette évidence insoupçonnée, insoupçonnable, de l'écorce et des branches, des feuilles. C'est à cause de cela, peut-être, que tu ne te promènes jamais avec un chien, parce que le chien te regarde, te supplie, te parle.[223]

---

221 | Perec (1967/2002), 227.
222 | Perec (1967/2002), 235.
223 | Perec (1967/2002), 237.

The student's indifference gradually becomes a state of mind, a cognitive function that could probably offer a response to the question of the absurd: "tu n'es qu'une ombre trouble, un dur noyau d'indifférence, un regard neutre fuyant les regards."[224] The narrator describes how the student feels displaced in his own life, an uncomfortable state of desperation, expressed as an absence of goals and social contact. While such feelings and experiences accumulate and as the experiment progresses, the student's determination to dissociate himself from any social life and abstain from it crystallises and presents itself as a solution to his existential crisis:

> Tu n'as guère vécu, et pourtant, tout est déjà dit, déjà fini. Tu n'as que vingt-cinq ans, mais ta route est toute tracée, les rôles sont prêts, les étiquettes: du pot de ta première enfance au fauteuil roulant de tes vieux jours, tous les sièges sont là et attendent leur tour.[225]

The success of the experiment entails a systematic abandonment of any self-development and of any social or emotional attachment and the cultivation of a flat zero existence instead which might lead to achieving "la vie annulée."[226]

> Ne plus rien vouloir. Attendre, jusqu'à ce qu'il n'y ait plus rien à attendre. Traîner, dormir. Te laisser porter par les foules, par les rues. Suivre les caniveaux, les grilles, l'eau le long des berges. Longer les quais, raser les murs. Perdre ton temps. Sortir de tout projet, de toute impatience. Être sans désir, sans dépit, sans révolte. Ce sera devant toi, au fil du temps, une vie immobile, sans crise, sans désordre: nulle aspérité, nul déséquilibre. Minute après minute, heure après heure, jour après jour, saison après saison, quelque chose va commencer qui n'aura jamais de fin: ta vie végétale, ta vie annulée.[227]

224 | Perec (1967/2002), 230.
225 | Perec (1967/2002), 238.
226 | Perec (1967/2002), 245.
227 | Perec (1967/2002), 244f.

At the end of the first part the project seems to be accomplished successfully as the student has reached a state of indifference, living happily in isolation free from desires and hopes, an outsider and loner:

> Tu vis dans une bienheureuse parenthèse, dans une vide plein de promesses et dont tu n'attends rien. Tu es invisible, limpide, transparent.[228]
> Nulle hiérarchie, nulle préférence. Ton indifférence est étale: homme gris pour qui le gris n'évoque aucune grisaille. Non pas insensible, mais neutre.
> [...]
> Maintenant tu es le maître anonyme, celui sur qui l'histoire n'a plus de prise, celui qui ne sent plus la pluie tomber, qui ne voit plus la nuit venir.[229]

Sometimes in extremely long sentences, other times in shorter expressions, the narrative takes the form of a continuous one-way flow, addressed to the student without any alteration of tone apart from the echo of a flat, affirmative utterance, implying that no reaction, answer or feedback of any kind is expected. It is worth mentioning that in the rhetoric of *Un homme qui dort* the experimental character of the text and the notion of hypothesis is implied; narrated emphatically as a narrative in process, presenting an evolving experiment and reflecting the simultaneous making of a person, Perec's text shows radical self-reflexivity. It chronicles the results of an experiment in indifference composed in an experimental narrative form (the narrative jigsaw puzzle).

> Vie sans surprise. Tu es à l'abri. Tu dors, tu manges, tu marches, tu continues à vivre, comme un rat de laboratoire qu'un chercheur insouciant aurait oublié dans son labyrinthe et qui matin et soir, sans jamais se tromper, sans jamais hésiter, prendrait le chemin de sa mangeoire, tournerait à gauche,

228 | Perec (1967/2002), 262.
229 | Perec (1967/2002), 272f.

puis à droite, appuierait deux fois sur une pédale cerclée de rouge pour recevoir sa ration de nourriture en bouillie.[230]

Its verbs appear mainly in the present tense or, exceptionally, in the future tense, with some forms in the infinitive. The dominating present tense adds to the fact that the experiment is in progress, like the narrative itself, that is the development of the student's narrative persona. These verb forms add to the sense of a bounded present and evoke stability and fixity of purpose. The inscribed contemporaneity of the discourse is not only an outcome of the text's grammar and the selection of the present tense but also derives from the employment of the second-person perspective. The use of the pronoun strengthens the sense of actuality and connotes an implication of face-to-face interaction and of a happening-now narrative, which the reader together with the student witnesses the moment it is narrated.

Non. Tu préfères être la pièce manquante du puzzle. Tu retires du jeu tes billes et tes épingles. [...] Tu n'écouteras plus les bons conseils. Tu ne demanderas pas de remèdes. [...] Tu ne sors plus de la maison, à peine de ta chambre.[231]

The future tense tends to be employed to convey guidelines supplied by the narrator. The excerpts in the future reflect determination, security and decisiveness, but as they are expressed in the future tense they tend to show aspiration rather than actuality. In such a view, the passages in the future tense – even in the first part of the narrative that is affirmative – affect the sense of fixity and imply doubt and openness to outcomes of the experiment other than success, altering the tone momentarily from affirmative to reassuring. By the time the experiment reaches its peak with the student becoming indifferent, the tone of the narrator changes again from

230 | Perec (1967/2002), 272.
231 | Perec (1967/2002), 239f.

affirmative to questioning, echoing a new sense of doubt, confusion and inquiry.

> [...] mais est-ce bien à toi de le faire? Ta place dans la hiérarchie, tes années de service ne te dispensent-elles pas de cette corvée?[232]

Meanwhile the aim and aspirations inherent in the experiment are constantly questioned ("Quels secrets cherches-tu dans ton miroir fêlé?"[233]) in a tone of high tension. The student appears confused and scared, unable to detach himself from his human needs, feelings and reactions. At the end of chapter 15 there is a strange pause in the narrative and a change to the third person, connected with a summary of another text (Melville's *Bartleby, the Scrivener*)[234] that is placed in the narrative in a descriptive and informative tone.[235] At this point the narrator breaks with the sequence and style that he had used throughout the text so far; going by the esoteric tone, he now takes on Melville's style, choosing a third-person perspective and an exoteric view of what is narrated. In a passage of radical intertextuality, Perec's narrator stops addressing the student, ceases the narrative and the experiment as such to summarise Melville's *Bartleby, the Scrivener* instead.

At that point *Un homme qui dort* reveals a direct dialogue with Melville's narrative. In doing so, Perec steps into the production of the meaning of his narrative and, at the same time, reveals and instructs the student and his own readership to turn to Melville to complete the experiment by reading the novella and taking into consideration a comparison with Bartleby. Thus, the narrator reveals –

232 | Perec (1967/2002), 275.

233 | Perec (1967/2002), 297.

234 | Herman Melville, *Bartleby, the Scrivener.* 1853. (Leipzig: CreateSpace Independent Publishing Platform, 2015).

235 | "Jadis, à New York, à quelques centaines de mètres des brisants [...] On le fit enfermer, mais il s'assis dans la cour de la prison et refusa de se nourrir!" Perec (1967/2002), 298f.

what Perec described in later interviews – the relationship of his text with Melville's and draws an implicit parallel between the student's fate and that of Bartleby, while the radical intertextuality demands an active reading engagement with the text.

The text therefore is presented as a production which, rather than being examined here and read individually as an absolute object, will be understood as a compilation of cultural textuality about indifference and heroes of the absurd. For Perec, Melville's *Bartleby* was a milestone in that tradition. Hence in *Un homme qui dort* we can identify both a vertical and a horizontal dimension in the dynamic of the narrative and the experiment; in the horizontal dimension, Perec's narrative *tu* reflects the process of developing a character in a story of an experiment in social detachment, similar to what we have seen in Butor. In the vertical dimension, the narrative *tu* reflects a dialogue with the anterior and synchronic literary corpus with which Perec is in dialogue. The choice of the narrative *tu* over any other narrative form enables Perec to maintain this duplicity throughout the narrative without breaking the coherence and flow of the text. It is the ambiguity and shifting quality of the second person that can embrace both the vertical and the horizontal axis of the narrative dynamic, as in traditional examples of intertextuality in a story that reflects the development of a character and chronicles both the formation of an *I* and a reading quest in a literary paradigm of emphatic self-reflexivity.[236]

It is important to note that after this direct reference to Melville, the narrative proceeds directly and swiftly to its end. The narrator's tone in this last part involves amplifying the tension with a faster rhythm (in the film version of *Un homme qui dort*, this is mediated through the background music). Sentences are enriched with additional punctuation and exclamation marks while some verbs are put in the imperative. The student now appears accessible as he gradually adopts the characteristics of an autonomous yet anony-

236 | Julia Kristeva, *Desire in Language: A Semiotic Approach to Literature and Art.* (New York: Columbia University Press, 1980) 66.

mous narrative figure. The narrator names and rejects as fake the literary heroes of his forerunners Jean-Paul Sartre, Albert Camus and Thomas Mann – "ne les crois pas"[237] – revealing what was only implicitly reflected in the persona of the student at the beginning – and adds a critical self-reflexive comment about literature and literary heroes.

Moreover, emotions and human needs that were suppressed in the first part of the experiment in indifference are revealed ("Tu as beau te serrer contre lui, haleter contre lui, le tilt reste insensible à l'amitié que tu éprouves, à l'amour que tu recherches, au désir qui te déchire"[238]), determination and effort wane ("Tu as perdu tes pouvoirs"[239]) and expectations are proven futile ("Mais il n'y a pas d'issue, pas de miracle, nulle vérité"[240]).

> Tu traînes, mais la foule ne te porte plus, la nuit ne te protège plus. [...] Comme un prisonnier, comme un fou dans sa cellule. Comme un rat dans le dédale cherchant l'issue. Tu parcours Paris en tous sens. Comme un affamé, comme un messager porteur d'une lettre sans adresse.[241]

The potential and limitations dictated by this experiment are expressed rhetorically in passages written either in the future indicative or including modal verb formulations and phrases that stress what the student can and cannot do, defining the frame and limits of indifference and its impact on him. The narrator removes the student from the possibility of reaching a further stage of indifference and acknowledges that the experiment in indifference and depersonalisation could never be accomplished. To this purpose, a

---

237 | "Tu n'es pas mort et tu n'es pas plus sage [...] Combien de Robinson, de Roquentin, de Meursault, de Leverkühn! Les bons points, les belles images, les mensonges: ce n'est pas vrai." Perec (1967/2002), 301.

238 | Perec (1967/2002), 280.

239 | Perec (1967/2002), 282.

240 | Perec (1967/2002), 282.

241 | Perec (1967/2002), 286.

symbolic nightmare is described that undermines the whole project: the detached, observing consciousness becomes a single eye, ever open, that cannot be deprived of its primary function of seeing, which means perceiving, its own *raison d'*être.

Tu n'es plus qu'un œil. Un œil immense et fixe, qui voit tout, aussi bien ton corps affalé, que toi, regardé regardant, comme s'il s'était complètement retourné dans son orbite et qu'il te contemplait sans rien dire, toi, l'intérieur de toi, l'intérieur noir, vide, glauque, effrayé, impuissant de toi. Il te regarde et il te cloue. Tu ne cesseras jamais de te voir.[242]

The necessity of performing even a single action contravenes the goal of indifference and becomes the line that cannot be crossed, marking it as unattainable. Subsequently, the strategy for a life of freedom obtained through social detachment is dropped, and the tone of the narrator gradually shifts from a questioning to a disappointed one, as hopes and desires expressed in the first part of the text are now abandoned.

L'indifférence est inutile [...] Mais ton refus est inutile. Ta neutralité ne veut rien dire. Ton inertie est aussi vaine que ta colère.[243]
Cesse de parler comme un homme qui rêve.[244]

At the end of the experiment the narrator initiates a sort of text-inscribed conclusion, summarising observations and assumptions in the form of a project review. Indifference proved to be in vain and, moreover, it had become a menace to the student who felt trapped in the attempt to reduce his life to a minimum. Still unable to act, the solution and exit from the labyrinth of indifference come naturally with time, without requiring any personal initiative:

---

242 | Perec (1967/2002), 278.
243 | Perec (1967/2002), 303.
244 | Perec (1967/2002), 304.

Le temps, qui veille à tout, a donné la solution malgré toi. Le temps, qui connaît la réponse, a continué de couler.
C'est un jour comme celui-ci, un peu plus tard, un peu plus tôt, que tout recommence, que tout commence, que tout continue.
Cesse de parler comme un homme qui rêve.
Regarde! Regarde-les. Ils sont là des milliers et des milliers, sentinelles silencieuses. [...][245]

The final words of the narrative describe the student at Place Clichy waiting for the rain to stop. As he never managed to become a transparent existence, his return to normality and ordinary human behaviour – to feel the rain and wait for it to stop – comes as a kind of closure moving away from indifference and bringing a positive end to the project and the narrative. The tone at the end of the text is positive and optimistic and stresses the fact that as long as the student is neither dead nor mad like some of the self-destructive heroes mentioned or implied in the text, life goes on, all possibilities remain open and he can restart his life.

The Script of Intertextuality

Pour mon dernier livre, qui s'appelle *Un homme qui dort*, j'ai fait la même chose en me servant principalement de deux auteurs, l'un est Kafka, l'autre est Herman Melville. Alors, si vous voulez, il y a, en ce qui me concerne, une image de la littérature qui se dessine et qui serait l'image d'un puzzle. Ça, c'est une... Butor a très bien expliqué cela. Butor a expliqué que tout écrivain était entouré par une masse d'autres [...] et, si vous voulez, ce puzzle qui est la littérature, dans l'esprit de cet écrivain, a toujours une place vacante, et cette place vacante, c'est évidemment celle que l'œuvre qu'il est en train d'écrire va venir remplir.[246]

245 | Perec (1967/2002), 304.
246 | Perec (2003), 83.

Un homme qui dort involves two scripts that interact and reflect one another: the one described in detail above summarises the experiment in indifference that the student undergoes and is narrated to him in the form of a direct address by the narrator; the other reflects on the rhetorical experiment of the narrative collage that Perec performs within it, making a narrative out of other narratives. While the first script is easy to follow as it evolves along with the experiment, the second script presents a challenge to the reader, since the references to other texts and heroes (fictional or historical) are numerous and appear in various forms: directly mentioned in the text or implied in quotations of text passages, text summaries, verses, words and descriptions. It would not be an exaggeration to say that almost every sentence of the narrative recalls another figure or text.

At the beginning the student is presented as a marionette, an experimental figure belonging to the project that he executes. Playing out the experiment in indifference and incorporating several literary figures, he lacks an identity of his own and appears to be more a combination of preformed identities, ones with which the reader is familiar as they echo major works and well-known heroes of world literature. As the narrative develops we thus witness a gradual development of his own identity (reflected in the rhetoric of the text within the second-person perspective) and we realise that within this process of performing, the student is actually *trying out* other literary figures that are eventually rejected.

The mining of intertextual references already begins in the title *Un homme qui dort,* extracted from Marcel Proust's À la recherche du temps perdu.[247] It is further established by opening the novel with Kafka's epigram from the *Zürau Aphorisms* [248] translated into

247 | "Un homme qui dort tient en cercle autour de lui le fil des heures, l'ordre des années et des mondes." Marcel Proust, *Du Côté de chez Swann.* (Paris: Gallimard, 1954) 11.

248 | "Es ist nicht notwendig, daß Du aus dem Haus gehst. Bleib bei Deinem Tisch und horche. Horche nicht einmal, warte nur. Warte nicht einmal, sei

French by the author and put at the beginning as a cover-quotation for the narrative:

Il n'est pas nécessaire que tu sortes de ta maison. Reste à ta table et écoute. N'écoute même pas, attends seulement. N'attends même pas, sois absolument silencieux et seul. Le monde viendra s'offrir à toi pour que tu le démasques, il ne peut faire autrement, extasié, il se tordra devant toi.[249]

The text finishes with an extended reference to Melville's *Bartleby, the Scrivener* that appears as a short summary just before the end. The two texts create the poles between which *Un homme qui dort* balances, while traces of intertextuality are scattered in between. By using the quotation from Kafka as a pre-text, Perec defines and justifies the style of his narrative, i.e. the esoteric tone and the choice of the second-person perspective. By using two intertextual allusions to frame his text and revealing within the narrative its literary influences and thematic precursors, the author conjures the technique of a narrative bridge, a clear reference to the Oulipian methodology of experimenting with radical intertextuality, and thus clarifies the way he generated the text.[250]

De la même manière, pour *Un homme qui dort*, la lecture à outrance, enfin, pendant des semaines et des semaines, d'une nouvelle de Melville qui s'appelle *Bartleby, the Scrivener* et des *Méditations sur le péché, la souffrance et le vrai chemin* de Kafka, enfin du journal intime de Kafka, m'a conduit

völlig still und allein. Anbieten wird sich Dir die Welt zur Entlarvung, sie kann nicht anders, verzückt wird sie sich vor Dir winden." Franz Kafka, "Aphorismen-Zettelkonvult". In *Nachgelassene Schriften und Fragmente II*. Ed. Jost Schillemeit. 1992. (Frankfurt am Main: Fischer Taschenbuch Verlag, 2002) 140.

249 | Perec (1967/2002), 217.

250 | Gascoigne (2006), 37.

presque nécessairement, comme à travers une espèce de voie à la fois royale et tout à fait étroite, m'a conduit au livre que j'ai produit.[251]

The theme of indifference and the silent abdication from choice and volition in response to the absurd have already been declared as an a priori hint to readers in the quotation from Kafka. These then expand within the narrative as numerous references to major literary works and allusions to authors of the absurd, and make up the second script of intertextuality, forming the so-called narrative collage of *Un homme qui dort*. The collage functions as a self-reflective element revealing aspects of the generation of the text that justify its style and narrative perspective, and although challenging, it actually gives the content a pattern and a certain structure and serves its coherence. As the experiment in indifference evolves, Perec's forerunners and their works appear in the text associatively, reflecting on the assumptions and results of the project itself.

Le collage pour moi c'est comme un schème, une promesse et une condition de la découverte. Bien sûr, mon ambition n'est pas de réécrire le Quichotte, comme le Pierre Ménand de Borges, mais je voulais par exemple refaire la nouvelle de Melville que je préfère, Bartleby, the scrivener. C'est un texte que j'avais envie d'écrire: mais comme c'est impossible d'écrire un texte qui existe déjà, j'avais envie de le réécrire, pas de le pasticher, mais de faire un autre, enfin le même Bartleby, mais en peu plus ... comme si c'était moi qui l'avait fait. C'est une idée qui me semble précieuse sur le plan de la création littéraire [...] C'est la volonté de se situer dans une ligne qui prend en compte toute la littérature du passé. On anime ainsi son musée personnel, on réactive ses réserves littéraires.[252]

251 | Georges Perec in Mireille Ribière (comp.), *Parcours Perec [travaux du] Colloque de Londres*. 1990. (Lyon: Presses universitaires de Lyon, 1998) 36f.

252 | Georges Perec in Ariane Steiner, *Georges Perec und Deutschland. Das Puzzle um die Leere*. (Würzburg: Königshausen and Neumann, 2001) 106.

Meanwhile other references to the poets of malaise and mythology appear in the narrative.[253] The student suggests a persona developing its own identity, addressed in the narrative by the second-person enigmatic narrator and enabling constantly shifting references to various literary heroes and their corresponding themes: he mirrors heroes of the absurd and reminds us strongly of Jean-Paul Sartre's Antoine Roquentin in *La Nausée* (1938) or Meursault, *'L'Étranger'* in Albert Camus' eponymous text,[254] pictured as an outsider, playing out Melville's *Bartleby* and *preferring* like him to stay out of any social environment. However, it is important to emphasise that Perec's intertextuality appears as a dynamic process in which patterns and themes that interrelate between texts and that appear in *Un homme qui dort* are embedded in the text, thus modified and reflected anew, in a way *re-narrated* by Perec.

Therefore, the student develops into a contemporary hero of the absurd by reflecting on the literary ancestors and by elaborating on the theme of the outsider, experimenting with the choice of living isolated and out of the social frame instead of repeating or echoing attitudes and characters of other narratives uncritically. The results of his experiment are announced in the text.[255] This example stresses the notion of self-reflexivity in intertextuality as a result of

253 | "[...] que vienne la nuit, que sonnent les heures, que les jours s'en aillent, que les souvenirs s'estompent" Perec (1967/2002): 227. and "Bateau ivre, misérable miracle: le Harrar est une attraction foraine, un voyage organisé." Perec (1967/2002), 238.

254 | "Combien d'histoires modèles exaltent ta grandeur, ta souffrance! Combien de Robinson, de Roquentin, de Meursault, de Leverkühn! Les bons points, les belles images, les mensonges: ce n'est pas vrai. Tu n'as rien appris, tu ne saurais témoigner. Ce n'est pas vrai, ne les crois pas, ne crois pas les martyrs, les héros, les aventuriers!" Perec (1967/2002), 301.

255 | "Non. Tu préfères être la pièce manquante du puzzle. Tu retires du jeu tes billes et tes épingles. [...] Tu n'écouteras plus les bons conseils. Tu ne demanderas pas de remèdes. [...] Tu ne sors plus de la maison, à peine de ta chambre." Perec (1967/2002), 239f.

a dynamic and productive *literary discussion* between authors and texts that generates the composition. We realise that intertextuality is presented at its most dynamic when we have a closer look at the main intertextual references in *Un homme qui dort*.

Melville's Bartleby is not reflecting *indifference* since he is actually stating his choice and preference *not to do* certain actions and duties in the office in which he is working, that it is his preference to stay out of the social environment.

> "Bartleby," said I, in a still gentler tone, "come here; I am not going to ask you to do any thing you would prefer not to do – I simply want to speak to you."
> Upon this he noiselessly slid into view.
> "Will you tell me, Bartleby, where you were born?"
> "I would prefer not to."
> "Will you tell me *any thing* about yourself?"
> "I would prefer not to."
> "But what reasonable objection can you have to speak to me? I feel friendly towards you."
> [...] "What is your answer, Bartleby?"
> [...] "At present I prefer to give no answer," he said, and retired into his hermitage.[256]

Bartleby represents the choice and conscious attitude of being indifferent, like the student who attempts the status of indifference as part of an experiment that involves several rules, choices and decisions. This choice that might eventually lead the student to reach indifference as a state of mind and not as a matter of selection and choice, is actually the kernel of the chronicled experiment of *Un homme qui dort* (that of the plot and that of the composition) that is reflected as an attempt and involves a paradox that will be discussed later in the chapter. Hence the student in that sense is quite different

256 | Melville (1853/2015), 20.

from the actual heroes of the absurd, who have reached a state of indifference: Sartre's Roquentin and Camus' Meursault.

Whereas through Roquentin, a shadowy character and solipsist, Sartre's *La Nausée* explores a world without meaning that reflects a world of nothingness, and Camus shows in Meursault a character ostensibly without consciousness, Perec's attempt at developing an indifferent hero resulted in the rejection of such archetypes, in the sense that indifference has no benefit other than indifference itself for the hero, who in the end was never able to reach it in a pure sense. At the obscure ending of *La Nausée,* Roquentin announces his desire to write a book, something beautiful, which would nevertheless make people ashamed of their existence: "Il faudrait qu'elle soit belle et dure comme de l'acier et qu'elle fasse honte aux gens de leur existence."[257] In direct contrast, Perec's ending in *Un homme qui dort* implies that re-socialisation reflects positivity and the rejection of the absurd.

In the last chapter (16) of *Un homme qui dort,* we encounter a reference to another hero in almost every sentence and utterance, in emphatic contrast to the student who has now acquired and developed his own identity, and describing also the failure of the experiment and the vanity of indifference.

Tu n'est pas mort et tu n'es pas plus sage.
[...] Les volcans miséricordieux ne se sont pas penchés sur toi.
[...]Mais toi, pauvre Dédalus, il n'y avait pas de labyrinthe. Faux prisonnier, ta porte était ouverte. Nul garde ne se tenait devant, nul chef des gardes au bout de la galerie, nul Grand Inquisiteur à la petite porte du jardin.
[...] Tu n'as rien appris, sinon que la solitude n'apprend rien, que l'indifférence n'apprend rien: c'était un leurre, une illusion fascinante et piégée.
[...] L'indifférence est inutile. Tu peux vouloir ou ne pas vouloir, qu'importe!
[...] Tu n'es pas mort. Tu n'es pas devenu fou.

257 | Jean-Paul Sartre, *La Nausée.* (Paris: Gallimard, 1938) 250.

> [...] C'est un jour comme celui-ci, un peu plus tard, un peu plus tôt, que tout recommence, que tout commence, que tout continue.[258]

The jigsaw puzzle of narratives consisting of different texts and authors adds to the text a richness of motifs and metaphors that appear as literary influences, and it enriches the script of intertextuality further.

One such motif is that of the broken mirror: in his dorm the student has a cracked mirror in which his face is split into three different parts. The cracked face reflects the inner and outer perspectives that coexist within the text and also the intertextual allusions, the other narrative personae that are implied or mentioned in the text.

> [...] Ceci, dans la glace fêlée, n'est pas ton nouveau visage, ce sont les masques qui sont tombés, la chaleur de ta chambre les a fait fondre, la torpeur les a décollés.[259]

Before focussing on the second-person narrative perspective and the way it interrelates and functions in both scripts, we will refer to the two paradoxes on which the text is based, one of which was briefly mentioned before. The first concerns the social roles and possible forms of revolt against convention that are presented or implied in the text and that appear predictable and banal. As intertextual implications these are already included in the narrative. While the protagonist refuses to identify with several fictional and historical (self-)destructive antiheroes – with Faust who sold his soul to the devil, Empedocles who threw himself into the crater of Mount Etna, Herostratus who burnt the temple of Artemis at Ephesus in order to immortalise his name, or even Sisyphus – his attitude initially leads to a negation of literary and cultural stereotypes but ends up being just another literary stereotype. Perec himself denounces his literary

258 | Perec (1967/2002), 301-304.

259 | Perec (1967/2002), 229.

precursors as dishonest by adopting the view that they express fascination with a life they aspire to discredit. In addition, the individual's refusal is exalted to the level of heroism, when indifference seems the only possible escape.

The second paradox is inherent in the core plot and in the experiment in indifference itself: performing the latter as a possible escape from and response to the absurd, the student becomes an elaborate version of an absurd hero, one of Perec's principal inspirations for this work that also challenges the myth of the outsider. However, as the experiment maintains the paradoxical goal of simultaneous mastery and passivity which suggests a contradiction, it is doomed to fail.[260] The novel defines indifference as a cancelling of life by minimising it to nothing, a notion that echoes clearly the abandoning of life interests and the lack of any excitement, thus alluding directly to Sartre's Antoine Roquentin.

We can see the same contradiction at the level of rhetoric and structure: the novel privileges a sense of randomness over casual links in its main part, evoking a sense of "anti-histoire" despite quoting numerous stories by other authors. As we saw earlier, the concept of a game might have had a paradoxical function as to the content, but it appears similarly in the rhetoric of the text as Perec does not present a project based on instincts, reflections and luck; on the contrary, he follows certain rules and narrative schemes to explore the limits of his narrative experiment.

It may seem that the script of intertextuality is a product of automatic writing, in the sense that the intertexts and references appear unexpectedly and with pretentious randomness, but because they align with the evolving experiment, it is clear that the second script follows the logic of the first and that it also has a certain structure, since different literary figures are recalled or commented on in accordance with the student's state of mind or a particular stage of the experiment. The strategy Perec employs against spontaneous

260 | Alison James, *Constraining Chance: Georges Perec and the Oulipo.* (Evanston: Northwestern University Press, 2009), 33f.

creation echoes the idea developed by the Oulipo movement that emphasises the importance of conscious control over the writing process, hence it highlights his remarkable technique and reveals a highly elevated style.[261]

The Narrative Perspective

As described earlier, *Un homme qui dort* borrows its title from Proust, its tone and style from Kafka and its theme from Sartre, Camus and Melville. No matter which hero the student acts out at each point of the text, the evolving narrative reflects a process of continuous reduction linked to the rejections of its forerunners, thus affecting the nar-ratorial perspective of the text. In the final chapter, the narrator reveals the major components of the script and admits to their rejection. Hence the evolution of the narrative reflects the end of the experiment in indifference (first script), the completion of the narrative collage (second script) and the modification of the narrative perspective while signifying reduction and determination.

The narrative *tu* evolves from an undefined apostrophic reference, a generic and collective *tu* in which several heroes coexist and which designates a developing narrative persona, to a rhetorical device of address for the eventually fully-shaped hero. Perec's *Un homme qui dort* is an example of second-person storytelling that employs the pronoun's perspective very differently from what we have seen in the previous examples of Christa Wolf and Michel Butor. Perec uses the pronoun as the main narrative figure of the discourse without reference to a definite person, even with problems of self-awareness.

Mais le héros d'*Un homme qui dort* est un interlocuteur muet: ce "tu" ne dit jamais "je". Le "tu" est d'autant plus insolite que ce pronom caractéristique de l'échange verbal renvoie ici à un sujet autiste. [...] Le recours au

261 | James (2009), 15.

"tu" dans la construction du récit ne fait que souligner encore davantage, dans l'histoire racontée, l'enfermement d'un personnage qui refuse toute communication.[262]

Couched in the second-person singular form *tu*, the text is endowed with a specific sense of intimacy, which also raises the issue of determining the narrative voice and its enigmatic relationship to the protagonist. As mentioned in the introduction to this chapter in connection with the film adaptation of *Un homme qui dort*, narrative voice and protagonist have no other relationship in the narrative than that of creator and executor.

The student is deprived of any sense of personhood; he just belongs to the project as its executor and vital component. He is introduced as a potential thus ambiguous, developing and thus undefined narrative figure, performing and being an experiment, addressed by the narrator in the second-person singular; the latter in fact designates the text's main narrative figure instead of the student due to the ability of the pronoun to encompass multiple addressees and to shift continuously between them, covering all the narrative forerunners, elements and needs mentioned above. Until the end of the narrative the student represents an (elaborated) combination of all other heroes implied or mentioned in the text, a hero made up of (the reflection of) other heroes but lacking personal identity.

The evolution of the *tu* throughout the narrative comes with a continuous reduction and limitation of digressions and references. As the project evolves, the narrative examples of indifference that are mentioned directly or indirectly are rejected, thus reducing the scope and range of address, whereas the student develops a concrete persona at the same time. When finally all the implications and literary paradigms are refused, the student stops being a cognitive entity (*topos*) of other figure-reflections and qualifies as a figure of indifference himself. By the time the project reaches its end and a new, complete version of an indifferent narrative hero is available,

262 | Perec (1967/2002), 213f.

one that has actually refused to be the outsider, the narrative *tu* finally acquires a definite sense and addresses the student and the person he has become exclusively.

Responding to the fundamental question of whether other pronouns might be appropriate for this narrative, the answer is negative. The complex narrative structure studied throughout this chapter would work neither in the first nor in the third person. For a start, the choice of the narrative's theme excludes the first-person employment, as it would be contradictory to the whole project of indifference, reflecting activity, initiative and requiring personhood instead of passivity and the cancelling of life. Such a choice would also mean that some decisions had already been made, i.e. the text would not chronicle an ongoing experiment but rather the result of an experiment already completed or expected to be completed. Had *Un homme qui dort* been written in the first person, it would also be impossible for the narrator and the author to incorporate all the narrative examples in the text and discuss them in order to form a narrative collage of references.

For similar reasons a third-person narrative would not work either. Should Perec, like Melville, have preferred the third-person perspective, he would have needed to limit the narration to the perspective of the outsider, leaving aside the reflections, thoughts and emotions that the narrator of *Un homme qui dort* reports. As mentioned earlier in connection with the (non)choice of the first-person perspective, no pronoun other than that for the second person would enable the narrator to keep the contemporaneity of his text and reflect the notion of an experiment in terms of theme and rhetoric. The same holds for intertextuality: a third-person perspective would eliminate from the theme and rhetoric of the text the significance of intertextuality, one that enables Perec to experiment with different figures until he forms his own version of the indifferent hero, thus contributing to the existentialist-philosophical literary discussion of the absurd. For the requirements of a third-person narrative, Perec, in order to introduce the text other than by *tu,* would need to have a concrete persona already formed; this would eliminate the self-reflexive aspect of the narrative and rule out the second script of *Un homme qui dort*.

It is the choice of the second-person pronoun that actually permits the combination of the external perspective needed by the narrator for the experience of the experiment in indifference that is chronicled, like Melville in connection with Bartleby's deliberate social detachment, while at the same time employing Kafkaesque tones for addressing inner thoughts without, however, affecting the sense of the impersonal.

> Dans *Un homme qui dort* toutefois, le personnage n'est pas aboli: c'est "tu". Il ne peut pas avoir un nom. Mais il est très présent, c'est quelqu'un qui murmure; c'est ce "tu" qui apparaît quand on se regarde dans un miroir, quand on se parle. Quand on se dit "tu" ... Il ne s'agit donc pas d'un "je", encore moins de "l'autre", d'une troisième personne.[263]

The employment of the second person for the dominant narrative voice generates duplicity in the novel by addressing simultaneously the actual project of indifference inscribed in the text through the student and the series of historic and fictional heroes who are compared to the actual hero and who deal with the same issues (indifference, the absurd, a sense of not-belonging). Perec's *tu* is a narrative choice which enables the author to compose in one narrative a double script and address all coexisting and implied figures and circumstances by implementing them in the narrative and processing them in it.

The author reveals in his cover-quotation that he follows Kafka in employing this form so as to benefit from the narrative ambiguity and resilience inherent in the second-person viewpoint. He thus manages to bridge different narratives in one discourse and succeeds in challenging the myth of the outsider and the theme of

263 | Georges Perec in Yvonne Goga, "Formes de l'autoréflexivité mallarméenne dans *Un homme qui dort* de Georges Perec." In Écrire l' Énigme. (Paris: PUPS, 2007) 135.

indifference by reflecting on it as a literary theme and existential resolution based on examples from fiction, mythology and history that are profound in the narrative and appear as its integral parts. It is only by using the second-person (singular) form that Perec adds a resilient and versatile narrative component to his text, one that enables him to pursue the project of indifference within an experimental text and thus manages to combine both scripts and aspirations, without putting the textual coherence at risk.

Conclusion

Un homme qui dort is a book devoted to the exploration of a world without meaning. It is a philosophical novel that does not propose philosophical arguments in the formal sense but dramatises them instead. It is also a document of its own making. Appearing in France in the sixties and written from a second-person perspective, *Un homme qui dort* is often linked to Michel Butor's earlier *La Modification*. However, even if the two novels share some profound similarities – for example reflexivity, the notion of a closed space and the obsessive attention to visual perception as well as detailed descriptions of surroundings – they do not offer a basis for any generic assumptions regarding the second-person perspective as they employ it quite differently in terms of form (Perec uses the second-person singular *tu* and not the plural *vous*), function and rhetorical properties.

What the two texts do have in common is their uniqueness *vis-à-vis* the movements that dominated the French literary scene upon their appearance. Butor's *La Modification* may belong to the *Nouveau Roman* period but involves elements from the traditional novel and therefore cannot be considered a pure and representative text of that movement; the same may be said for Perec and the place of *Un homme qui dort* in the works of the Oulipo group.

As with *La Modification, Un homme qui dort* constitutes an account of the formulation and failure of a project about human existence, an attempt to achieve re-orientation in life after a crisis. In the fictional frame both protagonists move from one state to another, creating the illusion that (here and now) they are prone to sharing their experience on an extra-fictional level. In both cases, the individual and his self-definition are brought to the fore, starting from an undefined sense of malaise, half-awake (Butor) or half-asleep (Perec). Butor's protagonist moves from a state of crisis and doubt to one of certainty, as does Perec's, with the difference that in his case the resolution comes unintentionally and naturally as time passes and his student has no authority or personhood to take action.

La Modification is a story of return and re-evaluation of that which exists, while *Un homme qui dort* tells the story of how being indifferent does not make any difference in the end. In his obsessive concern with objects, extensively enumerating itineraries and trivial actions, Perec elaborates a new version of the myth of the outsider, questioning the myth itself as his hero recognises the vanity of being excluded from any social constellation. In gathering examples of other literary outsiders from major works of literature, he rejects their vision of heroism achieved through self-destruction or sacrifice for the sake of ideals. Reading the text we follow an attempt at finding meaning in the meaningless, in a project where the suspension of time and the sense of isolation is striking.

Making the ordinary and the everyday a part of fiction reminds us, of course, of Butor and his protagonist Léon, who represents an ordinary man dealing with his life decisions with the fears, agonies and hesitations of a real person and not of a traditional fictional hero. Perec's story is of the banal and ordinary built on the accumulation of the insignificant, and it reflects the need to integrate in society and find meaning within a social context. After Butor's ordinary hero, Perec centres his story on the value of the *quotidien*. In this, he is influenced directly by Lefebvre[264] who was preoccupied with its theorisation during the late fifties.

264 | For a more comprehensive approach to the topic, see Henri Lefebvre, *La Production de l'Espace*. 1974. (Paris: Anthropos, 2000).

Ce qui se passe vraiment, ce que nous vivons, le reste, tout le reste, où est-il? Ce qui se passe chaque jour et qui revient chaque jour, le banal, le quotidien, l'évident, le commun, l'ordinaire, l'infra-ordinaire, le bruit de fond, l'habituel, comment en rendre compte, comment l'interroger, comment le décrire?[265]

It is Perec's achievement that he manages with his second-person account to expand the second-person narrative to extreme limits, beyond Butor's self-reflective *vous* or Wolf's self-analysing and self-examining *du*. Perec acknowledged the twentieth-century crisis in realist representation, rejecting the solution proposed by the *Nouveau Roman* (at least in its first phase, as represented mostly by Butor) and showing a solid faith in literary experimentation and even transformational procedures in his writing. For him, literature is revolutionary by nature as it demonstrates the need for social change through formal modifications.[266]

Perec's self-reflexive text may be read as an allegory of fiction writing undertaken in a mode of social detachment and pure observation, and as a comment on literature as a continuous exchange of ideas and inspiration: games of influence and favour between authors. Reducing the narrative to a minimum in terms of plot and personae and releasing it from any time constraints or specifications, Perec uses the second-person singular to narrate a story of non-action in total contradiction to the historic context in which he wrote the book, namely the tensions and agitation of 1968 in France.

Un homme qui dort demands an active reading: the more fully the intertextual allusions are decoded, the deeper the reader's appreciation. The author does not reveal to his audience the composition process of his text as much as Christa Wolf did, neither does he provide any sort of guidelines, encouragement or instructions on authorship as Butor did, for example. However, he does list his ancestors and literary influences and reveals his sources of inspi-

265 | Georges Perec, *L'Infra-Ordinaire.* (Paris: Seuil, 1990) 10f.

266 | James (2009), 24.

ration in the form of a literary index on the topic of indifference, adding to the self-reflexivity of his text. *Un homme qui dort* focuses on the experimental and hypothetical within the second-person viewpoint to explore a literary theme within a text that combines and urges direct contact with its literary companions.

Keeping to the sequence of second-person texts that are analysed here based on the complexity of the narrative perspective rather than chronological order, and having discussed Perec's liminal text that challenges the limits of composition and the scope of the second-person pronoun, the thesis will now focus on an earlier and even more enigmatic and experimental text, Ilse Aichinger's *Spiegelgeschichte.*

2.4 Ilse Aichinger's *Spiegelgeschichte*

At the End the Beginning

> "(In der Geschichte) gibt es ein Mädchen, das im Sterben sein Leben wie im Spiegel wieder erlebt, das einem Freund, als es ihn zum letzten Mal sieht, begegnet, und sich von ihm, als es ihn zum ersten Mal sieht, trennt, dem zuletzt die Zöpfe wieder wachsen und das bei jeder Prüfung immer mehr von dem, was es wusste, vergessen haben muss, bis es endlich im Augenblick des Todes zur Welt kommt."
> Ilse Aichinger

The Question Reversed

I will now turn to Ilse Aichinger's *Spiegelgeschichte,* the oldest text considered in this thesis and the one with which I will conclude the close-reading review of second-person narrative examples written during the post-war period and after. Aichinger's story is a narrative masterpiece with a remarkable symbolic character and richness in poetic and rhetorical properties. It offers a basis for drawing some final conclusions regarding the poetics of the second-person narrative perspective and expands the notions and concepts discussed in the previous parts of this thesis. Moreover, *Spiegelgeschichte* invites further investigation into philosophical, socio-political and gender themes that this chapter will gesture towards.

Spiegelgeschichte has the limited page range of a *novella*. Without involving or developing a narrative hero, at least in the traditional sense, it involves two parallel narrative levels assigned to two different narrators. From different perspectives, both narrative levels refer to and tell the same plot, namely a woman's life and her dying, but in a different way since they reflect different kinds of logic and connotations. Written in 1948-1949 in the aftermath of the Second World War, *Spiegelgeschichte* primarily deals with mortality, guilt and human experience and, implicitly, also with language, expression and narrative limitations. Praised for her striking narrative artefact, the thirty-one-year old author received the prize of the Group 47 for this text in 1952. Having joined the literary company of the canonical authors of German post-war literature very early in her writing career, Aichinger enjoyed continual respect and recognition from then on.

Spiegelgeschichte reveals its experimental and revolutionary character from the very start, beginning with a sentence in the conditional that correlates the opening of the story with its end, composing its unusual plot in a highly poetic and symbolic style and employing an uncommon structure of duplicity. Because of its cryptic language and challenging form, Aichinger's masterpiece was described as a "sperriges Sprachexperiment,"[267] and indeed, due to its striking content and innovative style that consists of formal experimentation and challenges the traditional themes of writing, it marked a turning point ("Wendepunkt"[268]) in the history of German literature. The author's language gives expression to a period of fear, anxiety and distrust and responds to the need for change and innovation in storytelling in order to voice aspects of a silenced and polemical reality. With *Spiegelgeschichte* Aichinger introduced the theme of reversal and transformation narrated within an alternative narrative strategy

---

267 | Wilfried Barner, "Ilse Aichinger: Spiegelgeschichte." In *Interpretationen. Klassische deutsche Kurzgeschichten*. (Stuttgart: Reclam, 2004) 76.

268 | Barner (2004), 77.

that develops in two streams, involves a number of innovations and reveals new possibilities in writing. The creativity of language is emphasised by giving words unexpected meanings and connotations, and incidents appear in an unforeseen order. Aichinger thus challenges the cause-effect relationships of a life narrated in a way that (re-)creates it, and that enables her to offer a new approach to philosophical questions about life and death and also the concept of beginning and ending.

Aichinger's text experiments with the limits of language and representation while thematising writing as a transforming dynamic that challenges traditional ideas and concepts. Examples are the association of death with the end and birth with the beginning; narrating as a means of forgetting rather than remembering; even the composition of a novel in which the main figure is unable to act. *Spiegelgeschichte* reflects events and perceptions of reality in different ways and with different connotations. It also offers a remarkable example of self-reflexivity, liminality and transgression in fiction as it employs the second-person viewpoint in a novel and totally unique way: once again the second-person perspective is employed for a self-centred story, though this time the story doesn't present a self-discovery process but rather the possibility and result of revisiting the past and recreating life at a poetic level. To do so, Aichinger invents an enigmatic mirror which reflects the events, but with distortions. What is seen in the mirror of *Spiegelgeschichte* is narrated by an enigmatic voice that employs the *du*.

Der **blinde** Spiegel mit den Fliegenflecken läßt dich verlangen, was noch keine verlangt hat.
[...]
Und da erschrickt die Alte. Und in dem großen Schrecken, in dem **blinden** Spiegel erfüllt sie deine Bitte. Sie weiß nicht was sie tut, doch in dem **blinden** Spiegel geling es ihr.[269]

269 | Aichinger (1954/1979), 47.

The following close-reading analysis of *Spiegelgeschichte* will focus first on its content and structure, concentrating on the two narrative levels of which it is composed; then discuss the mirror element as a catalyst for the theme and as a rhetorical tool; and finally examine and clarify the value and dynamic of the second-person pronoun as employed by Aichinger in a total reversal of what we have seen so far.

The Two Plots

Two narrative levels and plots referring to the same topic make up *Spiegelgeschichte*. It tells the story of the episodes of a life (and death) in three parts and from two different perspectives, which approach the topic according to their own logic and consequently select different parts of the life and death theme. *Spiegelgeschichte* generally refers to the life and death story of a young woman whose name is never revealed and who is dying in a hospital bed after a botched abortion. The first narrative level has a linear flow, reports the final stages of her life and the decline in her health, and is composed in the third person. This level shows the perspective of others, namely the hospital staff, regarding the woman's situation and her experience.

It appears in *Spiegelgeschichte* in only four sentences that resemble announcements as they inform us of the condition of the woman's health, and divide her life (and the novel) into three parts addressing the corresponding periods: that of suffering and death, that of a youthful period of love full of expectations and hopes, and that of childhood and infancy. The order in which these periods appear in the text is reversed, going against the forward flow of the narrative, and they belong as narrative-fragments to the second narrative.

The sentences of the first narrative are positioned at intervals in the novel. They signal the transition from one life-period to another and raise salient points which, although they cannot be subverted, are brought into question in the second narrative. The end of *Spiegelgeschichte* is emphatic as the second-person narrator, designated by the enigmatic voice, questions the death announcement by the third-person narrator.

> "Es ist zu Ende –" sagen die hinter dir, "sie ist tot!"
> Still! Laß sie reden![270]

The narrator of the second narrative level which prevails in the majority of the pages and covers the period from burial to birth, is an enigmatic voice that employs the second person and tells the woman of episodes of her life and death in reverse, as they are seen in the mirror mentioned earlier. The theme of reversal affects every condition of the narrative: it is apparent in the reverse flow of events that is followed, and impacts on their meaning and the ways in which those events correlate.

The *ordo inversus* influences the casual and temporal relationships of the narrated events, with reasons depicted as results, altered sequences and connotations. Manifesting the theme of reversal, the second narrative level describes a backward progress of reversing and thus transforming in the sense of undoing life events, and when at the end it refers to the woman's birth (coinciding with her death as per the other narrative flow) it questions this (her death) as well. Striking also is the condition of this route as a process of forgetting and unlearning, so as to reach a terminal point.

> Das schwerste bleibt es doch, das Sprechen zu vergessen und das Gehen zu verlernen, hilflos zu stammeln und auf dem Boden zu kriechen, um zuletzt in Windeln gewickelt zu werden. Das schwerste bleibt es, alle Zärtlichkeiten zu ertragen und mehr zu schauen. Sei geduldig! Bald ist alles gut. Gott weiß den Tag, an dem du schwach genug bist.[271]

In the end the two narratives reflect both terminal points (death and birth) which, though not identical, are treated equally in *Spiegelge-*

270 | Aichinger (1954/1979), 52f.
271 | Aichinger (1954/1979), 52.

schichte. They manage to deprive them of any positive or negative connotations. The story opens with the mysterious voice describing scenes of a burial and a funeral up until the final moment of death.

Wenn einer dein Bett aus dem Saal schiebt, wenn du siehst, daß der Himmel grün wird, und wenn du dem Vikar die Leichenrede ersparen willst, so ist es Zeit für dich, aufzustehen, leise, wie Kinder aufstehen, wenn am Morgen Licht durch die Läden schimmert, heimlich, daß es die Schwester nicht sieht und schnell![272]

The employment of the second-person perspective at the beginning has the more generic sense of describing a common, though strikingly unpleasant situation gesturing both towards the woman and the reader. Its syntax and content set reversal as a dominant theme and style of the (dominant) second-person narrative and establish the conditions for reading *Spiegelgeschichte.* Even in its title, the novel announces the key role that the mirror holds and implies its being a catalyst for the theme of reversal.

Aichinger assigns to the mirror a double role in *Spiegelgeschichte*: it shows the events that the voice has exclusive access to, and narrates and defines the structure and rhetoric of the text, since the events are narrated in a modified way because of the distorting mirror. The rhetorical value and ambiguity of the role the mirror acquires in *Spiegelgeschichte* is more prominent in the title's English translations. They show variation, *Life Story in Retrospect (Mirror Story)*[273] and *Story in Reverse,*[274] and they thus interpret the ambivalence and duplicity of the distinction between the two words more expressly and orientate the reading of the narrative and the reception of the

---

272 | Aichinger (1954/1979), 43.

273 | Ilse Aichinger, "Life Story in Retrospect." In *Ilse Aichinger.* Ed. J. C. Alldridge. Chester Springs: Dufour Editions, 1969. 65-77.

274 | Ilse Aichinger, "Story in Reverse." In *German Short Stories 1= Deutsche Kurzgeschichten* 1. Ed. Richard Newnham. Trans. Christopher Levenson. London: Penguin Books, 1964. 27- 51.

mirror in a rhetorical direction. Before we continue with the close reading of the novel, it is important to emphasise that the analysis of *Spiegelgeschichte* is based on the relationship between the "Spiegelndem" and the "Gespiegelten," a constellation that has an impact on all narrative conditions including plot, narrator and structure.

> Aber da hat er schon begonnen, der Vikar, da hörst du seine Stimme, jung und eifrig und unaufhaltsam, da hörst du ihn schon reden. Laß es geschehen! Laß seine guten Worte untertauchen in dem blinden Regen. Dein Grab ist offen. Laß seine schnelle Zuversicht erst hilflos werden, daß ihr geholfen wird. Wenn du ihn läßt, wird er am Ende nicht mehr wissen, ob er schon begonnen hat [...] Und sie nehmen den Kranz vom Deckel und geben ihn dem jungen Mann zurück.[275]

The reverse narrative involves words that validate its reversed logic: "zurück, wieder zurück, wieder hinauf"[276] and give the second narrative an uncommon character with a flow that is hard to follow, continuously challenging by reversing, undoing and then transforming and recreating the story of the woman's life. Actions, emotions and feelings are mostly recorded descriptively and in a consistently affirmative tone; meanwhile rhetorical, self-reflexive questions ("Was bleibt jetzt zu tun?"[277]) pop up.

At other points ("Er weint. Du bleibst nicht länger in der Leichenhalle. Warum weint er?"[278]), the tone is more intimate, subjective and comforting. Thus it creates a consultative and personal aura, one that characterises the proximity the voice has to the woman, taking the role of adviser sometimes; this also can be seen in a syntax full of subjunctive forms ("Du hättest ihn warnen können, aber um dieser Ehre willen ist noch keiner aus dem Sarg gestiegen"[279]); these forms

275 | Aichinger (1954/1979), 43.

276 | Aichinger (1954/1979), 43.

277 | Aichinger (1954/1979), 43.

278 | Aichinger (1954/1979), 45.

279 | Aichinger (1954/1979), 44.

reflect the unreal but fictionally realised process of revisiting the past. The future reflects the past, being already known, and is therefore articulated in an oxymoronic style as something definite and concrete ("Du wirst es später lange nicht mehr fertigbringen, so still zu liegen. Am nächsten Tag kommt der junge Mann wieder"[280]).

> Und sie haben dir das Tuch wieder um den Mund gebunden, und das Tuch macht dich so fremd. [...] Und ein wenig später werden sie dir das Tuch vom Kopf nehmen müssen, ob sie es wollen oder nicht. [...] Der Morgen wird schon dunkler.[281]

In the first part the voice describes moments after the woman's death, hence incidents that the woman could not have had access to while she was alive. This point raises additional doubts about the already controversial and enigmatic relationship the woman has with the narrating voice. Since, however, the discourse covers only the moment of burial, it is not that disturbing in the logic of the narrative. Regarding the relationship between the woman and the voice, which will be reviewed in the following section, this thesis prefers a rhetorical approach and will discuss it only in poetic terms avoiding any metaphysical or other types of approaches. The brief post-death period finishes when death is announced in the first out of the four sentences articulated by the people in the hospital.

> "Die Fieberträume lassen nach", sagt eine Stimme hinter dir, "der Todeskampf beginnt!" Ach die! Was wissen die?[282]

The almost ironic response of the voice gives a first hint about the relationship between the two narratives and the way they interrelate. From the moment the irreversibility of the woman's condition is declared, the voice continues the reverse narrative flow, but from

280 | Aichinger (1954/1979), 45.
281 | Aichinger (1954/1979), 45f.
282 | Aichinger (1954/1979), 46.

this point onwards describes events from her life, starting from its very last moments. The moments of suffering are depicted in detail; the tension and emotional intensity reach their peak with the experience of the abortion that, as we know from the beginning, is fatal and linked to feelings of disappointment with the young man who didn't meet the expectations of his lover.

Die Schmerzen jagen dich, den Weg wirst du ja finden. Erst links, dann rechts und wieder links, quer durch die Hafengassen, die so elend sind, dass sie nicht anders können, als zum Meer zu führen. Wenn nur der junge Mann in deiner Nähe wäre, aber der junge Mann ist nicht bei dir, im Sarg warst du viel schöner.[283]

At certain moments we detect traces of criticism and despair ("Wie soll denn auch eines davon dein Kind sein, wenn du zur Alten gehst, die bei der Kneipe wohnt?"[284]) that emphasise the personal tone and the insistent focus on the voice-woman relationship, the nature of their communication and connection, and that almost immediately dispel from the reader the sense of being addressed, inherent in the second person and offered at the opening of the narrative. The focus on the woman is emphatic as can be seen in the narrative's lack of any direct characterisation of secondary narrative figures, with the exception of the actual abortion, when the voice is permitted some negative observations about the old woman who performed it and who is described as an alcoholic who lives in a dirty haunted house.

Das weiß der ganze Hafen, wovon die Alte ihren Schnaps bezahlt. Sie steht schon an der Tür. Die Tür ist offen, und sie streckt dir ihre Hand entgegen, die ist schmutzig. Alles ist dort schmutzig.[285]

283 | Aichinger (1954/1979), 46.
284 | Aichinger (1954/1979), 47.
285 | Aichinger (1954/1979), 47.

The secondary characters are bare and mostly male; about the father, for example, very little is revealed. Children make an appearance more frequently and they signify the emotions associated with the abortion. Other characters simply provide the means to undermine social institutions: the priest, for example, is shown as a neutral figure who with his words represents a particular culture but poses no threat to the young woman. He is treated with implicit irony by the narrative voice while he conducts the funeral.[286] The same critical approach is found in the description of the woman's feelings towards her lover, spread throughout the narrative but without such indirectness: in the case of the lover, a lack of empathy and social understanding is emphasised.[287]

Sie lassen dich allein. So allein lassen sie dich, daß du die Augen aufschlägst und den grünen Himmel siehst, so allein lassen sie dich, daß du zu atmen beginnst, schwer und röchelnd und tief, rasselnd wie eine Ankerkette, wenn sie sich löst. Du bäumst dich auf und schreist nach deiner Mutter. Wie grün der Himmel ist![288]

Other people are referred to as hostile somehow, especially to the world of women, and they remain unnamed and distant. In terms of linguistics this is expressed in universal statements in an impersonal syntax while in specific parts of the discourse the collective term *Leute* is used to show the contrast between the woman and the rest of society. At a moment of high emotional intensity, the perspective of the text changes when the narrative voice begins to use the first person, adopting the voice of the woman so as to speak to

286 | "Er schüttelt dem jungen Mann heftig die Hand und wünscht ihm vor Verlegenheit viel Glück. Es ist sein erstes Begräbnis, und er errötet bis zum Hals hinunter." Aichinger (1954/1979), 43.

287 | Henry U. Gerlach, *Einwände und Einsichten. Revidierte Deutungen deutschsprachiger Literatur des 19. und 20. Jahrhunderts.* (München: Iudicium, 2002) 292-294.

288 | Aichinger (1954/1979), 46.

the old woman who performs the abortion, demanding that she try to, and succeed in (in the context of the second-person narrative) bringing her baby back to life, in other words, *undoing* the abortion.

"Mach mir mein Kind wieder lebendig!" Das hat noch keine von der Alten verlangt. Aber du verlangst es. Der Spiegel gibt dir Kraft. Der blinde Spiegel mit den Fliegenflecken läßt dich verlangen, was noch keine verlangt hat.
"Mach es lebendig, sonst stoß ich deine gelben Blumen um, sonst kratz ich dir die Augen aus, sonst reiß ich deine Fenster auf und schrei über die Gasse, damit die hören müssen, was sie wissen, ich schrei."
Und da erschrickt die Alte. Und in dem großen Schrecken, in dem blinden Spiegel erfüllt sie deine Bitte. Sie weiß nicht was sie tut, doch in dem blinden Spiegel gelingt es ihr.[289]

This moment is the climax of the narrative. It shows the profound difference between the two narrative streams and what they connote: what is done in the third-person narrative is altered and transformed in the second-person narrative. This climax also displays a key element of the narrative when the distorting mirror is mentioned for the first time, the one that we have described as a fundamental tool for the plot and thematic catalyst for *Spiegelgeschichte* right from the beginning and the one which is used for the composition and constellation of the dominant plotline in reverse. This mirror doesn't offer a true reflection of the objects but a reversed and modified one, therefore it is characterised as *blind*. In German, a *blind* mirror is one that has turned dirty and milky-white due to age and that therefore cannot reflect images placed before it. Such a description may suggest alienation and an obstacle to self-revelation, but it may also offer a chance to see things anew, from a different perspective, taking advantage of a temporally advanced and thus superior angle.[290]

289 | Aichinger (1954/1979), 47.

290 | Deborah Janson, "Ilse Aichinger's Spiegelgeschichte: Challenging the Symbolic Order." In *Frauen: MitSprechen MitSchreiben. Beiträge zur*

At this point we can explain the double function that the *blind* mirror has in the text: thematically it generates the plot of the narrative while formally it points to the mechanism that reverses the events of the past as they are reflected back, transformed, and thus defining the reverse rhetoric of *Spiegelgeschichte*. Of course, apart from what the mirror literally *does* in the narrative, it also suggests a metaphor and echoes self-reflexivity as it makes concrete in the narrative the reflective sense of literature and poetics as *poesies*, while at the same time it underlines the creativity and transformative properties of language.

Bevor er weiß, daß du das Kind erwartest, nennt er dir schon die Alte, bevor er sagt, daß er dich liebt, nennt er die Alte. Sei ruhig! Er weiß nicht, daß du bei der Alten schon gewesen bist, er kann es auch nicht wissen, er weiß nichts von dem Spiegel. Aber kaum hat er's gesagt, hat er es auch vergessen. Im Spiegel sagt man alles, daß es vergessen sei. Und kaum hast du gesagt, daß du das Kind erwartest, hast du es auch verschwiegen. Der Spiegel spiegelt alles.[291]

Omniscient and omnipotent (as per the limits of the woman's story), the mirror portrays the fantasy of undoing the damage caused by the entanglement of the woman with the young man. It may show nothing new, but by exposing the past to new perceptions and in a reverse way, it enables events to be judged anew, reformed and then forgotten as they recede into the future while the narrative progresses further into the past. By making true forgetting possible, the woman can revisit and re-experience her past in a new way and proceed to the end which actually coincides with her birth, a symbolic start and new beginning.

Coming back to the close reading of the text, the section dealing with despair ends with a sentence that marks the second sentence

literatur- und sprachwissenschaftlichen Frauenforschung. (Stuttgart: Hans-Dieter Heinz Akademischer Verlag, 1997) 500.

291 | Aichinger (1954/1979), 48.

of the third-person narrative following the reference to the mirror when, again, the voice doubts the ultimate meaning of death:

Was flüstern die in ihren hellen Hauben? "Das ist der Todeskampf!" Die laßt nur reden.[292]

From that point onwards the properties of the mirror and their impact on the second-person narrative are emphasised, especially in reference to the abortion, which is described as left behind and, with relief, forgotten.[293] The narrative in this part chronicles the period of love, including the despair of parting and revealing the expectations, hopes and eagerness for a bright future together with some irony as we know already how things have turned out.

Gib acht, jetzt beginnt er bald von der Zukunft zu reden, von den vielen Kindern und vom langen Leben, und seine Wangen brennen vor Eifer. Sie zünden auch die deinen an. Ihr werdet streiten, ob ihr Söhne oder Töchter wollt, und du willst lieber Söhne. [...]

Die Zukunft ist vorbei. Die Zukunft ist ein Weg am Fluss, der in die Auen mündet. [...]

Drei Tage später wagt er nicht mehr, den Arm um deine Schultern zu legen. Wieder drei Tage später fragt er dich, wie du heißt, und du fragst ihn. Nur wisst ihr voneinander nicht einmal mehr die Namen. [...]

Ihr werdet immer fremder. Von der Zukunft habt ihr schon lange zu reden aufgehört. [...]

Eines Tages ist er dir so fremd, daß du ihn auf einer finsteren Gasse vor einem offenen Tor zu lieben beginnst.[294]

292 | Aichinger (1954/1979), 49.

293 | "Du hast genug geweint. Nimm deinen Kranz zurück. Jetzt wirst du auch die Zöpfe bald wieder lösen dürfen. Alles ist im Spiegel (...) Im Spiegel tut man alles, dass es vergeben sei (...) Und das verdammte Haus bleibt hinter euch zurück." Aichinger (1954/1979), 49.

294 | Aichinger (1954/1979), 50.

Soon after this part is over, the third-person narrative sets in again with the hospital nurses announcing that death is approaching, thus introducing the third period of the woman's story that reflects childhood and infancy.

"Es dauert nicht mehr lang", sagen die hinter dir, "es geht zu Ende!"[295]

In this final episode the young man is now a stranger to the woman who is pictured as a girl getting younger and younger:

Ein Tag wird kommen, da siehst du ihn zum erstenmal. Und er sieht dich. Zum erstenmal, das heißt: Nie wieder. [...] Jetzt darfst du mit deinen kleinen Brüdern spielen, und du darfst mit ihnen den Fluß entlanggehen, den Weg am Fluß unter den Erlen, und drüben sind die weißen Schindeldächer wie immer zwischen den Wipfeln.[296]

In a sequence full of connotations and reversed metaphors, the girl begins school, unlearns how to write and, when autumn comes, accompanies her father to the cemetery to meet her mother, whose death – provocatively – allows her to join her little daughter in play and to help her with her siblings. The journey back stops after the years of infancy, and when the whole process of unlearning is completed as it reaches the moment of birth, it coincides with the hospital team announcing the death. The end of the narrative, though forming an oxymoron, underlines its duplicity and symbolism and highlights the reversal even more.

Bald kommt der Sommer mit den langen Tagen. Bald stirbt deine Mutter. Du und dein Vater, ihr beide holt sie vom Friedhof ab. Drei Tage liegt sie noch zwischen den knisternden Kerzen, wie damals du. [...]
Es ist gut, daß deine Mutter gestorben ist, denn länger hättest du es mit den kleinen Brüdern allein nicht machen können. Jetzt ist sie da. [...]

---

295 | Aichinger (1954/1979), 50.
296 | Aichinger (1954/1979), 51.

Das schwerste bleibt es doch, das Sprechen zu vergessen und das Gehen zu verlernen, hilflos zu stammeln und auf dem Boden zu kriechen, um zuletzt in Windeln gewickelt zu werden.[297]

The fourth and final sentence of the third-person narrative appears very close to the third sentence mentioned earlier, at an accelerating tempo reflecting both the tension and the agony of the imminent death. The moment the story reaches its conclusion and the woman the limits of her physical existence (death and birth), time speeds up, thus emphasising the extreme *Raffung* that characterises the text (*Erzählzeit* < *erzählte Zeit*).

Es ist der Tag deiner Geburt. Du kommst zur Welt und schlägst die Augen auf und schließt sie wieder vor dem starken Licht. Das Licht wärmt dir die Glieder, du regst dich in der Sonne, du bist da, du lebst. Dein Vater beugt sich über dich.
"Es ist zu Ende -" sagen die hinter dir, "sie ist tot!"
Still! Laß sie reden![298]

The two narrative levels run parallel in the text and form a symmetry that culminates in the voice announcing the birth of the woman and the nurses announcing her death at the end. The unequal amount of text assigned to each is striking as the reverse plot dominates the narrative while the third-person stream appears only in four sentences that interfere with the dominant second-person narrative stream. This phenomenon should be understood as part of Aichinger's narrative tactics rather than suggesting lesser importance. The sentences of the third-person narrative flow may be brief and few but they serve the structure of the whole story.What is described so far in terms of plot is displayed in the graphic below:

297 | Aichinger (1954/1979), 52.
298 | Aichinger (1954/1979), 52f.

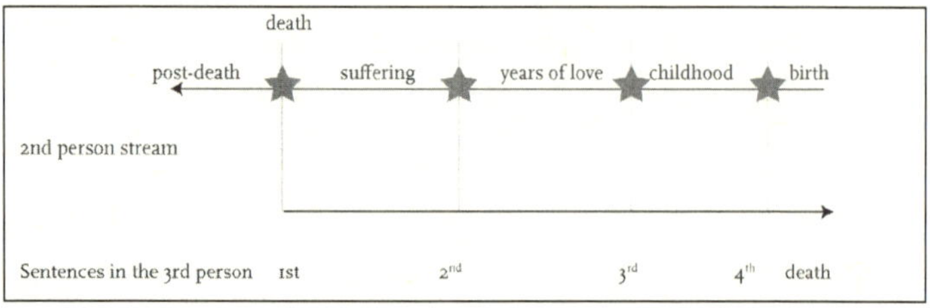

Spiegelgeschichte is a woman's story of life and death that develops between the two poles and that exceeds its limits by adding onto the first level of happening a second level that reflects that happening as a different plot, changed on the level of language. The second person stream designates the mode of language in which more possibilities are open; the third-person stream is the one describing the events that appear distorted on the other level. The two narrative levels may be contradictory in content and flow but they are complementary in that they inscribe two different yet coexisting narrative modes, and two kinds of logic referring to the same plot in a way that emphasises their differences while they reveal the possibilities of language and representation.[299]

299 | "*Spiegelgeschichte* erzählt von zwei unterschiedlichen Geschehnissen, deren Abläufe ineinander verschoben und gegeneinander ausgespielt werden. Auf der einen Ebene wird das Leben einer namenlos bleibenden jungen Frau im Rücklauf erzählt, auf einer zweiten Ebene werden die einzelnen Phasen dieser rückwärtig wiederholten Biographie zu den Stadien des regulär fortschreitenden Todeskampfes der Frau in Beziehung gesetzt. Die beiden Ebenen nehmen innerhalb der Erzählung unterschiedlich breiten Raum ein. Den vier umfangreichen Abschnitten, die den Lebensweg der Protagonistin vom offenen Grab bis zum Augenblick ihrer Geburt zurückverfolgen, entsprechen vier kurze Zwischenrufe, die den Beginn, den Höhepunkt, das Ausklingen des Todeskampfes und schließlich den Eintritt des Todes bezeichnen." Annette Ratmann, *Spiegelungen, ein Tanz, Untersuchungen zur Prosa und Lyrik Ilse Aichingers.* (Würzburg: Königshausen and Neumann, 2001) 76.

To that extent we could argue that the one narrative level suggests the reflection mode, in other words the plot, and the second reflects the poetic mode in which language is empowered by the mirror to recreate the plot. In contrast to the third-person narrative level which reflects traditional norms, forms and connotations, the second-person narrative level is more symbolic; it reflects the innovative and thus poetic properties of the technique that is used to explore the dynamics of language within the plot itself and that shows the story in reverse order in all parts and aspects: narrative flow, order of events, reasons and consequences.

In brief, the third-person narrative level expressed by the hospital staff stands for reality and reflects objectivity, while the second-person narrative level voiced and coming from an undefined origin reflects the personal aspect of the same story and appears ambiguous, subjective and even subversive. The third-person stream is more focused on the events and the object of the narration, while the second-person stream emphasises the way these events can be re-narrated and thus transformed in a process of recreation and metamorphosis, which is possible only at the level of language and representation. In the lines of the second-person narrative stream, Aichinger is able to approach themes, forms and metaphors from a reverse angle and explore the frames by challenging the limits of representation at the same time.

Die Kinder spielen mit den Kugeln am Weg. Du läufst in sie hinein, du läufst, als liefst du mit dem Rücken nach vorn, und keines ist dein Kind. Wie soll denn auch eines davon dein Kind sein, wenn du zur Alten gehst, die bei der Kneipe wohnt?[300]

Before we proceed to the next section of this chapter we need to add an observation. The way in which the voice is offered access to the past, telling it backwards while moving forward with the back turned to the future, is a concept similar to Walter Benjamin's study

300 | Aichinger (1954/1979), 47.

Über den Begriff der Geschichte and the historical and philosophical implications he draws from Paul Klee's famous painting *Angelus Novus.* [301] Benjamin's essay, written in early 1940 at the beginning of the War, involves a critique of historicism based on poetic and scientific analogies. One key criticism is the rejection of the past conceived of as a continuum of progress. Benjamin argues that to articulate the past historically does not mean to recognise it the way it really was but rather to seize a memory as it flashes up in a moment of danger. Aichinger, who wrote *Spiegelgeschichte* a few years later, alludes to Benjamin's ideas about historicism and thematises the representation of the past as a process that involves modification and alternation when seen from a temporally superior point of view.

301 | "Es gibt ein Bild von Klee, das Angelus Novus heißt. Ein Engel ist darauf dargestellt, der aussieht, als wäre er im Begriff, sich von etwas zu entfernen, worauf er starrt. Seine Augen sind aufgerissen, sein Mund steht offen und seine Flügel sind ausgespannt. Der Engel der Geschichte muß so aussehen. Er hat das Antlitz der Vergangenheit zugewendet. Wo eine Kette von Begebenheiten vor uns erscheint, da sieht *er* eine einzige Katastrophe, die unablässig Trümmer auf Trümmer häuft und sie ihm vor die Füße schleudert. Er möchte wohl verweilen, die Toten wecken und das Zerschlagene zusammenfügen. Aber ein Sturm weht vom Paradiese her, der sich in seinen Flügeln verfangen hat und so stark ist, daß der Engel sie nicht mehr schließen kann. Dieser Sturm treibt ihn unaufhaltsam in die Zukunft, der er den Rücken kehrt, während der Trümmerhaufen vor ihm zum Himmel wächst. Das, was wir den Fortschritt nennen, ist *dieser* Sturm." Walter Benjamin, "Über den Begriff der Geschichte" In *Gesammelte Schriften*. Vol. 1 - II. Eds. Rolf Tiedemann and Hermann Schweppenhäuser. (Frankfurt am Main: Suhrkamp, 1991) 697f.

The Two Narrators

Involving two narratives, *Spiegelgeschichte* also has two narrators. Whereas the third-person narrator(s) of the first narrative does not provoke any severe problems and challenges in the study of the novel, reflecting the *actual* life events from an external perspective to the woman and a linear and thus more orthodox description of the events, the situation is not the same for the narrator of the second narrative, a voice that remains enigmatic until the end and that challenges the reading of the story. The attempt to understand the voice and its function in *Spiegelgeschichte* is one that reflects on both narratives that compose the novel: being the narrator of the second-person narrative and commenting on the third-person narrative relies on the relationship the voice has with the woman and the narrative itself.

The fact that the voice is narrating post-death events rules out any interpretation of it being the woman's voice. The separation between the voice and the woman becomes more prominent through the fact that the voice tells the story to the dying woman though she is actually the person who has experienced the narrated events.

> Auf den ersten Blick scheint der Du-Erzähler die Funktion des Bewusstseins der Sterbenden zu erfüllen. Wie sich jedoch am Ende der Erzählung herausstellt, ist es nicht mit ihr identisch. [...] Es kann sich unmöglich um das erlebende und erzählende Ich allein handeln. Außerdem fällt auf, dass die junge Frau nicht in die gleiche Vergangenheit zurückgeführt wird, die sie bereits erlebt hat. Der Erzähler begleitet sie vom Grab bis zur Geburt, navigiert sie aber in eine neue vergangene Zukunft. Diese entsteht durch die verkehrte Kausalverkettung der Ereignisse und stellt die alte Vergangenheit in Frage. Die Sterbende scheint auf diese Führung angewiesen zu sein [...].[302]

---

302 | Andrea Nagy, *"Spiegelgeschichte" von Ilse Aichinger. Eine Analyse.* (Norderstedt: Grin Verlag, 2004) 5.

However, the esoteric tone of this narrative and the fact that the information revealed is more personal and subjective, reflecting an internal perspective on the story, implies that the voice shares some sort of direct association with the woman. Aichinger implies in *Spiegelgeschichte* that while alive, one engages in autobiographical self-talk in the second person. In her example the transcendence of the *I* to a *you* is a primitive and autonomous lifelong process. This phenomenon is elaborated on and embedded in the novel with the addition of the (distorting) mirror, located in between life and death and allowing this autobiographical talk to be seen. Since the voice has exclusive access to what is seen in the mirror, it is the one that narrates it in the same way that it generates the content and the form of the second-person narrative.

As for the question of the relationship between the woman and the voice, supported by the personal and intimate tone of the second-person narrative and the exclusive access to personal details, emotions and feelings that the voice enjoys, the argument maintained in the thesis is that the voice should be understood as belonging to the woman, even if it is not *her* voice. It suggests a non-identical reflection of the woman's silenced and deceased *I* which had been the *speaking I* while she was alive, performing a continuous second-person self-talk narrative about the events of her life which are now narrated transformed and reversed as they are reflected back to her in the *blind* (distorting) mirror. The way these life events are shown in the mirror and are narrated reversed allows the woman to re-experience them in this new context, composing in the end *another* life than the one that will soon come to an end.

The voice reflects an *I* in *off* modus, the one that has been performing this lifelong self-talk, and at the moment of death (or birth in the second-person narrative) which represents actual transcendence, is narrated backwards the way it is seen in the mirror. Hence the voice narrates the story using the second person in sequence with the lifelong *I-you* transcendence. The transformation of the *I* described above is pictured below:

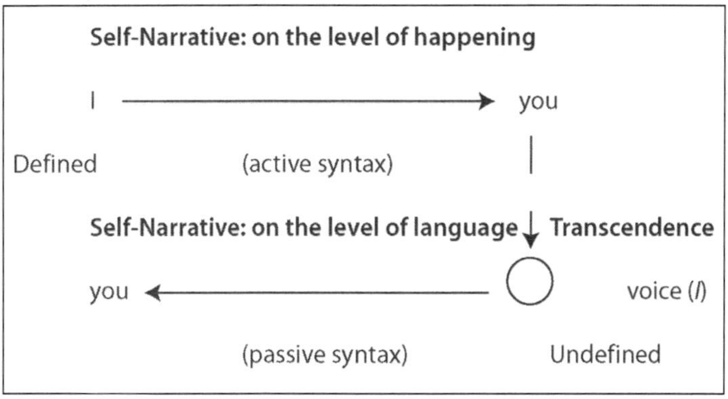

In the graphic above, we see that in such a constellation and with the second narrative generated in the mirror, we actually have two narrative *you-s* which, though related to the same plot and being reflections of the same events, are quite different. The second occurs after the mirror is used and this reflection is not only thematic/biological but poetic as well. At this poetic level and confirming the original meaning of the word deriving from the Greek verb ποιέω, which means to create, the events are re-created, oxymoronically, given that first they needed to be forgotten. The result of this process is the second-person narrative which addresses the themes of reversal and metamorphosis, and shows how plastic the properties of language are at a level at which a (re)creation of life (for example one without the failed abortion), is possible.

In this we notice an intriguing difference between Aichinger's narrative and Wolf's novel in terms of life-assessment and past access: whereas in *Kindheitsmuster* the main aspiration was related to remembering and employing the proper devices and mechanisms to examine and rectify memories in order to arrive at a genuine representation of the past, in Aichinger the process of dealing with the past is actually related to a process of forgetting, unlearning and undoing, reflecting the theme of reversing that dominates *Spiegelgeschichte*.

The notion of reversal is also expressed in the fact that the active syntax of the lifelong self-talk in which the *I* (the woman) was an active agent has transformed into the passive, as due to the condition of her health the woman is unable to act. She is but a passive recipient of the narrative, the one that the voice needs to narrate. Before proceeding to the next section of this chapter, which will be concerned with the structure of the novel and the way the reversal is linked to a so-called *poetics of metamorphosis*, it is important to raise an additional point: Aichinger expands and reverses constellations that were previously discussed in the other second-person narratives.

Her innovation lies in the following constellation: in *Spiegelgeschichte* the issue of determining the reference of the second-person pronoun that dominated our earlier close readings is reversed as it reflects the problem of determining the voice of a narrator who uses the second-person perspective throughout the text and not that of the addressee who is specified. In Aichinger's example the *du* is defined; in contrast to all previous novels, it is definitely referring to the dying woman and including the reader at the beginning of the narrative. What remains undefined until the end of the narrative is its origin, the mysterious voice designating the narrator of the second-person narrative. The voice remains ambiguous and enigmatic until the end, only the relationship with the woman and its role in the novel can be speculated on through the narrative, but even as a narrator, the voice designates an *off*-type that contains no existential status or autonomy of any kind, designating in the novel what the mirror actually does and shows.

In this total reversal that takes place in the mirror, not only the content, rhetoric and the narrative conditions are reversed and transformed, but even the syntax itself. *Spiegelgeschichte* challenges the readers throughout and especially by choosing the post-death period as the beginning of the story. The reverse narrative stream brings the terminal points very close to each other as we move from the end to the start and then back to the end again, which is actually the start. The narrative circle created reflects the notion of a loop, echoing that of the *life-cycle* and emphasising how close birth and death are, as with the end and the beginning, implying also that their meaning as well as their connotations are subjective.

Spiegelgeschichte challenges the norms of convention and, based on the relationship between "Spiegelndem" and "Gespiegelten" that we highlighted at the beginning of this chapter; how a plot, narrator and also a form and structure can appear differently in a *blind* mirror, that is at the level of language and representation. Aichinger presents not just a story of a distorting mirror that can reflect life back once it reaches its end; it is also a story that thematises the process of writing and that challenges the limits of expression and language itself. *Spiegelgeschichte* is a symbolic story about expression that experiments with its possibilities by applying the mirror as a key element for the plot and as an essential factor for the rhetorical strategy, adding to the structure of the narrative and showing on a separate narrative level the protean character of language and its dynamic.

The Theme of Reversal and Transformation

The theme of metamorphosis is fundamental to the second-person narrative stream and its rhetoric since the *ordo inversus* that the distorting mirror generates affects its content, structure and language in every respect. As a linguistic symbol the mirror represents the author's idea of language as subversive and transcendental, recasting the opinion that literature can serve to reflect reality by showing aspects of life often absent in conventional narratives and also different from the way they originally occurred.[303]

In the following, I shall analyse the rhetoric of the text, clarifying the meaning of the term "poetics of metamorphosis" as used in this chapter to describe the consistent reversal as a narrative technique Aichinger relies on, inscribed and legitimised in the text by the dis-

303 | Janson (1997), 500.

torting mirror and combined with the rhetorical and poetic properties inherent in the second-person narrative perspective that enables her to compose a story about, and also as reflected within, a mirror.

The rhetoric of metamorphosis is evident firstly in the way the content of *Spiegelgeschichte* is organised in the text. As we have seen in the previous section, the story involves both the reversed narrative of the woman's life as shown in the distorting mirror and the (post-) death episodes as well as the third-person narrative that chronicles the decline of the woman's health culminating in the ultimate reversal in which birth coincides with death, both leading to the post-death sequence. The reciprocity and narrative dualism with which the narrative attains the dynamics of (distorted) mirroring serves as a contrast between two poles, the inner and the outer, as well as the different order and logic they reflect; this is the main metamorphosis we witness in the text.

The second-person narrative technique assures the coherence of the text by initiating a sort of dialogue between the two (when the voice comments on the third-person sentences) and by keeping the two narrative levels together.[304] The technique of transformation and the rhetoric of metamorphosis are evident in the reversal of the life and death episodes and they have an impact on the time sequence and the cause-and-effect relationship which in the style of the second-person narrative stream justifies the dominance of subversive language: this figural reversal is the other aspect in which the rhetoric of metamorphosis manifests itself, affecting the narrative as a whole and also the individual components.

Aichinger's images are whimsical and perplexing on a first reading, and they contrast with conventional metaphors and evoke a sense of ambivalence. Words, metaphors ("wenn du siehst, dass

304 | "Durch die Simultaneität der Außen- und Innenperspektive erscheint die Biographie gleichermaßen individuell wie allgemein, ebenso speziell wie exemplarisch. Eine ähnliche Wirkung geht auch von der Protagonistin selbst aus – als ein "Du" rückt sie in vertraute Nähe und bleibt doch namenlos und distanziert." Ratmann (2001), 78f.

der Himmel grün wird")[305] and similes acquire contrary meanings and connotations; the sky and the sea, for example, are rather surprisingly associated with serious illness and the tragic fate of the woman. Infancy is associated with death since at the opening of the text the coffin brings birth and its decline through youth and rejuvenation. Happiness reflects pain and, as a ceremony, even the funeral is reminiscent of a wedding in several ways ("Und der Leichenwagen fährt fröhlich nach Hause").[306] It is as if the truths of life were fully realised only in retrospect.[307]

While these conventional figurative elements carry inverted connotations thereby challenging their customary positive and negative values, Aichinger manages to employ the same tactics in the syntax itself. *Spiegelgeschichte* is a text that portrays the experience of mortality on the verge of its limits, located on the threshold between life and death, depicting the sense of *not anymore* but still *not yet*. At this in-between temporal stage the present tense is the only legitimate choice for maintaining the coherence and balance of the text.

Spiegelgeschichte in its second-person stream challenges and reverses all the norms of tenses, resulting in the striking phenomenon that present perfect is used to describe future events while incidents of the past are described by future tenses, with the adverbs following the same principle ("Und ein wenig später werden sie dir das Tuch vom Kopf nehmen müssen, ob sie es wollen oder nicht. Und sie werden dich waschen und deine Hemden wechseln, und einer von ihnen wird sich schnell über dein Herz beugen, schnell, solang du noch tot bist"[308]). The only solid, definite temporal ground is that of the present tense ("Ihr werdet immer fremder"[309]); it establishes a sense of contemporaneity and of an evolving narrative while

305 | Aichinger (1954/1979), 43.

306 | Aichinger (1954/1979), 44.

307 | Carol Bedwell, "The Ambivalent Image in Ilse Aichinger's *Spiegelgeschichte*." In *Revue des Langues Vivantes* 33 (1967), 364f.

308 | Aichinger (1954/1979), 45.

309 | Aichinger (1954/1979), 51.

extending the time of the narration in the perception of the reader, delaying the moment of death.

The sense of contemporaneity and actuality is emphasised not only in the use of temporal adverbs ("jetzt") but also in the imperative syntax ("Geh jetzt! Jetzt ist der Augenblick!"[310]), the rhetorical questions ("Was soll jetzt werden?"[311]) and in the short sentences ("Und die Alte ist viel zu freundlich. Und die Treppen knarren auch hier. Und die Schiffe heulen, wohin du immer gehst, die heulen überall"[312]) that dominate the text and accelerate the tempo of the discourse.

The rhetorical function of metamorphosis extends to every single detail of the novel: sentences often resemble the structure of poetic verses; two phrases reflect one another, separated by a comma that functions as a line break between them; the phrases, while similar in that they involve repeated words, reflect a transformed meaning. What is stated in the first phrase is undermined or altered in the second ("Laß seine schnelle Zuversicht erst hilflos werden, daß ihr geholfen wird"[313], "so lassen dich allein. So allein lassen sie dich, daß du die Augen aufschlägst und den grünen Himmel siehst, so allein lassen sie dich, daß du zu atmen beginnst, schwer und röchelnd und tief, rasselnd wie eine Ankerkette, wenn sie sich löst"[314], "Der blinde Spiegel mit den Fliegenflecken läßt dich verlangen, was noch keine verlangt hat"[315], "Du wirst es nicht vergessen, wenn er es auch vergißt"[316]). Consistent with the same pattern and emphasising the rhetoric of metamorphosis, words are often repeated throughout the text ("da hörst, Trägern – Träger"[317], "blaß – Blässe, verdammte – ver-

310 | Aichinger (1954/1979), 46.
311 | Aichinger (1954/1979), 50.
312 | Aichinger (1954/1979), 47.
313 | Aichinger (1954/1979), 43.
314 | Aichinger (1954/1979), 46.
315 | Aichinger (1954/1979), 47.
316 | Aichinger (1954/1979), 48.
317 | Aichinger (1954/1979), 43.

dammt"[318]) or they come in opposing pairs ("Da reicht der Morgen noch lange in die Nacht hinein"[319], "darauf – hinauf"[320]).

Opening the text with a conditional sentence is also regarded here as an example of the rhetoric of metamorphosis. The first word (*wenn)* of the story suggests lexical ambiguity and creates a sense of unease and doubt that *Spiegelgeschichte* continues to provoke even after this first glimpse.[321] Rather than choosing a sentence with which to start her text on firm ground with an affirmative expression, Aichinger uses a doubtful *wenn* to open a sentence in which further ambivalence is created by the tense employed and which hangs between the temporal and the conditional.

> Wenn einer dein Bett aus dem Saal schiebt, wenn du siehst, daß der Himmel grün wird, und wenn du dem Vikar die Leichenrede ersparen willst, so ist es Zeit für dich, aufzustehen, leise, wie Kinder aufstehen, wenn am Morgen Licht durch die Läden schimmert, heimlich, daß es die Schwester nicht sieht - und schnell![322]

In German grammar *wenn* can be used as a temporal conjunction *(dann wenn)*, a hypothetical-conditional conjunction (*falls*) or as an iterative (*immer wenn*) conjunction. Consequently a reader of the initial sentence is puzzled by the lack of precision. In the context of *Spiegelgeschichte*, the temporal aspect may be dominant and correspond with the general lack of specificity, but since the two other functions coexist, the sentence acquires a hybrid ambiguous meaning filtered by the conjunction (*wenn*) and implying the experimental character of the text and its reciprocal structure: one narrative level is a modified version of the other, and is also the one reflecting the other.

318 | Aichinger (1954/1979), 49.

319 | Aichinger (1954/1979), 44.

320 | Aichinger (1954/1979), 43.

321 | Barner (2004), 78.

322 | Aichinger (1954/1979), 43.

The problem of determining the meaning of the opening conjunction is more evident in the English translations of *Spiegelgeschichte,* where we get different interpretations as no equivalent form exists that encompasses the functional ambiguity of *wenn.* One of the translations chooses a temporal interpretation:

When someone pushes your bed out of the ward, when you see that the sky is growing green and when you want to save the priest the trouble of holding a funeral service, then it is time for you to get up, softly, as children do when in the mornings the light shines through the shutters, secretly, so that the nurse doesn't see – and quickly![323]

Others, however, prefer a conditional interpretation:

> If someone pushes your bed out of the ward, if you see that the sky is turning green, and if you want to spare the curate the trouble of a funeral sermon, then it is time you got up, as quietly as children get up when the light shimmers through the shutters in the morning, stealthily, so that the sister does not see you - and quickly![324]

If the speculative conjunction is startling, the undefined subject *einer* further amplifies a sense of ambiguity as the sentence continues, creating a context of generic references as times, places and subjects are unnamed and remain so until the end.[325] The sense of impersonality and the lack in the narrative of any determining details encourage the reader to identify with the narrative *du.* However, this sense fades very quickly as the subjectivity and intimate tone of the narrating voice is not eliminated but rather orients itself increasingly towards the woman, shifting the focus onto the relationship between the woman and the narrative voice, thus also reflecting on the rhetoric of the text.

---

323 | Aichinger Trans. Alldridge (1969), 65f.

324 | Aichinger Trans. Levenson (1964), 29.

325 | Barner (2004), 78.

As early as the third word (*dein*) in the opening sentence, Aichinger establishes the second-person as the dominant narrative perspective for most of the story, with the exception of a first-person passage at the climax of the abortion, a passage that we have discussed earlier in the chapter, as well as the four sentences in the third person that also serve the rhetoric of metamorphosis. In *Spiegelgeschichte* we can observe how the notion of dialogue and the emphatic tone of address that characterise the second-person storytelling serve the ongoing metamorphosis, starting with the reversal of the roles of the narrator and addressee and then affecting all other conditions of the text.

The way the narrative is generated as pictured in the mirror, hence narrated unchanged from a second-person perspective, shows the voice to be impersonal, an inanimate figure that functions as a voice-over (off-screen) narrator positioned in an in-between place, at a middle point in, and superior to the world of fiction. The second-person narrative is the reflection of the self-talk the woman was performing as an active speaking *Ich (I)* while alive and which has now been transformed and transposed to a *gespiegelten du (you)* that reflects this narrative back to her reversed in order and meaning, keeping – though only formally – the same (second-person) perspective as both addressees (woman/reader) are unable to react or participate in any form of dialogue, in a novel where there is no narrative figure.

This reversal also implies that the syntax is subject to a transformation from active to passive, at least as long as it refers to the authority that the woman has on the narrative, shifting to being a passive recipient of the narrated events instead of an active speaker. The personal and intimate tone that characterises the voice and its association with the woman also explains why Aichinger preferred the more personal, singular form *du* to other pronouns like the more common but still distant (external) German *Sie*. Her choice is also bound up with an attempt to create a secret, coded language that resembles that of children and is unknown to adults, designating the *others,* who appear hostile to the woman throughout the entire narrative.

The voice taking over the second-person perspective in the text represents the central enigma of *Spiegelgeschichte,* that is the unique use of the technique to narrate a story in reverse in all single aspects and elements involved, based on the oxymoronic condition of forgetting so as to recreate the life and even reversing and moving the focus of interest, from the addressee of the second person and its reference to its origin and source. The second person here – as a narrative figure per se – reflects a duplicity and designates the transformation that the subject has experienced when reaching the limits of existence. Linguistically, it is the proposed narrative alternative that can be used effectively when the first-person perspective has become unavailable, having reached its own expressive limits. In other words the use of the enigma of the second person in the story is related to the reverse of the definite and indefinite, given the fact that whereas this *you* is a definite reference to the woman, it is then transformed into a *you* coming from the voice of the indefinite narrator.

Considering the innovative technique of *Spiegelgeschichte,* Aichinger's text may be situated in the dominant general atmosphere of distrust regarding language at the time. It answers the need for innovation in both literature and expression by offering a convincing narrative alternative. Aichinger's reflexive technique is also applicable to other art forms. In cinema we encounter it as *flashbacks, jump-cuts* and *voice-over* or even *off-screen narrators.*[326] In

326 | "Filmisch an der *Spiegelgeschichte* ist aber nicht nur diese Rückwärtsbewegung und die Ähnlichkeit mit einem Lebensfilm, sondern greifbar ist Filmisches auch in einer deutlichen Medienverschänkung und einer Palette von filmischen Verfahren, die intermedial eingesetzt werden: Visualisierung und filmischer Blick, Handlungsstrukturierung in visuell intensive Szenen und Parallelmontage, dazu das Sprechen aus dem Off, um die wichtigsten filmischen Elemente zu nennen." Peter Beicken, "Die Geschichte von Leben und Tod: Ilse Aichingers *Spiegelgeschichte* als intermediales Kino." In *Ilse*

Spiegelgeschichte Aichinger offers ideas relating to socio-political and philosophical problems, gender theory, historicism and revolt. The expansions in these directions that the narrative employs reveal that the theme of reversal and transformation, apart from a narrative quality that enriches the rhetoric of the text, affects meanings and interpretations on a level other than that of narratology, giving the novel a wider social dimension. *Spiegelgeschichte* is a remarkable narrative not only due to its unique composition and unusual theme but also because of its position regarding important issues of human life and social structure.

In relation to gender, for example, with its two impersonal narrators (that of the others and that of the voice) Aichinger's story may be of undetermined time, space and heroes, but it does have – to our surprise with regard to the subversive logic of the text – a clear and subjective tone stemming from an undoubtedly female perspective. Aichinger exploits the profoundly gendered grammar of German to compose a consciously female text: while thematically the narrative transgresses the limits of mortality and reverses and transforms traditional and conventional forms rhetorically, it still keeps gender – its definition and social limitations – bracketed and out of the reversing process.

Spiegelgeschichte investigates the distance between birth, death and after-death clearly from a female point of view. It is not only the themes of abortion and the seduction of a woman which dominate the plot that leave no doubt about this, but it is also the feeling of isolation that the woman experiences, especially compared to the other (mostly male) characters, and the compassion shown towards her that almost none but her deceased mother express.

As a reflexive text that echoes the female voice of its time, *Spiegelgeschichte* may be considered a precursor to the literary revolt of Julia Kristeva. In "Women's Time", Kristeva refers to the specific interaction between the symbolic and the semiotic modal-

---

Aichinger. Misstrauen als Engagement? Eds. Rabenstein, Retif and Tunner. (Würzburg: Königshausen and Neumann, 2009) 110.

ities expressed within each individual: the symbolic indicates the social contract to such an extent that the semiotic can be perceived only as a disruption, silence or absence. Recognising this phenomenon, Kristeva maintains that writers of the generation of the 1960s began searching for a means of expression closer to the body and the emotions, an endeavour that resonates with Aichinger's work. Their literature reflects "women's desire to lift the weight of what is sacrificial in the social contract from their shoulders, to nourish our societies with a more flexible and free discourse, one able to name what has thus far never been an object of circulation in the community: the enigmas of the body, the dreams, secret joys, shames, hatreds of the second sex."[327]

Aichinger's narrative exemplifies this literary revolt to the extent that it addresses semiotic aspects of reality that usually remain hidden, such as emotions, intuitions, physical sensations, grief, remorse: all the psychological processes the woman of the story undergoes, from pregnancy to illness and ultimately death. By illuminating the causes of the woman's demise, Aichinger confronts the patriarchal tradition of sacrificing the female so as to uphold a male unity as well as Christianity as a social institution, and with her specific, subversive use of language she offers a counter-perspective on death.[328]

Conclusion

So können alle, die in irgendeiner Form die Erfahrung des nahen Todes gemacht haben, diese Erfahrung nicht wegdenken, sie können, wenn sie ehrlich sein wollen, sich und die andern nicht freundlich darüber hinwegtrösten.

---

327 | Julia Kristeva, "Women's Time" in *The Kristeva Reader*. Trans. Alice Jardine and Harry Blake. Ed. Toril Moi. (New York: Columbia University Press, 1986) 207.

328 | Janson (1997), 501.

Aber sie können ihre Erfahrung zum Ausgangspunkt nehmen, um das Leben für sich und andere neu zu entdecken.[329]

To sum up, Aichinger presents a text structured on two levels, one reflecting and the other reflected at the level of language. She employs a distorting mirror to deal with boundaries and limits both biological and expressive in a fictionally credible way by discussing mortality, and the possibilities that literature offers as a means of recreating reality. By thematising the terminal point (death-people/silence-language), her story inverts it: *Spiegelgeschichte* is a narrative that discusses the poetics of the end by applying consistently the technique of reversal and the rhetoric of metamorphosis and implies that ends and endings, though existing in traditional forms and norms (as reflected in the third-person narrative), can always be approached and rediscovered as starting points (as reflected in the second-person narrative).

Aichinger revisits the terminal nature of death and accepts it as part of life without attempting any metaphysical interpretation, while her resilient and versatile symbolic narrative demonstrates that language offers inexhaustible ways of expression and re-creation. Considering the historical and cultural context in which it was written and published, *Spiegelgeschichte* may be considered as giving an optimistic twist to solving problems of literary expression that contemporary writers were facing during the Cold War, when the fear of espionage dominated social relationships.

Aichinger presents an innovative and striking text that provokes uneasiness due to its uncommon technique and theme but also admiration for its uniqueness and brilliance. Her *du* is inscribed in the text in a way that puts a spotlight on its properties and functions. Aichinger achieves this by combining two narrative levels in one and also by employing the third-person perspective as a break from

329 | Ilse Aichinger, "Das Erzählen in dieser Zeit." In *Ilse Aichinger: Der Gefesselte. Erzählungen 1948-1952.* (Frankfurt am Main: Fischer, 1991) 10f.

the dominant second-person narrative tactic which invites a comparison between the two.

This *du* stresses the rhetoric of metamorphosis that forms one level of the narrative in direct opposition to the other; a strong sense of dialogue since no reaction from or interaction with the addressee is possible; an emphatic sense of the present and of contemporaneity since all other temporal components are challenged by the reversal; reflexivity per se, triggered by the mirror and evident in the narrative; ambiguity and ambivalence due to being intimate and distant at the same time as it provides the impersonal tone in a subjective narrative of constant depersonalisation.

Spiegelgeschichte is placed last in this thesis because although older, it reflects aspects of all the other second-person narratives discussed earlier and also because of its narrative complexity: it is hoped that its reception and the understanding of the second-person employment have become clearer after having discussed these earlier in less complicated second-person texts. In Aichinger's text we witness a strikingly innovative story of an assessment of and reconciliation with the past, that is like but also unlike what is in Christa Wolf, that describes an emphatic modification such as in Michel Butor in the form of a total metamorphosis, and in contrast to Perec's creation of a person we find ourselves reading the unmaking process of dissolution.

The problem of saying *I* may be easier to trace in Aichinger as the woman is deceased and hence we can argue that the duplicity of the *Spiegelgeschichte* echoes the sense of reversal in its rhetoric as well. Since it involves a known though anonymous addressee the narrative contains no figure of *apostrophe* which is otherwise common in second-person narratives, but it does involve *prosopopoeia* in the way the voice acquires personal properties by narrating and the woman existential status through being addressed.

Also notable regarding the self-reflexive character of the text is that intertextuality may not be as fundamental and generative here as in *Un homme qui dort*, but here, too, it involves the influences and concepts of other authors such as Walter Benjamin. Moreover, intertextuality is also implied in the title, expressing the interrelation of literary works as an outcome of mutual reflection, thus commenting on the writing process. Aichinger's story is an outstanding example of second-person fiction, not only for its theme, striking rhetoric and structure, but also because despite its very small number of pages it contains implications and expansions that invite multiple readings and that demonstrate almost excessively the dynamics of language and the possibilities inherent in narrative expression focussing on the second-person narrative mode.

It is also a case of the second person enjoying its most symbolic and poetic narrative employment as it comes from an enigmatic and thus undefined voice that addresses a dying person, positioned in an in-between territory of life and death. Having discussed Aichinger's poetics of reflection, terminal points and the themes of reversal and metamorphosis, this thesis now enters its final stage. It will outline its conclusions regarding the second-person technique and try to list the major observations and assumptions, summarising what has been discussed so far in a comparative way. An overview of the fundamentals of second-person storytelling studied here based on milestones of literature will be offered, expanding and elaborating on the central arguments and observations and formulating some final conclusions.

Part 3
Assessment

Overview

Because of You: Understanding Second-Person Storytelling has explored a narrative technique through the analysis of four case studies. The novels selected for this thesis represent milestones in the history of literature not only because of their narrative perspective but also because of their decidedly elevated style, the way in which they elaborate on common themes and the richness of their poetic and rhetorical qualities. The aim of the thesis has been to further understanding of second-person storytelling as a technique though not as a genre, emphasising certain features that appear with great frequency and presenting key variations of second-person employment while avoiding any attempt at theorising or classifying texts that actually belong to different genres. This latter concern would have precluded consideration of the technique itself, one which shows rare resilience and versatility and offers authors narrative flexibility and potential.

The lack of a theoretical background to the second-person phenomenon throughout the history of literature not to mention its employment in poetry, drama and non-fictional narratives led me to pursue an inductive approach for the needs of my study. I decided to come back to the term itself and first of all attempt to clarify the categories of person and pronoun, tracing essential features of the technique in the fundamentals of grammar and rhetoric in order to enhance my case-by-case research of the texts themselves.

In the study of my primary sources I used the same approach, progressing and gradually deepening. Starting at the first level of understanding such as plot and structure, I moved on to a consideration of rhetoric and the impact of the technique on different aspects of each narrative in such a way as to reflect back on my initial study of grammar and rhetoric. This individualised approach, however, did not prevent me from drawing some more general conclusions useful for a broader view of the phenomenon. It actually revealed to me the intertextuality of second-person narratives, since their composition and rhetoric in various manners and to different degrees involved links and references to other narratives, emphasising the notion of a literary dialogue and the ludic possibilities inherent in second-person storytelling.

As for the selection of the texts themselves, the novels discussed in the project centre on common themes such as the post-war experience, a love-triangle, human indifference and the issue of life and death, but they tell their stories in an uncommon way. Not only do they employ the unusual second-person technique but they use it in a way that affects the narrative with its ambiguity in content, structure and rhetoric. Due to the second-person technique these narratives make possible an additional space of ambiguity and openness within which plot, rhetoric and poetics can expand and develop.

The employment of the second person, for instance, enabled Butor to present a narrative that reflected the story narrated and its written representation simultaneously; it permitted Perec's hero to develop within the narrative and made it possible for Aichinger to apply the theme of reversal to all parameters of *Spiegelgeschichte*. Also important to mention here is that the technique associated with both intertextuality and a highly elevated rhetorical style frequently adds self-reflexivity to the discourse and a sense of present tense and contemporaneity which is, perhaps, its most striking quality. It is the factor that enables and strengthens *ambiguity* and thus the richness and depth of second-person storytelling.

Christa Wolf's *Kindheitsmuster,* Michel Butor's *La Modification,* Georges Perec's *Un homme qui dort* and Ilse Aichinger's *Spiegelgeschichte* all employ the second-person narrative perspective either partly or throughout. They all show a lack of first-person singular perspective in the traditional sense, meaning that the first person is silenced, disguised or non-applicable for reasons explained in detail in the corresponding chapters. Also, although they share some thematic associations concerning self-discovery, self-awareness, reconciliation with the past and with writing, they do benefit in different ways from the rhetorical and poetic implications of the technique and reflect its primary qualities and thus contribute to the understanding of the phenomenon as a whole.

The uncommon elaborations on common themes can be summarised as follows: in Wolf, a narrator is writing her autobiography but, alienated from her past, chooses the third person to do so as well as the second for presenting the reflection inherent in the narrating; in Butor, a man on a train reflects on a decision he has made though ultimately reverses, so that his entire journey is actually in vain unless he announces his intention to transform this experience into book form, namely the one we readers have in our hand; in Perec, a student, following the examples of other narrative heroes confronted with the same problem of indifference, experiments with social detachment with the guidance of a voice-over narrator until he realises the uselessness of the experiment. In Aichinger, a mysterious voice narrates to a dying woman her life episodes in reverse. The narration covers, in this order, the moments from her burial until her birth, thus affecting their meaning and how they relate. The voice speaks that which is reflected in a distorted mirror, while the hospital staff interrupt the narrative by announcing the woman's progression towards death.

Second-person stories call for an active reading stimulated by the inviting, almost engaging, force of the narrative *you* and one that reflects on multiple meanings and patterns simultaneously. A study of this technique could variously expand on these. In this thesis I have tried to stay as close as possible to the text and to narratology, aiming to demonstrate a clear understanding of the narrative mode without any admixture of other interpretations or disciplines. In the chapter that follows I will explain the method I have employed to complete this study.

Methodology

The methodology I followed for this study was inductive and experimental: I developed it "from scratch", starting from the basics. As both theory and criticism on the topic were limited in volume and scope and sometimes misleading in being too technical or one-sided, I had to undertake consistent research starting with the fundamental components of the term in order to comprehend first what the pronoun and second person meant in terms of grammar and rhetoric and second in my aim to contribute to the understanding of second-person storytelling and narratology. After turning to second-person texts and having reviewed the employment of the technique throughout the history of literature, I selected four examples on the basis of which I would discuss and analyse the phenomenon aspiring to drawing more generic conclusions.

The resulting selection of second-person texts revealed an intriguing diversity in both theme and structure as well as genre classification. As my focus was less on (traditional) theory and more on the texts themselves, the methodological question shifted towards selecting interesting examples for this study. Looking into the history of the technique, my main observation proved to be that the technique, though used consistently throughout the history of storytelling, enjoyed a popularisation and increasing attention during the post-war period after the 1950s. I therefore decided to choose texts from that more recent period, assuming they would present aspects of the technique in a more striking way that would also justify the popularisation as such. Hopefully they would also enable me to make more generic or collective assumptions about the entire group of second-person texts, as they were composed more recently yet embodied elements from earlier texts in which intertextual relations could be spotted.

The texts were selected to involve a clear second-person narrative level of transgressive and self-reflexive character, representing for me *pure* second-person storytelling, without any first-person singular narrative in the traditional sense. Examples such as Günter Grass's *Katz und Maus* would not qualify for this study because the second person is clearly used to address a narrative persona in the fictional world, thus implying a stable meaning and reference for the second person, with a first-person narrative level present. Rather I have tried to focus my research on texts that through complex rhetorical schemes and structures emphasise the ambiguity of the technique and its potential, elaborating on the *ambiguity* of the *you* and offering significant narrative depth. Consequently, the quest for an understanding of the essentials of the technique within a close reading of the texts started with a text that presented a second-person narrative level in a comparative way, coexisting in the narrative with a third-person and a first-person plural narrative. Wolf's *Kindheitsmuster* offered a remarkable example with which to begin this comparative analysis.

Michel Butor proved even more attractive, since his is the text that triggered the second-person discussion among the theorists of the fifties and sixties and demonstrated the total employment of the technique in a narrative. *Un homme qui dort* involved a striking *tu* designating a narrative figure per se and representing a unique manifestation of intertextuality that is a key feature of the technique. Aichinger's *Spiegelgeschichte* is the earliest narrative in this thesis and the most symbolic. The way it employs the technique to present the story of a dying woman in reverse, including events taking place after her death and ending with her birth, represents a total reversal of all narrative conditions and the dominance of a mysterious voice that designates this entire process of reversal. Aichinger's novel enabled me to explore the limits of language and representation in a setting where an enigmatic voice dominates the discourse using the *du*, reversing the quest of investigating the second-person reference to that of aspiring to understand and identify where this *du* comes from.

At the end of my study, aiming to provide answers and draw conclusions that would benefit an overview of second-person storytelling as a whole, I tried to understand the case studies as intertexts. Given that these examples involve elements of awareness and thus belong to a kind of group of similar literary texts, experimenting as they do with the technique and commenting on the process of writing, my final observations were more focused on specifying and clarifying their contribution to the development of the phenomenon as a whole. Finally, this approach helped me define the three main ways in which the second person is employed in narrative: as a means of reflecting *apostrophe* and multiple addressees; as a way to adopt a middle distance in special narrative circumstances; and as a mode to convey an ambiguous figure that invites multiple interpretations and readings.

Observations Regarding the First Part

The objectives of the first part of the study were the clarification of the fundamental properties of second-person storytelling; that is, to emphasise those elements that may appear too obvious or even too simple to be considered part of an academic study of storytelling. These include the categories of person, pronoun and the historic development of the technique. Using this approach, the thesis has arrived at the following conclusions:

- Person is the deictic category that defines the role of the participant in the speech situation (according to linguists). Fundamentally, the second person refers to the addressee in the speech act.
- One way to express person and personal reference is by use of pronouns. The way a pronoun functions in the discourse defines its grammatical classification: the second-person pronoun refers to the addressee in a speech situation but does not necessarily refer to a specific person. Hence the pronoun can be more of a placeholder than a personal reference in the communication process. The narrative implications of this are that if a pronoun is used instead of a noun, this indeterminacy of the placeholder pronoun contributes to narrative elements such as the verisimilitude of dialogue and a sense of ambiguity.
- The second-person pronoun is linked to attributes that are better understood when reviewed in comparison with the other personal pronouns. The second and first person reflect the category of person, whereas the third person stands for the absent agent, reflecting the *non-person*.

  Between first and second person, the second person designates the more objective pole, which the first person aspires to within the dialogue; the objectivity inherent in the second person and the transformation of the narrated to a less subjective version justify the choice of the second-person perspective in narratives with an aspiration of authenticity. In that sense, the second person designates the *Other* more so than the third person does (contrary to what one might expect). This explains the frequent use of the second person in autobiographical writing and self-discovery stories, reflecting an aspiration towards depersonalisation.

- Second-person narratives are particular to each language due to the formal variations that the pronoun enjoys in different language systems. In English, second-person narratives involve the generic *you* on all narrative occasions; in French, on the other hand, the author can decide between *vous* and *tu* to reflect different narrative circumstances. Similarly in German, *du*, *ihr*, but also *Sie* can appear as second-person forms since attributes and features of the second person can be expressed in non-second person forms as well, especially in the polite form.
  The use of the pronoun in a given discourse reveals the social code that operates within a speech community and functions as a relationship marker for the participants in the speech act. When using, for example, the second person plural in French for singular reference, i.e. by conducting the discourse in the polite form, such use connotes a certain communication environment and particular circumstances.

The second person was also noted in a wide variety of rhetorical functions. Among these, the figure of *Apostrophe* is dominant in second-person narratives. Apostrophe, having its origin in epic poetry in the invocation of the Muse, reflects the notion of addressing absent or unavailable beings. It is mostly linked to the formal feature of starting the narrative *in medias res*, thus emphasising the notion of an episode and having implicit self-reflexivity, revealing as it does the origin of the discourse and aspects of its generation process. An observation facilitated by the use of apostrophe is that the concept of the double audience is inherent in the use of the second person in general. Turning to a *you* can imply addressing more than one being simultaneously, splitting the audience into primary and secondary; in most cases, the fictional *you*, though addressing a narrative figure or situation, also refers to the reader, one who varies across time, space and culture, and creates in him/her the feeling of being invited to engage in the discourse.

Mise-en-scène, the rhetorical figure of staging, is associated with the rhetoric of apostrophe and the sense of dialogue and contextuality. *Mise-en-scène* implies a certain deixis in the manner of face-to-face communication and contemporaneity, at the same time it initates a poetic act. Deictic elements, in addition to pronouns such as the second person, can also be adverbs and imperatives, and they likewise reflect mutual presence. Therefore, *mise-en-scène* enables time and space transitions and transgressions at least at the level of language. Emphasis on this staging and a sense of concurrence is a tactic of formal realism that is often encountered in second-person texts. Balanced with an extreme attention to environmental details, it helps readers to familiarise themselves with the fictional world. Butor and Perec used these formal realist strategies to convey a sense of actuality that helps readers to feel more familiar with the text, inviting them into the world of fiction, as it were.

Prosopopoeia is also frequently found in second-person stories: inanimate figures become physical entities, taking the shape and properties of a literary persona the moment they are addressed. This happens, for example, in *Spiegelgeschichte* where the narrative *du* designates the reverse narrative voiced by an enigmatic source, positioned somewhere between life and death, reflecting the life episodes of a dying woman. The fact that the dying woman is being addressed allows her the qualities of a person despite her poor health. Here, as we have explained in the relevant chapter, the narrative shows the unmaking of a narrative persona until the final point, that is the birth of the person. In the other texts examined the second person reflects the reverse: the making of a narrative persona in an elaboration of a *Bildungsroman*.

The process of creating a narrative persona as the narrative develops is often aligned with an indirect characterisation of the heroes through their actions and thoughts *(dialogismos* and *sermocinatio)*. Therefore, in cases such as Léon Delmont or the student, we develop a profile of the hero gradually through their actions and observations rather than from traits disclosed by an omniscient narrator (*Ethopoeia*). Second-person stories designating a dramatised version of the present often involve voice-over narration, reflecting a narrator who is present only as a voice in the story and resembling other paradigms such as film narrative or the process of *hypnosis*. The constellation of a voice-over narrator reinforces the sense of a narrative in progress, as readers witness the narrator guiding the hero (and implicitly the reader) through the story.

A key observation of the first part of the thesis is that traditional theorists treated the second-person narrative mode with some ignorance and regarded it as rather experimental as they were unable to fit it into their dichotomous studies. More recent theorists, by dealing with the mode in greater detail, contributed significantly to the discussion, though not without some flaws. Attempting to theorise the technique and classifying a large number of texts reflecting different themes and periods into one and the same group proved to be a regressive project; the same holds true for those theorists who tried to develop a theory without building it on a narratological basis.

Such efforts ended up either as forced attempts to apply the structures that Genette and Stanzel had introduced, or their suggestions appeared too technical, leading to classification schemes that did not cover every case or focused more on other angles of interpretation. Consequently, by observing throughout the thesis the history of second-person narratives starting with ancient sources, I have arrived at the following conclusions:

- Second-person narratives tend to reflect themes that relate to the past and the self and they involve transgression, transitions and turning points. Consequently, they are often used in autobiographies or in stories involving self-discovery and self-awareness. It is an appropriate mode for a process of re-evaluating the past with the goal of gaining self-awareness and reconciliation with that past.

- In all second-person narratives the issue of the reader's identification with the narrative *you* arises. The employment of the second-person agent in the narrative inevitably invites readers to engage more actively with the text as they are continuously accepting or rejecting identification with the narrative *you* and the role of addressee.
- One major finding of this study was that the second person is a grammatical element designating a role in the speech and narrative act, one that can be taken over by various persons rather than being a marker of personal reference. The involvement of an element that enables a continuous shift in reference and context adds narrative depth to the discourse. This ambiguity enables transgression and transition between agents who belong to different narrative levels that coexist in the discourse.
- Second-person narratives are self-reflective, some of them emphatically so, thematising their own generative process. Thus, they challenge writing and narrating as such while, in intertextual dialogue with their ancestors, revealing aspects and benefits in terms of self-knowledge. Perec's example clearly shows how to convey self-reflexivity through intertextuality, a concept that echoes the notion of ambiguity and the benefits of lacking a stable meaning or reference. It connects to an infinite literary dialogue and the origin of the narrative within a literary constellation that exceeds the limits of time and space in the eternal always-current literary dialogue.

Observations Regarding the Second Part

The second part of the thesis involved the close reading and analysis of four key second-person texts. The texts presented in this part were organised according to their complexity and the way the narrative technique is employed rather than chronologically or thematically. The first text discussed is also the most recent. Published in 1976, Christa Wolf's *Kindheitsmuster* offered grounds for exploring the impact of the second person in comparison with other narrative perspectives.

Wolf presents the story of a narrator in the process of writing her childhood autobiography. The fact that the narrator's childhood memories contain experiences of a guilty past (the Nazi period in Germany, witnessed from the perspective of the survivors) and evoke feelings of uneasiness, shame and discomfort, lead to her extreme estrangement from her own past. She therefore tries to write her childhood autobiography from a third-person perspective, thus making a narrated persona out of her past self. Using the second person, she performs a cross-examination while reflecting on the writing process and therefore on the narrated past. She also uses the first-person plural to express experiences and thoughts in which she identifies with her contemporaries.

Through the agency of cross-examination, Wolf uses the second person to add the perspective of the outsider (the Other) to her personal reflections thereby attempting to authenticate the memories of the insider: the alienated *I* who experienced the narrated events. Accepting the fact that there is neither reliability nor absolute truth in the process of remembering and reviewing one's own past, Wolf employs the technique to strengthen the reliability and authenticity of the discourse. Along with other means employed (such as the reference to authentic material and the trip the narrator takes to her birthplace), it is a control mechanism presented within the novel. In the second-person narrative, Wolf reveals aspects of the narrative's process of generation, emphasising its self-reflective character and commenting on the writing process.

In *Kindheitsmuster*, we witness the employment of the second person to reflect a sort of middle-distance. Calling to mind Grimsley's thoughts and explanations from the first part of this thesis, *Kindheitsmuster* by drawing on all narrative perspectives, presents various distances from the narrated. For the estranged past and absolute distance where Nelly is located (*prosopopoeia*), the third-person narrative perspective is employed; for the closer distance of the narrator to the writing process she selects the second person, a mode that enables the cross-examination of memory and that emphasises self-reflexivity and the notion of re-creation. What is interesting in Wolf's narrative is that the use of the first-person plural equals the impersonal.

Unable to employ the first person due to her relationship to the past, we see a first-person-plural narrative perspective in *Kindheitsmuster*. The closeness and subjectivity of the personal aspects of her childhood past are not rejected as such when narrated in the first-person plural, but *depersonalised* and made part of a collective identity that is reflected in the narrative *wir*. The use of the impersonal *man* that appears at the same narrative level has a similarly depersonalising effect. It echoes ideas and assumptions more generically articulated and functions in the same way as the first-person plural.

A similar yet quite different situation is found in Butor's double narrative in which the difficulty of saying *I* dominates the narrative and encourages the employment of another narrative perspective. This time, however, there is no reference to trauma and therefore no necessity to employ the third-person perspective also. Butor published *La Modification* in 1957, representing a mind in flux. His novel, set on a train from Paris to Rome, describes the development of a decision by a middle-aged man to change his life.

Emerging during the *nouveau roman* period, the novel blends features of the movement with formal innovations and the less common second-person technique, which Butor explained was appropriate to a narrative told to someone who is not fully aware of his own story. *La Modification* tells the tale of Léon Delmont *to* himself, starting the moment he boards the train and ending with his arrival in Rome. Butor presents a novel starting *in medias res,* and he uses the second person almost exclusively (with some rare exceptions in the first person.) He shows excessive attention to detail (formal realism), which strengthens a sense of contemporaneity and the notion of concurrence that the narrative evokes. Another unique characteristic of this novel is that the narrator uses the second-person plural (polite) form *vous* to address Léon, reflecting the social coding of France as well as the distance necessary to realise the process of self-knowing.

What Butor adds to the study is primarily the extent to which the technique is used in the text and the coexistence of two narrative levels within it. Whereas in Wolf we observed the second person occupying a narrative level that improved textual coherence, in Butor we witness two parallel narrative levels, that of happening (Léon's adventure) and that of writing (the book), told from the same narrative perspective, thereby emphasising the rhetoric of *apostrophe* inherent in the technique and revealing some additional properties of the second-person perspective.

The fact that Butor uses the same narrative voice for both levels and also for communicating the theme of modification leads to a combination of form and content which gives the impression that changes happen within the writing itself, traced up to the final modification. This helps the hero to understand himself and his choices, and he is therefore able to transmit his experience in the form of a book after the journey of self-awareness is completed. His story of self-discovery and self-awareness is emphatically self-reflexive, leading to a written representation of the actual experience. In other words, the modification in Butor's example suggests not only a modification of content but also of form, both of which happen simultaneously, reflecting on one another, coinciding and coexisting in the narrative *vous.*

Without direct characterisation though presenting an indirect understanding of Léon through his thoughts and his memories of life incidents (*ethopoeia*), Butor's *Modification* expands the theme of self-discovery, chronicling the route towards certainty. As for the narrators, we experienced an *Erzählfigur* in the discourse in Wolf, a narrator who narrates her own actions within the story and who is the key protagonist in the narrative. In Butor, we encounter a voice-over narrator who is leading Léon towards a solid sense of self-awareness and certainty as he develops authority over his own choices.

In his case, similarly to Wolf's, the particulars of the central narrative figure (name, gender, situation) do not allow for a strong feeling of identification between the narrative *you* and the reader, at least in a traditional sense. However, just as Wolf opens up her narrative to having a more general meaning, presenting a childhood pattern and depersonalising a personal story, the fact that Léon's story is transformed from an actual experience to a version of it, namely the version we read, also suggests a certain depersonalisation and invites further elaborations and representations (writings) of the story. It opens the narrative *vous* towards a more generic notion of person, a collective entity that Léon could reflect in each of the versions. Hence *La Modification* presents throughout the novel a manifestation of the rhetoric of apostrophe in the second person as it enables the shifting between the two narrative streams that continually coexist in the novel.

After considering the two novels by Christa Wolf and Michel Butor, this study moved on to more symbolic second-person narratives in which the technique draws attention to rhetoric. These latter narratives provided the study with examples rich in metatextual properties, and they show the ability of the second person to designate the narrative figure per se in a text where no person has such consistency. Beginning with Georges Perec's *Un homme qui dort,* the study entered the territory of liminal and experimental second-person narratives. Written in 1966, in the later period of the *nouveau roman,* Perec's text is characterised by striking intertextuality, involving so many allusions and references to other texts and authors that it might be read as a narrative jigsaw puzzle. *Un homme qui dort* is a minimalist story that shows a student performing an experiment in social detachment. Starting *in medias res* and covering the time from the beginning of the experiment to its end, the narrative involves no other information or details either about the student or any other person.

The story is narrated in the singular form *tu* and may well have autobiographical origins in Perec's own student life. Within the pages of the narrative, Perec, like Butor, introduces a voice-over narrator who guides a student through the various stages of an experiment in social detachment, which appears to be a solution to the indifference that the student experiences and a way in which the student can find his identity and place in the world. This novel also offers an interesting contrast to Butor since it emphasises the personal and intimate tone of the *tu* and expands on the theme of self-discovery by introducing a character who is playing out the possibilities of living as several other narrative heroes until he acquires an identity of his own.

Perec contributes an example of narrative collage to this study of second-person narratives, adding a ludic character to the text and revealing intertextuality as a vital element in writing and a key quality of second-person storytelling. Perec's second-person narrative reflects both varieties of the technique (that of shifting and that of taking a middle-distance, expressed rhetorically through *apostrophe* and *prosopopoeia*) and presents a narrative artefact of intertextuality. As we have seen in the corresponding chapter, the narrative *tu* in *Un homme qui dort* shifts continuously between different heroes and narratives that echo aspects of its theme and form while addressing the developing student, until at the very end he has established his own character.

Un homme qui dort chronicles the making of a persona, neither as a narrative within the narrative as in Wolf, nor as a representation of such a process, as we have seen in *La Modification*, but rather as a choice among possible *you-s*, those addressed throughout the narrative that belong to Perec's literary ancestors. The process of self-discovery related to the experiment shows the making of that persona in actual concurrence with the discourse and also through pieces from and traces of other narrative personae from world literature. Therefore, the narrative *tu* reflects all potential (and rejected) identities the student might adopt, until at the end of the text he finds his own after the experiment has failed. As a text that develops at the level of the narrative itself, chronicling the evolution of the experiment but doing so by reflecting sentences, behaviours and parts of other narratives, we may argue that *Un homme qui dort* not only reflects the development of a hero and his experiment in social detachment but also suggests a narrative that reflects the reading of other narratives on that topic.

Un homme qui dort is a text that evokes a sense of being in progress and highlights a feeling of the present tense. Most importantly, Perec's novel suggests an example of using the second person as a narrative figure per se. The fact that the student acquires an identity only when the experiment, the narrative and also this implicit reading reach their final point, proves that through the student's changing of personae and developing of a personality, the narrative *tu* is the only narrative figure through which all this potential could be gathered and addressed. The way in which Perec employs the second person to articulate emphatically his literary version of indifference convinces us of the association of intertextuality with second-person storytelling.

We witness the same liminality with the use of the second person as part of a narrative characterised by an *ordo inversus*. Ilse Aichinger's *Spiegelgeschichte* is again a highly symbolic text that in 1952 won the prize of the Group 47. Written in 1948/49, Aichinger's *Spiegelgeschichte* is the oldest text studied here, and it is the most obscure and challenging of the narratives. This difficulty is due not only to the way the second-person narrative technique is employed but also to the uncommon theme and structure of the novel and the reversal it brings to all aspects and conditions of the narrative transforming one life event of a woman into another.

Spiegelgeschichte tells the story of a (distorted) mirror mostly from the perspective of that mirror. The mirror reflects episodes from the life of a woman dying from a botched abortion; the episodes in reversed order as reflected in the mirror are narrated by an enigmatic voice and interrupted by the comments of the hospital staff announcing the woman's progression towards death, that is the second narrative level of *Spiegelgeschichte*. The two levels that compose Aichinger's text, though parallel, have different functions and informative character, one presenting the life events narrated by the voice to the woman as seen in the distorted mirror until her birth, the other in total contrast showing the progression of the woman towards her end.

Aichinger's *du*-narrative covers the period after the death of the woman back to her birth. *Spiegelgeschichte* expands on the structure of multiple narrative levels coexisting in the same story. The narrative involves two levels: that of the voice and that of the *Others*, enriched with imperatives and a single first-person passage at the crucial moment of the abortion when the narrating voice takes on the woman's voice. Aichinger's story mirrors a process of reconciliation with one's past but in the extreme paradigm of a woman dying and dissolving her life rather than in an autobiographical frame, as encountered in Wolf where the pieces of the past are brought back together. In her text we witness an emphatic use of *prosopopoeia*, which lends the novel an esoteric tone and describes details about feelings and intimate moments that no external narrator could. The narrative *du* that the enigmatic voice addresses remains a mystery until the end of the story, intriguing like the mirror itself, thus enabling the story in reverse.

The emphatic symbolism and enigmatic character of the text don't affect its reception and quality negatively but, realised poetically within the second-person narrative mode, rather make it feasible and even attractive. *Spiegelgeschichte* reveals the potential of the technique to enable the reversal and transformation of reality at least at the level of language. Linguistically Aichinger's text achieves the reversal of all meanings and connotations and even challenges the notions of life and death themselves by adding to them expansions and implications. The *ordo inversus* witnessed in the text is made possible by the employment of the second-person technique which offers the grounds for performing a transition of time and for constructing levels of ambiguity needed in order to generate the narrative.

> "Es ist zu Ende -" sagen die hinter dir, "sie ist tot!"
> Still! Laß sie reden![330]

Aichinger presents a radical expansion of the second-person technique related to the notion of autobiography in this liminal text, reversing the concepts of beginning and ending, and setting forgetting as the condition for the generation of her story, contrary to Wolf. Also, the concept of the representation and the narration of a life are transformed. While this reminds us of Butor's text and the implication to see the world anew instead of changing its conditions, it emphasises even more the concept of representation and contributes to the self-reflexive character of the second-person stories as it further introduces the rhetoric of metamorphosis, revealing the dynamics of language.

Among the texts discussed, Aichinger's is the richest in terms of rhetoric and symbolic values: it involves an interaction between two non-compatible stages (life and death) and centres the story round a *blind* mirror and the notion of reversal, and a *du* that has a specified referent but comes from an enigmatic, thus unspecified, voice. It also makes possible the personification of a liminal addressee, designated by the dying woman (*prosopopoeia*), and applies the entire concept of transformation, enabled by the mirror and spoken by the *du* at all levels of the text, content and grammar alike. Here again we see an emphasis on the time frame and the notion of episode. *Spiegelgeschichte* elaborates on the concept of time by exceeding all temporal levels, even that of the present, expressing a sense of contemporaneity in a form of eternity, refusing to accept death as an ending and birth as a starting point. The text, following a pattern of constructing and recreating a life parallel to and triggered by the deconstruction and dissolution of the same life, implies that nothing is over yet, especially at the level of language and representation where the potential is richer and the grounds to explore and create are infinite.

330 | Aichinger (1954/1979), 3.

The complexity of narrative and the concept of life being the material for different narratives, accompanying our existence to its physical end and, as presented in *Spiegelgeseschichte,* extending it, appears in the disguise of *we* instead of the ambiguous *du* of Peter Brooks' narrative theory:

Our lives are ceaselessly intertwined with narrative, with stories that we tell and hear told, those we dream or imagine or would like to tell, all of which are reworked in that story of our lives that we narrate to ourselves in an episodic, sometimes semiconscious, but virtually uninterrupted monologue. We live immersed in narrative, recounting and reassessing the meaning of our past actions, anticipating the outcome of our future projects, situating ourselves at the intersection of several stories not yet completed.[331]

What Brooks describes and explains above is what we have examined as a lifelong interaction and interrelation between the *I* and the *you,* describing a type of lifelong narrated self-reflective autobiography, which is reversed in Aichinger. The narrative impulse in human nature that Brooks identifies, the desire, the need and the ability to narrate is what allows us to summarise and retransmit experiences and events in other words, forms and media. What Brooks describes as a continuous *I*-to-*I* interchange of narrative material that defines, affects and distils our life and *I,* is in the end what second-person stories elaborate on. By transferring the *I* to a *you* in the case of second-person storytelling, the concept of addressing and the notion of productivity in which our lives are re-created and revisited from the distance secured by the *you* are emphasised.

All the narrative heroes discussed in this thesis are addressed in Brooks' quote; when dealing with second-person storytelling we are confronted with narratives that emphasise their self-reflexivity and the narrative process. Brooks' *we* contains the *I-you* narrative pairing that follows the process of development and evolution in narrative

331 | Peter Brooks, *Reading for the Plot.* (Cambridge: Harvard University Press, 1984) 3.

terms, linked with constructing characters and figures, especially in cases where our *I* is challenged (Butor), in doubt (Wolf), in progress (Perec) or unavailable (Aichinger).

The relationship between the pronouns and the narrative conditions as stated in Brooks' quote, is reflected in the writing/reading act as well. In the second person narrative examples, the author, the writer and/or the narrator of the text are all part of the *reading*. In the production of the texts but also in their reception, the interaction and interchange happens between an expressing and an expressed pole, in other words an addressing and an addressed. This possibility to revert and shift between the first person and the first that comes as a disguise of the second - in this reflecting process - is the key to understanding not just the reasons why the use of the second person is so associated with the use of the first, but justifies also the choice of the second person pronoun in cases where issues with identity occur. This is what we have been experiencing in all texts treated in this book.

In summary, the second-person technique is appropriate to stories in which the narrator cannot use the first person for various reasons, a narrative level that is missing from all the texts under discussion, with the exception of Wolf's *Kindheitsmuster* where the narrator in a depersonalising manner eventually employs the first person plural and, at the very end, the first person singular due to convention and necessity. As it turns out, the use of the second person rather than a problematic first person comes with more complex ideas and patterns in terms of narrative and it requires a decidedly elevated style. This may be the reason why the authors seem to use the technique only once in their writing career. As for readers, the challenges of understanding such complex narratives and the continuous urge either to identify with the narrative *you*, or not, defines their reading preference and is connected to different levels of identification that they can enjoy each time. As unique texts, second-person narratives generate either enthusiasm or total rejection. The above considerations affect publishers as well, causing them to adopt a decidedly cautious approach or one that is perhaps almost too supportive and enthusiastic.

It should be stated at this point that the observations contained in this thesis are based on examples from two German novels as well as two French novels, the German texts written by female authors and the French ones by male authors. Each presents characters of their own gender. The influence of the gender of the narrators on content and style is profound, as both German and French reflect gender in grammar and also syntax, an aspect that would be interesting to compare with its rendering in the English translations of these texts.

Impact and Continuity

I would consider a key accomplishment of this study to be its focus on fundamental principles vital to an understanding of the second-person technique, for example the category of person and pronoun that are often neglected elsewhere. Moreover, my historic overview of the second-person texts showed that the technique should not be treated either as a formal novelty or as a postmodern feature but as a narrative mode that, albeit infrequently deployed, has always been trusted to reflect equivocal and special narrative situations involving multiple parallel narrative levels, emphatic self-reflexivity and ambiguity. Further research should be done on the notion of representation in second-person narratives, focussing especially on the concept of self in autobiographical texts and with storytelling per se as a representation of a life event, modified and altered at the level of language where possibilities are multiplied.

A more focused comparative study on the way the second-person technique is adjusted when translated from one language to another would be a further topic for discussion and investigation. Studying various translations of a second-person novel would shed light on additional areas more associated with linguistics and grammar, emphasising formal variations and the nature of the second person in different language systems. Since the second person has proven to be more of a grammatical issue than a personal reference, a more *linguistic/translation* oriented approach would serve an understanding of the technique better in terms of form and adaptability and clarify issues such as the possible roles of a second-person form and how additional information such as gender and number are conveyed in languages that lack formal variation or declination.

Another interesting field for expansion would be the recent blossoming of second-person publications and the popularisation of the technique as well as its association with and proximity to non-fiction forms and other media. From the 1980s onwards we observe increasing numbers of second-person narratives appearing mainly in the Anglophone world for reasons that are worth examining. This phenomenon could be studied in the context of a general shift in the social codes and communication schemes that have developed. Of course, the fact that in English the second person is reflected only in the general form *you* increases the occasions on which the *you* can be used and the references it can have, leading to a wider use of the pronoun as a storytelling technique, as with, for example, the impersonal *man*-syntax in German.

Limitations of This Study

It should be borne in mind that this study has a number of limitations, mainly reflecting the selection of texts for the close-reading section. Several second-person narratives could not be read in the original. Thus, although they might have offered further grounds for investigation, the fact that they could be reviewed only in translation which meant that I was unable to focus on the employment of the second person in the language in which they were originally written, led me to eliminate them from the final selection. Italo Calvino's popular *Se una notte d'inverno un viaggiatore* is such an example; I had to keep it out of the second-person text corpus not only due to my limited knowledge of Italian that prevented me from analysing and fully understanding the employment of the technique in the novel, but also due its theme and structure that would have shifted the focus of the study more towards the reader and reader response theory and the question of his/her identification with the narrative *you*.

The latter omission reveals another important limitation of this thesis. The case-by-case approach in the process of unravelling the enigma of the second-person technique suggests that the quest for understanding it would only be complete when all texts thus written would have been taken into account. Of course, it would be impossible to analyse every text written in the second person, so although I attempted to select some good examples in terms of complexity and richness, the topic is only covered in part; there are many themes and elaborations reflected in other texts that must go unmentioned here. Instead, my study offers an investigation of the technique that emphasises the rhetorical and poetic implications arising from the use of the second person in each text, highlighting some key variations of the phenomenon while omitting long references to other possible aspects and themes that are not directly linked to the second-person technique.

Therefore, the analysis of each text provided here should not be understood as a close-reading review of these works generally but, specifically, as a critical approach to their narrative technique and the impact of the latter. Regarding the limitations, it is interesting to note the challenges that I encountered during this study. The most serious was the process of selecting the *right* texts for the thesis. During my years of work, the texts I had to read to make a final choice were hard to come by due to availability and the problems with publishers mentioned at the outset. Moreover, my own critical reading remained challenging as I was forcing myself to resist the inviting power of the *you* and to maintain a critical approach towards the text in front of me.

The impact of the technique on me as a reader made a distanced critical approach extremely hard, but was in itself an important piece of evidence proving at first hand the appealing character of second-person narratives and the engaging relationship they build with the reader. Reading *La Modification, Spiegelgeschichte, Un homme qui dort* and *Kindheitsmuster* often had a hypnotic effect, inviting multiple readings so as to explore the texts from different angles, readings that were always challenged by the double role I had to take on, that of reader and that of critic.

There were insufficient secondary sources and critical reviews and a lack of theoretical input addressing the enigma of the second-person technique in a similar way to the approach taken by this thesis, that is: not as an experimental case, a novelty or an exception, but as a technique used consistently throughout time to address certain narrative themes and occasions. This posed a problem at the beginning, in the sense that there was no starting point, but on the other hand, it has proven of benefit to the study and its substantial character as it led me to review aspects that are often neglected as too obvious, imbedded as axiomatic. This drove the study increasingly to focus on the texts and to find in them answers to the questions that provoked the thesis in the first place.

Trying to find the words to conclude this book on second-person storytelling, I realise even now the broad range of possible expansions and implications this topic could have and how many themes and issues of narratology could be discussed in relation to each example written in the second person. In the quest for unravelling the enigma of second-person storytelling and aspiring to improve its understanding, this project contributed most regarding its relation to the first person and highlighting the narrative occasions and necessities in which the *you* is more appropriate because either the first person is unavailable or impossible or, referring to the last example of *Spiegelgeschichte*, transformed and reversed. It is indeed fascinating that this *you-centric* study in the end revealed as much about the *I* as well.

As for why authors tend to use the second-person technique only once, the answer has been given by the themes and situations that we have seen narrated in the examples of the second part. Though everyday stories, the ones reflected in the narratives of Wolf, Butor,

Perec and Aichinger involve an uncommon parameter in their plot which requires a compelling though fascinating and rich narrative mode to be expressed and represented, most often calling for an active reading in which the reader is supposed to mine information, references, hints and tricks so as to understand and enjoy the reading better. Understanding the second-person technique has proven to be related to an understanding of writing and creating through its self-reflexive character.

Witnessing infinity in the limits of language and representation, the second-person technique reclaims its enigma each time an aspect of it is brought into focus and explained. This may be quite a challenge for academic research, but it is fascinating for literature itself and for what it stands for in our lives, our positioning in the world, our self-perception and the opening of infinite possibilities in the process of writing in terms of creation, re-creation and representation. This seemingly small gesture from the authors, a minor tactic to employ the second person to tell a story, does have a major impact on the richness and rhetoric of the narrative and keeps reminding the readers of their place in the literary interaction and of its eternal and inexhaustible character. *Because of You* the limits of telling are never reached, and the same holds true for the reading experience.

This is quite a reason to love (or hate) second-person storytelling.

List of Works Cited

Aichinger, Ilse. "Story in Reverse." In *German Short Stories 1= Deutsche Kurzgeschichten 1*. Ed. Richard Newnham. Trans. Christopher Levenson. London: Penguin Books, 1964. 27- 51.

——. "Life Story in Retrospect." In *Ilse Aichinger*. Ed. J. C. Alldridge. Chester Springs: Dufour Editions, 1969. 65-77.

——. *Spiegelgeschichte. Erzählungen und Dialoge*. 1954. Leipzig and Weimar: Kiepenheuer, 1979.

——. "Das Erzählen in dieser Zeit." In *Ilse Aichinger: Der Gefesselte. Erzählungen 1948-1952*. Frankfurt am Main: Fischer, 1991. 9-12.

Augustinus, Aurelius. *Selbstgespräche. Von der Unsterblichkeit der Seele*. Ed. Harald Fuchs. München und Zürich: Artemis Verlag, 1986

——. *St. Augustine's Confessions: with an English translation*. Eds. William Watts. and W. H. D. Rouse. Trans. William Watts. London: W. Heinemann; Cambridge: Harvard University Press, 1950.

Auster, Paul. *Winter Journal*. New York: Henry Holt and Company, 2012.

Barner, Wilfried. "Ilse Aichinger: *Spiegelgeschichte*." In *Interpretationen. Klassische deutsche Kurzgeschichten*. Stuttgart: Reclam, 2004. 76-88.

Barthelme, Frederick. *Moon Deluxe. Stories*. Harrisonburg: Penguin Books, 1983.

Beckett, Samuel. *Imagination Dead Imagine*. 1965.Trans. by the author. London: Calder and Boyars Ltd. 1967.

Bedwell, Carol. "The Ambivalent Image in Ilse Aichinger's *Spiegelgeschichte*." In *Revue des Langues Vivantes* 33 (1967): 362-368.

Beicken, Peter. "Die Geschichte von Leben und Tod: Ilse Aichingers *Spiegelgeschichte* als intermediales Kino." In *Ilse Aichinger. Misstrauen als Engagement?* Eds. Rabenstein, Retif and Tunner. Würzburg: Königshausen and Neumann, 2009. 109-123.

Benjamin, Walter. "Über den Begriff der Geschichte". In *Gesammelte Schriften*. Vol. 1 - II. Eds. Rolf Tiedemann and Hermann Schweppenhäuser. Frankfurt am Main: Suhrkamp, 1991.

Benveniste, Émile. *Problèmes de linguistique générale I*. Paris: Gallimard, 1966.

Behn, Aphra. *La Montre, or The lover's watch by Mrs. A. Behn*. EEBO Editions ProQuest, 1686.

Bertens, Hans. *Literary Theory. The Basics*. London and New York: Taylor and Francis Group, 2nd ed., 2008.

Brogan T. V. F. and Alex Preminger, eds. *The New Princeton Encyclopedia of Poetry and Poetics*. Princeton: Princeton University Press, 1993.

Brooks, Peter. *Reading for the Plot*. Cambridge: Harvard University Press, 1984.

Butor, Michel. *A Change of Heart*. 1958. Trans. Jean Stewart. New York: Simon and Schuster, 1959.

——. *Répertoire II*. Paris: Éditions de Minuit, 1964.

——. *La Modification*. 1957. Paris: Éditions de Minuit, 1980.

Calvino, Italo. *Il Libro, i Libri*. Buenos Aires: Nuovi quaderni italiani, 1984.

——. *Se una notte d'inverno un viaggiatore*. 1979. Milano: Oscar Mondadori, 1994.

Carter, Ronald and Michael McCarthy. *Cambridge Grammar of English: A Comprehensive Guide: Spoken and Written English Grammar and Usage*. Cambridge: Cambridge University Press, 2006.

Clarkson, Carrol. "Embodying 'you': Lévinas and a question of the second person." In *Journal of Literary Semantics* 34/2 (2005): 95-105.

Cohan, Steven and Linda M. Shires. *Telling Stories: A Theoretical Analysis of Narrative Fiction.* London and New York: Routledge, 1998.

Coffman, James Burton and Thelma B. Coffman, eds. *Psalms 1-72. Vol. 1. Book 1.* Austin: Abilene Christian University, 1992.

Drosdowski, Günther. *Duden: Grammatik der deutschen Gegenwartssprache.* Mannheim: Dudenverlag, 1995.

Duffy, Jean H. *Butor. La Modification.* London: Grant and Cutler Ltd, 1990.

Eakin, Paul John. *Fictions in Autobiography: Studies in the Art of Self-Invention.* Princeton: Princeton University Press, 1985.

Faulkner, William. *Requiem for a Nun.* London: Chatto and Windus, 1919.

Fludernik, Monika. "Second Person Fiction: Narrative You as Addressee And/Or Protagonist." In *Arbeiten aus Anglistik und Amerikanistik* 18/2 (1993): 217-247.

——. *Erzähltheorie: eine Einführung.* Darmstadt: WBG, Wissenschaftliche Buchgesellschaft, 2010.

Gascoigne, David. *The Games of Fiction. Georges Perec and Modern French Ludic Narrative.* Bern: Peter Lang, 2006.

Genette, Gérard. *Figures III.* Paris: Édition du Seuil, 1972.

Gerlach, Henry U. *Einwände und Einsichten. Revidierte Deutungen deutschsprachiger Literatur des 19. Und 20. Jahrhunderts.* München: Iudicium, 2002.

Goga, Yvonne. "Formes de l'autoréflexivité mallarméenne dans *Un homme qui dort* de Georges Perec." In *Écrire l'Énigme.* Paris: PUPS, 2007. 127-138.

Grass, Günter. *Im Krebsgang.* München: Steidl, 2002.

Grevisse, Maurice. *Le Bon Usage. Grammaire française avec des remarques sur la langue française d'aujourd'hui.* 1936. Gembloux: Éditions J. Duculot, 1975.

Grimsley, Jim. *Winter Birds*. 1984. Chapel Hill: Algonquin Books, 1994.

Jakobson, Roman. *Russian and Slavic Grammar. Studies 1931-1981*. Berlin, New York, Amsterdam: Mouton Publishers, 1984.

Jespersen, Otto. *Selected Writings of Otto Jespersen*. London: George Allen and Unwin Ltd, 1962.

Hawthorne, Nathaniel. "The Haunted Mind". In *Twice-Told Tales*. Ohio: Ohio State University Press, Centenary Edition, Vol. IX, 1974. 304-309.

Homer and Theodore A. Buckley. *The Odyssey of Homer: With the Hymns, Epigrams, and Battle of the Frogs and Mice*. London: Henry G. Bohn, 1853.

Homer and Augustus T. Murray. *The Iliad*. Cambridge: Harvard University Press, 1891.

Hörnigk, Therese. *Christa Wolf*. Göttingen: Steidl, 1989.

James, Alison. *Constraining Chance: Georges Perec and the Oulipo*. Evanston: Northwestern University Press, 2009.

Janson, Deborah. "Ilse Aichinger's *Spiegelgeschichte:* Challenging the Symbolic Order." In *Frauen: MitSprechen MitSchreiben. Beiträge zur literatur- und sprachwissenschaftlichen Frauenforschung*. Stuttgart: Hans-Dieter Heinz Akademischer Verlag, 1997. 500-513.

Kacandes, Irene. *Talk Fiction: Literature and the Talk Explosion (Frontiers of Narrative)*. Lincoln and London: University of Nebraska Press, 2001.

Kafka, Franz. "Aphorismen-Zettelkonvult". In *Nachgelassene Schriften und Fragmente II*. Ed. Jost Schillemeit. 1992. Frankfurt am Main: Fischer Taschenbuch Verlag, 2002.

Kibort, Anna. *Grammatical Features Inventory: Person*. University of Surrey. 2008. Date accessed 21 September. http://dx.doi.org/10.15126/SMG.18/1.03. 2017.

Kristeva, Julia. *Desire in Language: A Semiotic Approach to Literature and Art*. New York: Columbia University Press, 1980.

——. "Women's Time" in *The Kristeva Reader*. Ed. Toril Moi. Trans. Alice Jardine and Harry Blake. New York: Columbia University Press, 1986.

Lausberg, Heinrich. *Handbuch der Literarischen Rhetorik. Eine Grundlegung der Literaturwissenschaft*. München: Max Hueber Verlag, 1960.

Lausberg, Heinrich. *Elemente der Literarischen Rhetorik*. 1963. München: Max Hueber Verlag, 1990.

Le Sage, Laurent. *The French New Novel: An Introduction and a Sampler*. Pennsylvania State University Press, 1962.

Lefebvre, Henri. *La Production de l' Espace*. 1974. Paris: Anthropos, 2000.

Leiris, Michel. Afterword: "Le réalisme mythologique de Michel Butor." 1958. In Michel Butor, *La Modification*. 1957. Paris: Edition Minuit, 1980. 287-314.

Levinas, Emmanuel. *Totality and Infinity: An Essay on Exteriority*. Trans. Alphonso Lingis. Dordrecht, Kluwer Academic Publishers, 1991.

Lydon, Mary. *Perpetuum Mobile: A Study of the Novels and Aesthetics of Michel Butor*. Edmonton: Alberta University Press, 1980.

MacIntyre, Gwynplaine F. "*How like a God*, by Rex Stout (1929)." In *Fantasy and Science Fiction - Curiosities*. Date accessed 21 September 2017. January 2008, SF Site spot art, www.sfsite.com/fsf/2008/cur0801.htm.

McInerney, Jay. *Bright Lights, Big City*. London: Bloomsbury, 1984.

Melville, Herman. *Bartleby, the Scrivener*. 1853. Leipzig: CreateSpace Independent Publishing Platform, 2015.

Moore, Lorrie. *Self-Help*. London: Faber and Faber, 1985.

Nagy, Andrea. *"Spiegelgeschichte" von Ilse Aichinger. Eine Analyse*. Norderstedt: Grin Verlag, 2004.

Oppenheim, Lois. *Intentionality and Intersubjectivity: A Phenomenological Study of Butor's "La Modification."* Kentucky: Lexington, 1980.

Perec, Georges. *L' Infra-Ordinaire*. Paris: Seuil, 1990.

——. *Un homme qui dort*. In: *Romans et Rêcits*. 1967. Paris: La Pochothèque (Le Livre de Poche), 2002. 211-304.

——. *Entretiens et Conférences I: 1965-1978*. Eds. Dominique Bertelli and Mireille Ribière. Nantes: Joseph K, 2003.

——. *Parcours Perec [travaux du] Colloque de Londres*. 1990. Comp. Mireille Ribière. Lyon: Presses universitaires de Lyon, 1998.

Pfeifer, Wolfang and Wilhelm Braun. *Etymologisches Wörterbuch des Deutschen*. Berlin: Akademie-Verlag, 1989.

Plato. "Meno". In *Meno and Phaedo*. Ed. David Sedley. Trans. Alex Long. Cambridge: Cambridge University Press, 2011. 1-41.

Pound, Ezra. *Lustra of Ezra Pound, with Earlier Poems*. New York: Alfred A. Knopf, 1917.

Proust, Marcel. *Du côté* de chez Swann. Paris: Gallimard, 1954.

Ratmann, Annette. *Spiegelungen, ein Tanz, Untersuchungen zur Prosa und Lyrik Ilse Aichingers*. Würzburg: Königshausen and Neumann, 2001.

Rechtien, Renate. "From Vergangenheitsbewältigung to Living with Ghosts: Christa Wolf's *Kindheitsmuster* and Leibhaftig." In *The Self in Transition. East German Autobiographical Writings Before and After Unification*. Eds. David Clarke and Axel Goodbody. New York: Rodopi, 2012. 123-145.

Reitan, Rolf. "Theorizing Second-Person Narratives: A Backwater Project?" In *Strange Voices in Narrative Fiction*. Eds. Per Krogh Hansen, Stefan Iversen, Henrik Skov Nielsen and Rolf Reitan. Berlin: De Gruyter, 2011. 147-174.

Richardson, Brian. *Unnatural Voices: Extreme Narration in Modern and Contemporary Fiction*. Columbus: The Ohio University Press, 2006.

Robbe-Grillet, Allain. *Pour un Nouveau Roman*. 1963. Paris: Les Éditions de Minuit, 2013.

Sartre, Jean-Paul. *La Nausée*. Paris: Gallimard, 1938.

——. *Huis Clos suivi de Les mouches*. Paris: Gallimard, 1947.

Schaumann, Caroline. *Memory Matters. Generational Responses to Germany's Nazi Past in Recent Women's Literature*. Berlin: Walter de Gruyter, 2008.

Schaper, Christine. *Christa Wolf: "Kindheitsmuster". Epische Struktur und Gehalt* (Doctoral dissertation). Halle, 1980.

Sheringham, Michael. *Everyday Life. Theories and Practices from Surrealism to the Present*. Oxford: Oxford University Press, 2006.

Sloane, Thomas O., ed. *Encyclopedia of Rhetoric.* Oxford: Oxford University Press, 2001.

Snyder Hook, Elizabeth. *Family Secrets and the Contemporary German Novel: Literary Explorations in the Aftermath of the Third Reich.* Rochester: Camden House, 2001.

Stanzel, Franz K. *Theorie des Erzählens.* 1979. Göttingen: Vandenhoeck and Ruprecht, 2001.

Stawarska, Beata. *Between You and I. Dialogical Phenomenology.* Athens: Ohio University Press, 2009.

Steiner, Ariane. *Georges Perec und Deutschland. Das Puzzle um die Leere.* Würzburg: Königshausen and Neumann, 2001.

Stout, Rex. *How Like a God.* 1929. New York: Pyramid Books, 1963.

Weinrich, Harald. *Textgrammatik der Französischen Sprache.* Stuttgart: Klett, 1982.

Wiesehan, Gretchen E. *A Dubious Heritage: Questioning Identity in German Autobiographical Novels of the Postwar Generation.* New York: Peter Lang, 1997.

Wolf, Christa. *Lesen und Schreiben: Neue Sammlung.* Darmstadt: Luchterhand, 1980.

——. *Kindheitsmuster.* 1976. Berlin und Weimar: Aufbau Verlag, 1987.

——. "Kindheitsmuster." In *Text + Kritik, 46.* München, 1980.

Interview

"Paul Auster interview - *Winter Journal* preview." In: *Time Out London,* www.timeout.com/london/books/paul-auster-interview. Date accessed 23 September 2017.

Films

Un homme qui dort. Dir. Georges Perec and Bernard Queysanne. Dovidis/Satpec, 1974. Film.

Europa. Dir. Lars von Trier. Nordisk Film Biografdistribution, 1991. Film.